D0759131

# ORCHESTRATION

## A MEMOIR

Saundra Henderson Windom
———née———
CHANG, BANG SUN

New York

# ORCHESTRATION

## A MEMOIR

ORCHESTRATION



First Edition

ISBN: 978-1-946274-55-7 (Hardcover)
ISBN: 978-1-946274-56-4 (eBook)

Library of Congress Control Number: 2020948860
Jacket design by Omomato
Interior Design by Amit Dey

Published by Wordeee in the United States, Beacon, New York 2021
Website: www.wordeee.com
Twitter: twitter.com/wordeee
Facebook: Facebook.com/wordeee
e-mail: contact@wordeee.com

Hope and faith are the twin rulers of the life I have lived. If there is one thing I've learned throughout my life, it's that *Arirang* (hope) springs eternal and, as noted in Hebrews 11:1, "*Now faith is the substance of things hoped for, the evidence of things not seen.*"

The bottom of my professional communique states my motto:

"*What really counts in life? It's not where you come from or where you start—it's where you go, what you do, and who/how you impact your fellow man along the way.*"

# Advance Praise for Orchestration

Fifty years ago, in our freshman dorm at Stanford, we knew her as Sandy Henderson, a dynamic, beautiful spirit straight outta Compton. What we never knew—and what she barely knew—was her extraordinary history. Her cinematic book —"Annie" for our times —tells that story.

—Glenn Kramon,
former assistant managing editor,
*The New York Times*

An affecting memoir that intelligently unpacks an experience of cultural dislocation. The author's story is as remarkable as it is moving, and she furnishes an exceedingly thoughtful reflection on a life that was full of both misfortune and luck.

—Kirkus Review

"Poetic. Haunting. Hopeful. Historical. *ORCHESTRATION* is a profound testimony of faith, identity, resilience and self-determination. Brutality. Neglect. Denial. All unmatched by the infinite power of the human spirit. Bang Sun is my new personal hero!"

—Dr. Lamman Rucker
Film Actor/Producer - Activist - Educator - Entrepreneur

A fascinating story of perseverance, love for family and God's beautiful *orchestration*.

—Susan L. Taylor,
Editor-in-Chief Emerita of Essence Magazine
and Founder of the National CARES
Mentoring Movement

A vivid depiction of hope in the belly of despair rests a child so curious about life that inquisitiveness keeps her alive. This riveting true story lends solutions to society about surrender and survival in real-time. If you dare to dream and wonder again, do so through the eyes of a child with the substance of things hoped for and the evidence of things not seen. Saundra Windom "Bang Sun" is real life goals for a world that could use a little bit of hope.

—Enitan Bereola II,
Believer, Best Selling Author, Black Dad

*Orchestration* is a beautifully written memoir that exposes yet another complex layer of the African diaspora. Saundra Windom reconstructs her history exploring identity through the lens of African American and Asian cultures at the intersection of adoption. The reader will discover what can become of a life that was designed to be silenced when it learns to scream.

—Michelle Gipson Publisher,
Written Magazine, Host of 'Wine and Words'

Ms. Windom gives a new meaning to the word transcendent as her life story spans beyond the range of the normal human experience. It has been an honor and privilege to be a part of her amazing life's journey! Be prepared to be captivated as she shares this masterpiece of tragedy and triumph of a life well lived!

—Dr. Lateshia Woodley,
KCPS Assistant Superintendent
Student Support Services. Award-Winning Educator
& Author of Transforming Alternative Education

From the beginning until the end, the extraordinary details bring us headlong into the narrative and hold us there, wanting more. The day-by-day account of your loss of Gibran creates a feeling of immediacy, being there with you. Reliving past events through writing is sometimes like tearing the skin from a deep wound; it ain't easy.

—Jacqueline Henry Hill,
author *Jennie Wren, Memories of Mommy*

*Orchestration* is a moving account of how an orphaned child of war was led and guided by a loving God to live a life that touched and impacted many in her family and community. The story of Saundra Henderson Windom provides many inspirational messages, including how to transform pain into perseverance, trials into triumph, frustrations into faithfulness and obstacles into opportunities.

—Marilyn Gavin,
Retired Principal

The inspirational and enriching story of Chang Bang Sun to Saundra Henderson Windom speaks to the goodness and resiliency of the human spirit and the faith of mankind. It is a story that will enrich the life of the readers and a story everyone should read.

—Amy Enomoto-Perez, Ed.D,
Retired School Superintendent

Bang Sun-Saundra's sweet spirit touches everyone she meets. But reading about her rich, often haunting, heritage brings tears of sorrow for all that she endured and tears of joy for The Almighty's *orchestration* of her symphonic life.

—Paris Brooks,
Policy Writer/Editor

WOW, Phenomenal Read!

My ROOMIE's memoir was not only a history lesson but an awesome account of the amazing person that she has become despite her humble beginnings.

—Melonie Gibbs, M.D.
#4ever friend & family

# Table of Content


Dedication ............ xv

Introduction ............ xvi

Chapter 1 Me, Bang Sun—You, Boy ............ 1

Chapter 2 Every Child Deserves a Home ............ 9

Chapter 3 Foreign Land: Coming to America ............ 23

Chapter 4 Straight into Compton ............ 29

Chapter 5 Identity Crisis: *Korea* Is a Bad Word ............ 51

Chapter 6 My Family ............ 59

Chapter 7 Young, Gifted, and Black-ish ............ 73

Chapter 8 Taking the Reins ............ 91

Chapter 9 The Joker's Wild ............ 106

Chapter 10 The Past Becomes the Present ............ 143

Chapter 11 Grandma Holt Is Alive? ............ 158

Chapter 12 A Family of My Own ............ 167

Chapter 13 Lost ............ 203

Chapter 14 Found/Full Circle ............ 221

Chapter 15 Confirmation Voices Breathing Life into the Past ............ 239

Epilogue ............ 251

Acknowledgments ............ 254

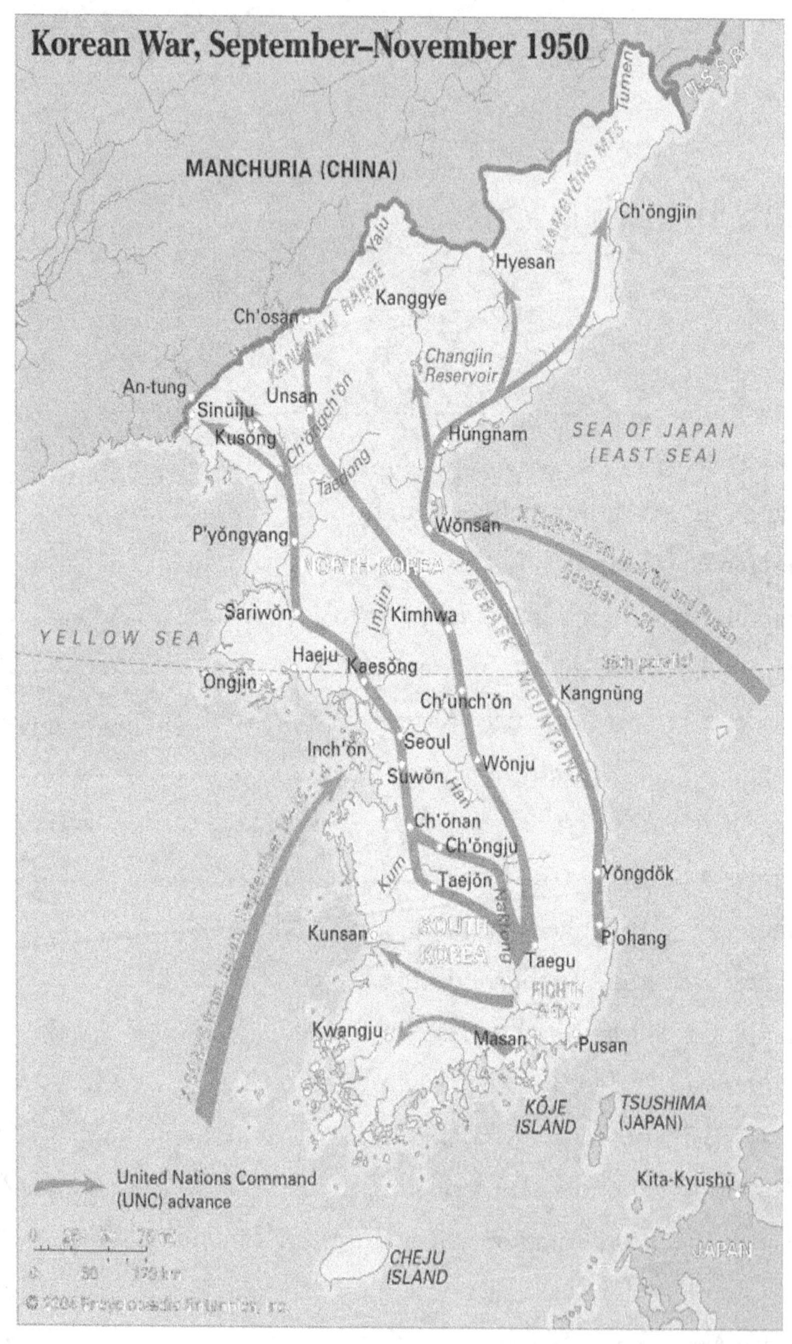


Courtesy of US Military

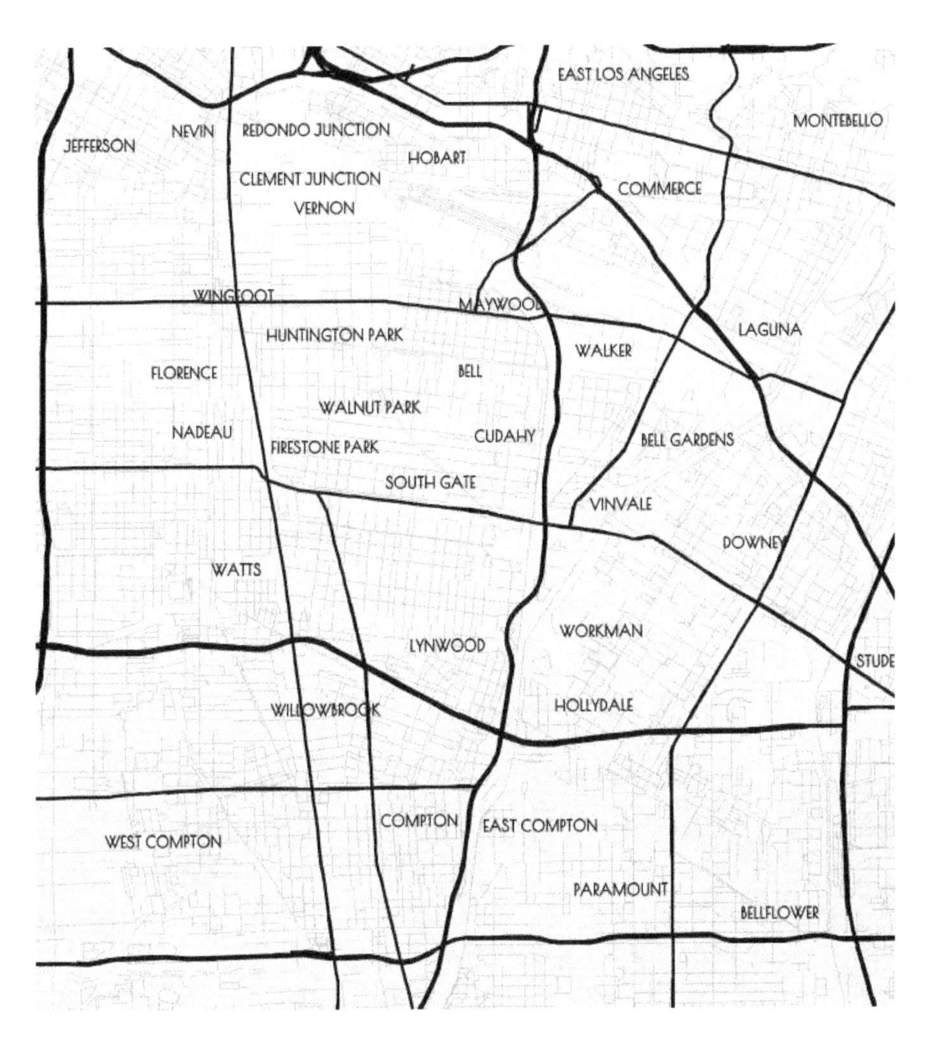


Map of Compton area

# Dedication

THIS BOOK, a labor of love and love's commitment, is dedicated to The Holts, Harry, Bertha, and Molly; my parents, James and Clemmie Henderson, and my godmother, "Nanny" (Berneatha Wade). To God, my Heavenly Father, Jesus my Lord and Savior and the Holy Spirit, my Comforter. All helped to lead me to know "who I am and whose I am."

To my children: Gibran, Ravi, Amir, the ultimate blessings in my life, and to my grandchildren who put pep in my step and a smile on my face: Mariah, Aiyanna, Mackenzie, Skylure and Athan.

# Introduction

FOR CENTURIES, the Korean Peninsula, because of its geography, was of great importance to Asia. It shared a reluctant history with both China and Japan, which in turn influenced and solidified its own culture, social beliefs, religion, language and trade. Picturesque with high mountains, clear seas, incredible natural beauty, and unmatched morning serenity, Korea's very moniker was coined by an emperor of China's Ming Dynasty on his 1934 visit. He called South Korea the Land of the Morning Calm.

In the early morning of June 25, 1950, with the invasion of the 38th parallel—the artificial line that now divides the once beautiful country of Korea into North and South—the serenity of the morning calm was destroyed. Over the next three years, war devastated the country beyond recognition, leveling cities, orphaning millions, destroying lives, and forever splintering families. A direct result of the Cold War between the Soviet Union and the United States, the Korean War split Korea into two sovereign states—one communist and one capitalist. Both governments of the new factions refused to accept the artificially imposed borders, and each claimed legitimate governance over *all* of Korea. Because of the constant border clashes between the splintered nations, when the North advanced on the South that fated morning in June, they had the full backing of Russia and China while the United States sided with the South.

Two months of fighting left South Korea's military might spent. Stepping up their support, the United States deployed its military to defend against the allied North's communist regime. Ninety percent of the military personnel came from the United States, but in actuality, twenty-one United Nations soldiers fought the battle for the soul of South Korea. Unimaginable at the time, when the order to aid Korea came down from President Harry S. Truman, right on the heels of World War II, there was reverberating shock.

Facing overwhelming odds, U.S. troops poured into the Chosin Reservoir's frozen tundra to fight this new war. No one expected it. Certainly not the young men first sent in to stem the crisis. At seventeen or eighteen years old, many had only enlisted in the armed services with hopes of seeing the world, and most had never faced conflict. In their wildest dreams, they would never have imagined going into combat so soon after World War II.

With the influx of Americans, impoverished farming and fishing villages near the military bases rapidly transformed into service towns for the Yankees. It wasn't long before they turned them into honky-tonk towns of shops, saloons, and prostitution that catered to the soldiers. The reality of Korea in the 1950s is that it was deathly poor—one of the world's poorest countries. In a culture of poverty, one longing for transformation from despair to hope, optimism rose with the influx of American dollars. Many poor Korean women and others from countries such as Indonesia, Russia, and Kazakhstan, trying to better their lives, flooded the military camp towns called Kijich'ons. The comfort women, as the Americans called them, were nothing more than prostitutes of a sanctioned sex trade that catered to the big spenders from the West. The Korean government, recognizing these women were bringing in close to twenty-five percent of its gross national product (GNP), expanded the "program" to ensure the servicemen were kept happy. This guaranteed a continuous flow of American dollars. On the premise of containing the spread of disease, both the Korean and American governments justified the "imprisonment of these prostitutes" by confining them to campgrounds. Despite these restrictions, as military bases expanded within South Korea, more and more women rushed to register as prostitutes, many migrating to the expanding army bases.

As the war raged on, soldiers digging foxholes fully understood those same furrows could become their graves. Facing daunting odds, many sought moments of solace in the arms of the comfort women. For soldiers facing death around every corner, eking out any moment of joy seemed harmless. However, in reality, those moments of joy led to a lifetime of sorrow for those left behind. Indeed, the Korean War left more casualties than the wounded and dead soldiers whose wives, mothers, and girlfriends will forever mourn their loss. It left behind unintended collateral damage of thousands of destitute, starving, and broken children with no hope of a better future and no country to call their own.

The historically closed patrilineal Korean society, at the time, was headed by Syngman Rhee, the first South Korean President. He'd been the last president of the Korean Provisional Government before its split and reelected after disunification. American-educated Rhee (George Washington University, Harvard, and Princeton) is pro-American, an ardent nationalist, and a dictatorial leader. His tyrannical philosophy, *ilguk ilmin*—one nation, one people—endorses racial purity. Rhee is non-negotiable about supporting bastard children of war. Known to tolerate zero opposition, he stridently encouraged women with mixed-race children to abandon their progenies for the good of the country. With this order, he put in motion one of the worst human rights atrocities in history. Duplicitously, but not apologetically, mothers, whose bodies were legislated to soldiers, were stigmatized and ostracized by the very regime sanctioning them. Unable to get work or receive social services for their offspring, they abandoned their flesh and blood—some out of love, some out of repercussions of disobedience and others from the fear of the stigma that comes with being unwed, or worse, being identified as a sex worker. For their own "good," many mixed-race children were killed by drowning, desertion in the mountains, or by abandonment in one form or the other. The more benevolent mothers flooded orphanages with their children.

Since Korea's strict family bloodline registry and social support system is for citizens, and since children get their citizenship from their father, mixed children of war under Rhee's regime could only look forward to a lifetime of discrimination and taunts. Soldiers who were willing to take their paramours and children home found it impossible as interracial marriage in the United States was banned. Forced to leave their children behind, many funneled their dreams and hopes for them into supporting the orphanages that would ultimately care for them. Massive numbers of abandoned children began overflowing the few orphanages that existed before the war. As orphanages ballooned past capacity with *Twigis* (mixed-race children), a new plan was devised. With the help and support of American servicemen and women, many G.I. orphanages began springing up. By the end of 1954, there were more than four hundred registered orphanages in the Republic of Korea.

When, even one year after the war ended, an estimated one thousand children a month are being sent to orphanages, the galled Korean government acted. Reaching a win-win agreement with the United States, they began the systematic process of racial cleansing, an exodus of Korean mixed-race children to America. At its height, a massive exportation of more than one hundred thousand children are adopted by American families. Adoption, much like the decreed sex trade, proved to be a financial boon for Korea. Since the 1950s, it's estimated that more than two hundred thousand full-blooded and mixed Korean children were adopted the world over.

But who benefited from the death of innocent civilians, higher than in World War II and Vietnam or the nine million displaced Koreans, the splintering of families to the North and South, the one million Korean children under the age of eighteen forced to fend for themselves with no family left, or the two million who died? What of the forty thousand mixed-race children born of war who suffered unimaginable hardships and became victims of loneliness, loss of identity, hunger, fear, and death? Or the five million servicemen and citizens who sacrificed their lives in the name of freedom? The war set the stage for new social issues that would come to scar South Korea's soul for years yet to come. The question of who was to blame can never be answered because such is the travesty of war. However, in a country where racial purity trumps humanity, the repercussions of the Korean War remain deep in the marrow of loss, grief, discard, and shame. As the war memorial in Washington so aptly says, "Freedom is never free." A deafening silence around the Korean War remains to this day. Much like the children it spawned, the Korean War, often itself orphaned by history, was one of the deadliest wars ever fought.

I can only piece together the story of my life from fragmented memory, broken stories, legal documents, and my birth country's history. Allegedly, I was born in 1953 in the Land of Morning Calm, except for my life; it was the Land of Mournful Calamity. A mother I'll never see gave birth to me during a time of strife. I'm mixed-race—African-American and Korean. At the end of the war, my foreign-soldier father could've returned to his previous life. But, of course, he also could've been rotated back to the United States following an injury, or he could've been a casualty of war. The truth is, I don't know the fate of my father or mother. Just more mystery to add to the pile that makes up my interrupted life. Either way, I was in Korea without a mother or father.

The invisibility of Black Korean adoptees is a narrative rarely explored, even when the silence is breached. "*Because of its mountains,*" says David Halberstam in his book, *The Coldest Winter: America and the Korean War*, the irony is, "*if there is a shade that describes Korea, it would be shades of brown.*" Dubbed the Forgotten War, none who was there would ever forget the carnage and brutal reality of the Korean War, including me.

Unlike many, I am one of the "lucky ones." I survived. A Korean War's collateral damage expelled on one of the early Babylift flights of over one hundred thousand Korean children exported to America; I am one of the Black, mixed-race children who has a story to tell. For many, my story could be an ordinary one of a Black child growing up in America in the 1950s, yet for five years—old enough to have my identity shaped—I was a Korean child.

Over the years, as I've recounted my story, I'm often asked, "How on earth do you remember some of the details of your early life, and why mourn Korea?" My answer is always, "We hold on to what we don't want to let go of." I never wanted to let go of Sonyeon, my savior and youthful companion, or Korea.

# CHAPTER ONE

## Me, Bang Sun—You, Boy

LEGEND HAS IT I'm found tied to a tree. What happens between the tree founding and my first recollection on this earth is the mystery of my life. By age four, I'd come to understand fate has not dealt me the best cards for a winning hand, but it's not until I'm an adult that I could patch together the pieces of my jagged memory.

My first memory is of the Prussian-blue sea, ebbing in the afternoon sun, stretching out before me like a calming blanket. It's the kind of blanket I appreciated on chilly Korean nights when temperatures plummet below zero, so cold that even the stars refuse to come out to play or one I throw off in the summers when temperatures top more than ninety degrees. The sea holds magic for me. It embraces me in its arms, washes me, and bears gifts that are saving my life. For many not as lucky as me, it has become their watery grave and final resting place.

I am in a sea town, one that could have been on the Sea of Japan, the East China Sea, or the Yellow Sea. Truthfully, I have no idea which one. But in my sea town, *Naneun haengbokhada*, I am happy. Happy because that's where I meet Boy. *Sonyeon,* which means boy in Korean, is what I've taken to calling the boy who has suddenly appeared in my life, much like Tarzan called his new son.

Sonyeon is my constant companion with whom I spend every day. When I close my eyes at night and think back on our day, I'm indeed always happily giggling next to him while dizzily bouncing along the foam-covered sea with its lulling, metronomic waves. The shoreline is in constant motion as we race along, and that, too, makes me happy, for we are in search of dinner. I don't know his real name. I don't know from where he's come. I don't know who he is, but I wonder if he's my *oppa* (older brother) who's finally come to find me. An *oppa* would make me happier because, as far as I can tell, I'm alone in the world.

Something about Sonyeon at first gives me pause. My complexion is much darker than his, but he, too, has a special look. His skin is olive, a few shades darker than most Koreans. It doesn't seem to bother him that I'm darker than he is, though others call me darkie, I don't ponder on it much. Sonyeon's eyes are expressive but narrow. Those small slits, flanked by lush lashes, could open wide, however, showing the full circumference of his big, dark brown eyes when he is mad or surprised. He often gives me a "bucking" look when I do something to alarm or amuse him, which I often do. He doesn't seem to mind either that I'm a girl.

Though I live on the street, I'm not street smart. Invariably, I do things that threaten our safety, like wave at the men in jeeps.

"What you doing?" Sonyeon scolds in our native language.

Ashamed, I hold my head down, knowing very well tears could flow at any moment. Tears are my enemy. Sonyeon does not like it when I cry. As I silently sob, I'm careful not to make a sound because sound, too, is my enemy.

"*Shush,*" Sonyeon would scold again if I can't silence my sobs. "You cry, they take you away. Don't you see, you have to be careful because the soldiers in trucks will take children who look like you and me away."

Every opportunity Sonyeon gets, he discourages me from doing anything to draw attention to myself. To distract him from his constant reprimands, I make him show me his big, little, and missing teeth. He obliges, and we burst into laughter because his baby teeth are giving way to his permanent teeth. Hastily skipping our way out of sight of anyone who poses a danger for us, we head to meet our only friend—the sea.

Our base is near the seashore. When nature calls, the sea again becomes our refuge. One day, I have an emergency and urgently need to go potty. Running out of sight, I go to handle my business. The stench of rotting seafood leaving my body makes me scrunch up my face in disgust, and to my horror, I get a little on my finger. I come running out, pointing my finger toward Sonyeon.

*"Ugh."* He grimaces. Repulsed, he begins to run away from me though I can see from his disappearing eyes he's amused. He is running faster and faster and chanting, "Dung Girl, Dung Girl." I take chase like a dog romping after its master. Neither of us can hold our laughter as we head toward the sea, which is where I need to be to cleanse my soiled body. Sonyeon leads the way with authority. He demands I wash myself, especially my hands. I plunge my soiled fingers deep into our savior, swirling them back and forth in the cool water. I take time to enjoy the gentle waves before burrowing my feet into the floury sand underfoot, which is tickling my small toes. Sonyeon is waiting for me a distance away while I wash. When I'm done, I hurriedly dash over to where he is standing. Clean and new, we head toward the rocks in search of the sea morsels—our meal—hiding beneath them. Sonyeon is wise beyond his eight or so years, and he's teaching me how to harvest seafood to eat so we can stay alive.

We are street kids—urchins, society's discards—forced to survive by sucking out tasty morsels we find in the conelike shells in the sea, and Sonyeon is an expert at it. Come nightfall, we bundle up under a blanket of stars. Sonyeon becomes my entire life. We are out and about at all times of the day and night. Often as we make our way into town, whenever my four-year-old legs are too tired to go farther, Sonyeon bends down and lets me climb onto his back for a piggyback ride. For me, this is sheer bliss, but for him, I'm guessing it's the nimblest way to move through the crowd during our excursion to the village market of street vendors.

The smell of the market, overpowered with hanging twines of garlic and onions meant to ward off evil spirits, means we are nearby. The closer we get, the stronger the odor of fishy fish. Stacked on top of each other, their briny smell fills the air. There's not much of a selection, but that doesn't stop the flies from lighting on and basking in the oozing juices of the un-iced fish. The disharmony of smells contrasts with the distinctive spicy scent coming from the dark brown barrels of fermenting *kimchi.*

The vendors at the market, poor and hustling, are trying to sell their goods to the equally poor. The burst of machine-gun fire is no longer heard, but the aftermath of war is everywhere. Though over, the impact of the war has devastated us peasants. We watch people come to the market from the hills, from across paddies, and along bombed-out roads looking for their next meal. Just like Sonyeon and me, they are suffering. Maybe like us, too, their visits to the market will include the pilfering of vendor's goods, which for us will necessitate a speedy escape. Most are gaunt like Sonyeon and me, and we are all wearing the tattered year-round standard peasant attire of white pants and flimsy blouses, hardly enough against the winter but enough in the summer air.

Today, the village market is crowded. Each food stand attendant wears something that represents what they sell. The fisherman's apron, for example, is covered in fish scales, blood, and fish fluids, creating a tie-dye–like pattern in its light cotton fabric. The fruit and vegetable farmer has bits of wheat, straw, and dirt woven into his attire and has shearing utensils to cut goods, if needed, hanging from his belt or stall. The merchants' hope always is for the foreigners to come driving up in their army jeeps. Those days, they'll be sure of selling some wares.

On this particular day, while we're at the market, the jeeps arrive. When they drive up, Sonyeon pulls me back into the shadows and whispers, "Stay calm, and do absolutely nothing to draw attention to yourself." He's nagging again. He says we have to be careful of the soldiers because we don't know who is friend or foe, so we have to keep out of sight until they leave the market. Curiously, I'm watching from my hiding place as the strangers strut about the market. They don't look Korean. Some have pale pink skin and funny hair, while others have dark skin with funny hair too. I don't associate my likeness with the dark ones. I don't know that one of the dark men, most likely a Negro soldier from the 24th infantry, could be my father. I'm mesmerized and captivated when I see these strangers, but Sonyeon prevents me from getting any closer.

Regardless of the weather, the men seem to wear a lot of clothes—hats, shirts tucked neatly into their pants, jackets with gold buttons and black boots that reach their ankles. Black or pale, they are dressed alike. The dark soldiers fascinate me most because, like Sonyeon and me, they have different shades of skin color, from yellow like most Koreans to dark umber. Under their hats, their hair is also very different and ranges from wiry to curly. I have never seen wiry hair before—if only I had a mirror. The pale ones have different color hair, too, underneath their hats. Some have a yellowish color while others have mousy brown, red, or black hair, but none wiry like the Negro soldiers. I stare hard at the pale ones because some even have cat-colored eyes. What the pale and dark soldiers have in common is that they are in groups of their own kind, they all smoke cigarettes, and they are all loud and playful.

I sneak to get a little closer. Sonyeon, who misses nothing, sees me, taps me on the shoulder, and gives me the stink eye. I obey him and retreat, my gaze fixed on the soldiers. My grumbling stomach distracts me and brings me to a more immediate reality: the fear of starvation. Sonyeon and I are among the many peasants looking for our next meal by any means necessary. My senses are overstimulated with all that is happening as we walk through the market after the soldiers leave. Trying to keep up with Sonyeon is hard, and I stray, drawn to the color pallets of burnt orange persimmons, pale yellow pears, and the deep purple eggplants at the fruit and vegetable stall.

Sonyeon pulls me by the arm. As we approach, the farmer stares at us, knowing full well we aren't contributors to the economy. We press on, and I now have my eyes on the candy stall. The smell of the candy is delicious, and my mouth is watering, imagining the taste of its sweetness permeating the north, south, east, and west of my mouth. Sonyeon is cool as a cucumber, but the vendor can undoubtedly see my wishes from the lust in my eyes. I want his candy! We move on without the candy, me in a state of sadness. We would go hungry this night.

Another market day Sonyeon and I find favor when a jewelry vendor setting up his stall drops his bag of loose beads. He is very old and can barely see. He usually creates new necklaces and bracelets with his beads throughout the day, but now he's distraught because the beads have scattered and are camouflaged by the dirt and broken glass on the ground. Sonyeon and I happen to be in the right place at the right time, and the old man, in a state of panic, offers Sonyeon enough *won* to buy something to eat if he will quickly gather the beads. Sonyeon instructs me on what to do, and together we enjoy the task of gathering the beads, even turning it into a game. We find all the colorful beads that had our customer so upset and prance off with our reward.

It is on this day I have my first gourmet meal—grasshoppers. Hungrily I chomp down on half of the tasty, hardened yet soft body of the fried or sautéed cicadas. It is such a distinct taste. I love the salty, yummy taste, so I devour the other half with haste. The Korean *hwan (won)* is only enough to buy one wooden spear of four. Because I'm a slow eater, Sonyeon eats three of the skewered grasshoppers, and I only get one. I'm still hungry. Unfortunately, we only have enough money for the one skewer, and it's time to head out of the village. On our way out, we pass the candy man. When we get close to the stall, Sonyeon stoops down for me to get on his back. A four-year-old on foot is definitely a hindrance to Sonyeon's escape plan, without question a disadvantage because speed is required when he steals food, which he frequently does. I'm delighted to be on Sonyeon's back for another reason, too: It helps me avoid all the animal dung on the streets and saves us from enduring unbearable smells for our journey home.

The man who owns the stall is busy clipping off a piece of his goods with giant shearing scissors for a customer while watching us like a hawk. What he is selling is a taffy-like candy called *yeot*. It is sweet and sticks to the teeth. Because I'm always lusting after his candy every time I visit the village market, the *yeot-jangsu* knows me. Now we're on our way home, and I'm already sad that we won't have any candy again today. At the very end of the table is some sheared candy, and I wish the vendor would just give it to us. Sonyeon sidles up close to the stall. While I'm dreaming of the candy gift, Sonyeon suddenly takes off like a bullet, me lurching backward as he runs full speed away from the market. I can hear the man hurling bad words at both of us, which only makes Sonyeon run faster.

When Sonyeon makes it to a clearing far enough away from the village, he bends down, and I get off of his back. He collapses to the ground, panting, trying to get his breath. I still don't have a clue what is happening. Finally, Sonyeon raises on his elbows and calls over to me.

"Bang Sun, come here."

Head bowed, I make my way over to him, afraid I've done something wrong again. He is now sitting up, but instead of scolding me, he says, "Close your eyes and open your mouth."

An explosion of sweetness—north, south, east, and west—enters my mouth. It is *yeot*. I'm in heaven as the taffy-like candy sticks to my teeth, prolonging its sweetness. It is a rare treat, one that makes our long day special. The delicious dessert helps my hunger go away, and I forgive Sonyeon for eating three grasshoppers.

More than anything, it seems Sonyeon and I are often on some food-acquiring adventure. But one day, that changes when we visit a home that leaves an indelible memory in my mind. It is a small space—probably a shanty. In the one-room house, there is a strikingly beautiful woman with long black hair and ruby lips. I'm mesmerized by her red lips and imagine this woman to be my mother. How delightful would it be if I now have a brother and my own *eomoni* (mother), no longer alone in the world?

The shiny tube with the ruby red paste that paints perfection on the woman's lips catches my attention. Hoping to paint myself red, too, I grab the tube from the dresser, trying to conceal it in my tiny hands. Unfortunately, I'm caught, and the woman with the red lipstick scolds me. I start to run over to Sonyeon but not fast enough as she grabs me by the collar, her long nails leaving a gash on my back. That faint scar still reminds me of red lipstick. That is the last memory I have of Sonyeon and the woman with the red lipstick.

# CHAPTER TWO

## Every Child Deserves a Home

I'M ABOUT four-and-a-half years old when I arrive at Mah San Orphanage in Masan, Korea, in 1957. I have no idea how I got there. All I know is that the day before, I'm with Sonyeon and the lady with red lipstick, and then I wake up here. I suspect I was brought by a soldier who found me sleeping by the sea or left here by the red lipstick woman.

"What is your name?" I'm asked.

I don't know who I'm supposed to be or how I happen to be here, so I simply say, "I'm called Bang Sun." I'm not sure either if it's my real name, but it's what Sonyeon calls me. If I was given a name at birth, it's an okay name with me because I like to fantasize that my name is special. You see, there is an indigenous plant in South Korea that proudly displays bright orange-red flowers called Bong Soong-ah. True or not, it gives me comfort to think my name might have been adapted from this flower because my mother, despite it all, wanted to plant my Korean identity inside of me.

The Mah San Orphanage is a simple wooden structure with one large room and a flimsy door. It has gaping holes between the slatted walls. I can't count past twenty, but it seems there are many, many more than twenty kids crowded in the barren space. Most are brown like me, so I'm no longer the odd one out. Almost daily, a good number of orphans are brought in by soldiers. Finally, it dawns on me that this might be why Sonyeon insisted we should be careful around them. The heart-broken servicemen who bring in hungry, homeless, destitute orphans left at sentry posts or picked up on the streets of Masan are not at all scary to me. It seems they go out of their way to find and bring in the sick children of war who live in ditches, in caves, and under bridges. Practically naked, even in terrible weather conditions, children often arrive diseased and riddled with parasites. Many are in worse shape than I am—or so I think because I don't realize that I, too, am diseased and riddled with parasites. In addition to the children, the soldiers bring bags of food and clothing. They also give money to the orphanage staff. Sometimes they take time to play with us older kids and bounce babies on their laps at other times. I'm now wondering if mine and Sonyeon's fears were misplaced.

The inadequacy of the Mah San Orphanage is better than the gutter, and I can see appreciation in the eyes of the daily arrivals. Maybe I'm in a better place, too, but I don't feel as grateful since I'd rather be with Sonyeon. Until I arrived at the orphanage, like the destitute kids, I'm walking down a path that likely leads to my demise. I'm emaciated with the typical kwashiorkor belly of the malnourished, and I have a huge head. I'm sad, cold, and hungry. I can't imagine where Sonyeon is. I'm hoping he'll show up, but after days he's still nowhere to be found. I wonder what has happened to him. Did he get captured too by the soldiers? Was he taken somewhere else? I miss Sonyeon more than ever and wish I could run off and look for him more, but I am more scared of being out in the streets alone. Losing Sonyeon—my everything, up until this point in my short life—becomes a haunt, and I cry often. My arrival at Mah San introduces me to loss.

At Mah San, I settle into the routine of the orphanage, the same every day. With each passing day, it amazes me how suddenly, snippets of memory are anchoring full recall of times, places, people, and experiences. I'm becoming conscious for the first time of continuous memory and time. So far, no place in my brief life has given a comfort star rating, but here at Mah San, I give it a one star. I feel the direness of my circumstance, probably because I feel trapped. The ramshackle building, cold and drafty, barely has space for all the children in the house. At bedtime, we scramble to find a spot on the floor. A flimsy blanket folded twice on the concrete flooring is my mattress, literally defining a "Hard Knock Life." Through the patched, leaky roof, I see no blanket of stars above to distract me, nor do I hear the lulling waves of the sea that allow me to drift off. Bodies huddling up against each other do nothing to stem the cold winds torturing our skeletal frames. The thermostat of the concrete floor has three settings: cool, cold, and cruel. I shiver uncontrollably. Folding my arm at the elbow and placing it between my head and the floor is the first pillow I proudly devise all by myself. Though I'm skinny, the fold creates a nice cushion—that is until my arm begins to tingle and go numb. Having to change position interrupts my hard-won sleep.

Caregivers always dashing here and there to attend to children's scraped knees, hunger cries, or wheezing chests are overworked. There are not enough of them to care for us all. Older kids like me have to fend for ourselves while they tend to the babies. Days drag on endlessly, and waking hours are too long for me because I don't want to be here. I'm becoming increasingly sad. I now regret losing my carefree life of skipping rocks over seashore. I guess I should be thankful I'm not injured or dead, but being imprisoned and away from Sonyeon and the sea is really hard. Maybe I should go and try to find Sonyeon.

To be honest, I'd rather be out scavenging for sea morsels, a challenge that always excites me; the fun of the hunt and unpredictable finds. When amply rewarded with edible sea morsels, I'd feel a sense of victory knowing I'd not go hungry that day. Today, however, I'm listlessly standing in a line, my tin cup in outstretched hands, waiting for my turn to receive whatever nourishment will be poured or plopped into my cup. The meal that day and most days is a thin soup or broth, which does nothing to satisfy the growl from hunger churning in my bloated belly. Becoming more aware of my confined circumstance and the likelihood it might not change and that I might never see Sonyeon again, I redirect my sorrow into survival to protect my mental and emotional well-being.

I find I like being alone with my thoughts, and I spend much of my time observing what's going on around me. Experience wise, I'm far older than my chronological age of four and a half. Over time, I begin morphing into a serious thinker, and most of all, I'm becoming assertive. I'm still not social, but little by little, I venture outside to experience nature's comforting caress—the warmth of the sun's rays on my emaciated body; the breeze that whips through my sometimes unruly, matted hair, seeing the haunting views and still scarred beauty of the ravished, broken surroundings that proudly hold on to the majesty of its mountains. Facing the mountain, I take it all in. The orphanage seems to be in the middle of nowhere.

On the day of my resolve that this will be my future, I inhale deeply and exhale down to the last wisp of air in my lungs. "At least I'm alive! I AM ALIVE." A new spirit enters me, and I spryly move around to prove it. Other children are outside, but on my emotional island, I come face-to-face with a new version of myself Chang Bang Sun. It's as if adding Chang, which is the name all the adoptees who rotate through Mah San get, has made me a new person. That name, Chang, happens to be the last name of the head of the orphanage.

The orphanage, swarming with hungry mouths to feed, finds new ways to relieve the overcrowdedness and meager means. Non-Korean adults begin coming to visit pretty frequently. The first time they come, they take a few children with them. They come again and again, and the process is repeated. As left-behinds, we can feel that being chosen by these adults is a ticket to a better future. Welling in me now is a desire to be one of the chosen ones to go with the visitors. Desire turns into hope, and I begin to dream about being part of something—who knows what. My curiosity and imagination ignite and begin to burn brightly from the spark of being a part of whatever that something is. Deep inside, the loss and separation I feel for Sonyeon is transforming into a yearning for the chance to explore the dreams and hopes that such an opportunity might bring. *Arirang*, a six-hundred-year-old song, captures the indomitable spirit of Koreans. It is a song of the mountain that speaks of the belief in hope unseen, of having faith no matter how in despair one may be. The age-old folk song and the anthem of Korea genuinely reflect the deep Korean belief of transforming sorrow into hope, and so would I. I now embody the spirit of *Arirang*.

I further develop my assertive qualities. I *need* to be one of the children chosen to go with the visitors. One day, a new non-Korean man I've never seen arrives. He has a black mustache and deep-set, gentle hazel eyes that stare lovingly from under thick, bushy black eyebrows. I'm in acute observation mode, far more attuned to the world than most would expect. Hardship, you see, makes one grow up fast. My eyes are peeled, noticing everything about this man. I want to go with him. When he leaves, some of the children go with him, but I'm not one. The second time he shows up, I boldly push my way toward him. Standing in front of him, I make eye contact. I want him to *see me*. I want him to choose me. I'm so excited that I unblinkingly keep staring at him until he smiles at me. He has a friendly, gentle manner, and he genuinely seems to care about us. I can feel his love, compassion, and his deep need to help us radiating from him. Not just in a mechanical way, but with sincere love and kindness.

Sensing his power to change my circumstances, I follow him around like he is holding the glass slipper to my better life. All at once, everyone is clamoring at him, begging him to take them away with him. That day I'm not chosen, but the mustache man returns again and again. With each visit, my hope surges, and I get bolder and bolder. Unfortunately, I'm not chosen over and over. However, I'm learning patience and faith. After a few more visits, my time finally comes. I'm one of the fortunate selected by the mustache man. I've been living in faith every moment of every day since I first met him, knowing that one day, he will choose me.

On July 7, 1957, I embark on a journey with the mustache man and the two others who are with him. I have no idea what to expect or where I'm going, but I'm glad to leave behind the cold, hard floors of the Mah San Orphanage. Dressed in my best orphan outfit, a hand-me-down floral tunic a size or two too big for me, I jauntily accompany Mr. Mustache and his helpers. From Mah San, we visit several orphanages between Masan and Busan, two cities in the district of Changwon in the Province of South Gyeongsang. By the time we leave Changwon, there are more than twenty children and babies in tow. We pile into a waiting vehicle and are taken to the train station, where we're bound north to Seoul—the 330-kilometer life-changing train ride we hope will help us escape our miserable existence of simply being born.

The two non-Koreans and the one Korean man in our party usher us onto the train. We settle in, and I'm getting very encouraged. This is for real! Many of the kids are restless and noisy, but not me. I sit quietly, feeling thankful. Often on our excursions, Sonyeon and I would see trains rumbling along. When we did, I would pester him about the metal boxes connected to each other that seemed to go on forever. The rattling noise and the loud *woot, woot* sounds they made delighted my senses, making me more curious about who or what was inside them. Now, here I am, inside one! I sit back and take great pleasure in experiencing this form of transportation, which is much faster, even if noisier than Sonyeon's back. I'm aware I'm going farther and farther away from Sonyeon, and I feel guilty for being this happy. I wish I could tell Soneyon what the train actually carries. I miss him so much.

I shift my thoughts. Now I'm torn between taking in the scenery outside the train window and observing the new strangers in my life. Outside will only be the barren, battered, bedraggled, and bombed-out scenery of the ravages of war, with miles of forlorn people walking down the dusty roads, heavy loads on their heads and babies tied to their backs. Would I trade places? The babies, snuggled up against their mothers' back, even under dire conditions, are feeling the heartbeat of love, something I will never experience. I avert my eyes from the window. The strangers in my life are winning the battle of my decision.

All three chaperones have dark hair, not yellow or wiry like the military men I'd seen at the village market in our sea town. The Korean man speaks English and Korean, and I like that he can one moment communicate with the foreigners in English and then, without blinking, speak to us in Korean. In Korean, he tells some of the kids to stay seated and not talk too loudly. I'm hardly listening as I'm fascinated by the talk of the mustache man and young woman. I know this language from before when Sonyeon and I were near the soldiers. What they are saying, however, I don't have a clue.

Like the soldiers, their bodies are fully clothed, and unlike us, they are proportionate—no big bellies or heads or stick arms and legs. I'm wondering how they get their food and clothes when one of the babies begins crying, interrupting my mental inspection and curiosity. The lady hushes the baby whose cry is likely from the severe cough that's making it miserable. Reaching into her bag, she squeezes some red stuff in its mouth. Holding the baby over her shoulder, she massages its back. The other adults are also tenderly holding babies. Their affection, even from my distant seat, is heartwarming. I want to say something but don't have language. Noting my intense stare, the mustache man smiles, making his thick, unruly eyebrows go up into a mountain peak. The baby he is holding gives universal approval and smiles too while reaching its little hands to touch the man's mouth. I have never seen this kind of attention or empathy being paid to children like us.

When I arrive at the Holt Orphanage, I'm surprised. From the squat brick buildings, three or four bungalow-type structures, a chimney juts from the roof. There are many windows and doors. From the windows, the picturesque mountain range looks untouched by war and is calming. On clotheslines, rows upon rows of white diapers flap in the sunlight.

In comparison to Mah San, this orphanage is sturdy, beautiful, and welcoming. Huge inside and out, many friendly faces welcome us.

More importantly, the rooms are warm; the sleeping quarters have bunk beds, and in the kitchen, several workers are cooking. Eating never excites me because I'm used to little or no food, which is what I know and expect; however, the aroma from the kitchen makes my mouth water. By my standards, I give this new residence a five-star rating.

Along with the other kids who arrive with me, I'm taken to be processed into the system. I weigh a mere twenty-eight pounds for a kid nearing five-years-old and have a big distended belly. There is no information from Mah San specifying any date of birth or who might have brought me there. Many kids arrive at orphanages with notes pinned to their flimsy ware, but not me. So, based on my teeth, height, and verbal abilities, which are quite advanced for my age, the young lady who was on the train with us and now wearing a nurse's uniform gives me a random birthdate; April 1, 1953. Go figure. Later, another document surfaces with a recorded date of August 1, 1953. This suggests, either way, that I was conceived during the wartime of 1952. My exact birthdate is unknown.

After the check-in process, I'm shepherded to another room. There is some kind of gadget that has an eye all set up. It has a big light on top. What I'm about to do, I'm told, is take my very first photo. This photo will eventually become my passport picture to a new future, they say. Sometime later, while looking at the photo, I wondered why I looked so sad. Perhaps it's from fear of the light apparatus (camera) that I'd never seen before, or possibly because as the light flashes into the mirror to my soul, through my eyes, I can no longer hide my yearning for Sonyeon.

As it turns out, the man I traveled with to Holt is Harry Holt himself, founder of Holt Orphanage. The woman who wears glasses that accompanied him is his daughter, Molly, and she has the same warm, welcoming smile as her father. The translator, David Kim, is a Korean man. Born in China during his father's work as a Presbyterian minister, his family fled back to South Korea during the cultural revolution. As time rolls on, I learn to live in the moment. That turns out to be easier than I expected because at the Holt Orphanage there is a sense of family. The feeling of warmth and kindness I observed on the train ride is embodied by all the staff; they care for us unconditionally. Unlike Mah San, they don't feel like people just doing a job, but like family looking out for each other, effortless and steady. These are the people holding our space in place of parents, and I did not feel like a burden as I had at Mah San, but then maybe it was me—not receptive to receiving care from anyone but Sonyeon.

When the mustache man is at the orphanage, it's not unusual to find five or six of us grabbing for his hand while others straddle his legs and neck. We even call Molly and Harry by family names. Harry Holt is *hal-abeoji* (grandfather), and Molly is *eonni* (big sister). We love *hal-abeoji* and *eonni*. In fact, Molly is our everything. The official orphanage nurse, she has many other jobs: teacher, kitchen help, negotiator, and premier toilet trainer.

As new arrivals, in addition to our passport pictures, we are given medical exams. There is a concern about me. I'm not sure of what, but I know I'm sick. I remember *hal-abeoji* taking me on many trips to the hospital in his station wagon. I love getting into the back of his car, lying flat on my back, looking up at the sky I know so well. As we bounce along, this is the closest feeling to freedom I get, compared to the sea of my past.

I don't like the medical exams that much. I'm made to stand on a scale, stick out my tongue, and have things poked in my ear. I jump at the cold stethoscope on my skinny chest. As it turns out, in addition to being severely malnourished, I have to be monitored for shadows on my lungs. The doctor thinks that I might have a type of tuberculosis. I'm not contagious or too far advanced in the disease to be quarantined, so I just keep going back and forth to the doctor. With each visit, I begin to feel better and better. I also start putting on weight. Waiting to be cleared of the shadow on my lungs, I get to stay longer than most at the Holt Orphanage. I don't know how long because I have no real concept of spans of time. However, time by its nature, adds up.

Many of the kids who arrived with me are now gone. I don't know to where, but I don't feel the need to hurry away. I suppose if I stay at Holt forever, it would be okay because I'm content. Having found my social self, I'm having lots of fun with the other kids. I especially enjoy singing the ditties of every Korean child's childhood, like *Nabiya*, a song about butterflies. How appropriate since, in Greek mythology, *butterfly* means *psyche*, and I must keep my mind intact. While singing, I put my right thumb on my nose's tip while my left thumb touches the pinky finger of the hand, touching my nose. Then I flutter both hands in the opposite direction imitating the wings of a butterfly.

Merriment and laughter fill the air at Holt as we hoist each other on the seesaw where a child jumps on one end of a longboard, lifting the other child upward toward the sky. Inescapable, however, is the sad reality of orphanage life, which is never far away. There is death all around me. I watch as Molly cares for sick children too listless to move, eat, or cry—children too far gone to be saved. I'm beginning to understand that when they don't move, talk, cry, or eat anymore, they will never come back from the little boxes they're put in. With each death, a little piece of Molly dies, and poor Molly is always so sad. I feel her sorrow, though my nearing five-year-old mind can't grasp what sorrow is. I wonder how she's able to grieve for every lost child when she has to focus on the survival of so many discarded children. In my mind, I devise a plan so Molly won't have to worry about me: keep moving. And moving I do all the time, so she'll see I am fine. Much like at Mah San, for as many children who die, many new ones arrive.

Holt's grounds are vast, and there are many activities to keep all of us children busy during the day. We play outside when we don't have to study or go for meals. By the end of the day, I'm ready for bed. I love my stacked bunk bed. When the orphanage is overcrowded, we have to share them. A new girl arrives. My bunk is where she's assigned.

Much taller and older than me by two or three years, her face is always in a scowl. Mean and ornery is kind in describing her disposition. I don't interact with her much because of this attitude. One night, while we are on the bed, she pinches and scratches me for a reason I can't fathom. I yell out, snatching away my arm. I turn and stare at her. From the look on her face, I realize it's no accident, so I ask, "Why did you do that?

"Be quiet, be still, and go to sleep, you little runt," she says.

"I am not a runt," I whisper, turning my back toward her. "You are a mean giant."

She then digs her fingernail into my shoulder and begins to shake me. "Go to sleep, runt."

With my back still turned away from her, I silently shed tears. I haven't done anything to deserve this. I want to retaliate, but survival mode sets in. Our bunk is a few feet off the floor. If we tussle in the cramped space, I will surely fall to the hard floor and be the victim. I decide then and there to remain still.

I often lie awake at night, trying to analyze the "whys" of life and the actions and reactions I'd observed that day. Tonight, I'm wondering why she felt the need to hurt me. Did I fall asleep and accidentally hit her with my arm or foot? Was she mad because she's been forced to leave someone she loves? Did someone leave her? Whatever the reason for her snarky behavior, the thought of it didn't help soothe me. We all have pity party stories because all of us at Holt either were left or had to leave someone. I don't tell anyone about our ugly encounter, and perhaps because I don't, she leaves me alone. We are able to get through a few more nights before a bed becomes available for her. Soon, like many who come, she leaves for her new life. Thank goodness!

It seems I'm recovering well. I'm also eating well. I'm full all the time, and the usual growling noise from my stomach is now gone. I can never associate Holt Orphanage with hunger or lack as I did Mah San. I'm soldiering on, getting healthier and healthier, and feeling happier and happier. I have not and will never forget Sonyeon, but

I'm adjusting to this new life. I'm mainly grateful for the good food because my skinny legs and arms are filling out, and even though I have no neck, my head is falling into proportion with my size, but my belly remains huge and distended. It makes me look disproportionate. Food is my medicine, and it's the first time in my life I haven't been hungry. Eagerly, I join in singing grace, thanking God for our daily meal. Before every meal, our voices, mine loud and clear, rise in unison—*Nalmada uriege yangshiekeul jooshineun* (For the meal you provide for us daily).

I particularly love breakfast. One snowy morning, I'm holding my bowl for Molly to empty the usual heaping of porridge (oatmeal or Cream of Wheat) that will warm my insides. While spooning the piping hot porridge into my bowl, some of it splatters on the back of my hands. I let out a primal scream as two blobs of hot cereal sear my skin above my index and middle fingers, and my skin begins to balloon. The pain is intense. Crying out loudly, I drop the bowl, porridge splattering all over the table and floor. At the calamity, the other kids stop eating and gasp when they hear my scream. They see the bowl flying across the floor. Molly immediately drops the spoon and runs to the other side of the table where I'm sobbing to comfort me.

"*Tteugeowo. Tteugeowo*" (It's burning. It's burning), I scream, tears streaming down my face. Molly, who is as distraught as I am, whisks me over to the sink and runs my hands under icy cold water to soothe the burn. She puts an antiseptic salve which stings on the wounds. Both my hands inflate into watery mounds that turn into ugly oozing blisters. My ballooning hands scare the kids senseless. They scamper away, insisting I have the cooties. Molly, who wears her emotions on her face, is sullen and distraught the entire day.

My hands now look disfigured, and the other children refuse to play with me. I soon find loneliness as I'm forced to play by myself. The cold from the winter snow, thank goodness, soothes my pain so naturally, I befriend it. I take to nursing my wounds by patting freshly fallen, soft, white snow dust on my bubble-looking hands. Being slippery and all, the snow trips me up. Trying to break my fall, hands first, puts me in an even worse predicament. With my hands fully immersed in the snow, my blisters take a beating. Finally, after a few falls, they bursts, and my deformed hands begin to look somewhat normal though the burns have left ugly scars on both of them. To my joy, my friends return to play, and my life goes on as before.

I'm growing stronger, infinitely healthier, and it seems now it's my turn to get ready to leave Holt. I didn't know when I arrived like the others who'd already left, I, too, was destined to become the "little girl" of some American Christian family. I am *not* happy. I begin to put up quite a fuss. Molly tries to explain the adoption process to me, but I don't care to hear it. Molly, who is just learning Korean, is the first person to give me a no-nonsense, one-on-one, face-to-face, eye contact, heart-to-heart talk. Constantly peppering her Korean with English words, I still understand. What it all means is I'm going to an adoptive family in another country. I don't even know what another country means, so I'm even more unhappy. She assures me I'll be well taken care of there, more so than I have been at the orphanage.

I don't see how that's possible as I love Holt. I'm having mixed feelings—sad ones—because what she is saying inevitably means separation again. I have separation anxiety, but the way she is explaining America is intriguing. As days go by, I'm beginning to look forward to something I can't imagine—a long-lasting, forever family, one that will never leave me or send me away. It's all beginning to sound wonderful. Still, I'm glad when my scheduled December 1957 date to go to the United States comes and goes because I don't have medical clearance. That doesn't deter plans because Molly is now showing me pictures of the couple who will become my new parents.

I inspect the picture intently, my almond eyes narrowing. They don't look anything like me! In fact, they look entirely different from any Koreans I've ever seen, and they don't look like the Holts either. I study each of their features carefully. The lady is stout with a large bosom, quite a departure from the slightness of Koreans. Her skin is darkish brown, even darker than mine, and her nostrils flare into a broad nose. Her eyes are double lidded and seem small for the rest of her face. Her hair is swept back from her face and piled on top of her head. Though unique to my eyes, she is pretty. The man is of a beige-ish complexion. He, too, has a broad nose, but the tip points downward. His eyes with clearly defined brows and his mouth are proportionate to his face. His hair is wavy, and he has what seems like huge ears to me. I've never seen anyone who looks like the brown woman, but the man looks a lot like the brown soldiers I spotted with Sonyeon at the village market.

Molly excitedly tells me my new family is very eager to have me and that when I arrive in America, they'll have a coat and dolls waiting for me under their Christmas tree. I smile reassuringly for Molly's sake, but I'm not upset that health-wise, I still can't travel. Now I'll have more time with the Holts. Every time I fail my TB clearance and physical is a good day because it postpones my departure. In January 1958, to my disappointment, I'm finally cleared to travel. Yet, I'm aware of something else creeping in, a curiosity. So, I find myself emotionally conflicted between the despair of leaving the Holts and the intrigue of what's ahead. I'm listed along with ninety-nine other children to go to the United States—the land of the free and home of the brave. I suppose I should be glad humanity exists for war orphans, but I'm not, and as I would come to find, neither are the people of my color in the United States of America.

# CHAPTER THREE

## Foreign Land: Coming to America

I'm leaving Korea, and I'm taking with me a most unforgettable memory, the porridge scars on my hands. They were prevalent enough to be listed as distinctive marks on my naturalization documents when it arrived later. Instead of associating them with pain, they now remind me of my sweet and loving times with the Holts and of my gratitude for their orphanage.

On the day of our travel, we arrive at Gimpo International Airport and board a big plane. The DC 9 charter, outfitted with wicker baskets holding four babies in each, takes up half the cabin space, making the aircraft seem more like a cargo plane. More space is eaten up by the rows and rows of cardboard boxes in the aisle holding formula, diapers, clothing, and other necessities, making moving around difficult. At first, since Korean adoption is about race-based evacuation, most of us on board are mixed-race G.I. babies. There are about a hundred of us crammed in between all the supplies on the flight. We are going to America, wherever that is.

As soon as we settle on board, there seems to be constant yelping from a crying baby or whiny toddler in need of care. The weaker wails, mere whimpers, are coming from the sickly babies. Molly and the other six caretakers on board, including *hal-abeoji* and Mr. Kim, are continually attending to the brood—changing diapers, feeding the hungry, and sticking pacifiers in mouths to stop never-ending crying. I'm one of the older kids. I get to sit by the window, and as always, I'm in observation mode. Clueless about what happens next, I feel okay about it all as *hal-abeoji* and Molly are on board.

A few hours in, everyone is complaining about something. Children are pulling and poking at their clogged ears, probably to relieve tickling, painful sensation from air pressure or maybe even from ear infections, that register their complaints with loud squeals. The flight crew is gagging at the smell of soiled diapers and spoiled milk piling up. Adult caretakers, working themselves to the bone, are also voicing their displeasure at the loud noise the plane is making.

At some point mid-flight, there seems to be more chaos than usual. The plane, it is announced, is going to make an unplanned stop in Wake Island, a tiny island in the Pacific Ocean between Guam and Honolulu. I can't imagine us picking up more passengers as we did on the way from Mah San. There is just no room. The plane lands, but initially, we do not get off. *Hal-abeoji* spends a lot of time talking back and forth with the crew and getting on and off the plane.

Finally, women from the island arrive to escort the older children off the plane. They entertain us with songs, dance, and play. Some ladies also become angels to Molly as they help clean and feed the babies on the plane, giving the six caretakers a short break. Back on the plane, I help Molly a little, too, by holding and feeding a baby. Amid it all, voices rise in laughter and song. One of the songs is my favorite, *Nabiya, Nabiya*—Butterfly, Butterfly—so I join in. A welcomed joy and a peaceful lull is on the plane. It's been more than twenty-four hours since we left Korea. We are on the plane for what seems like forever, and though I'm doggedly tired, I'm fighting sleep for fear of missing out on anything I can see or hear. Let's just say I'm the curious rather than nosey type, as being aware of my surroundings serves me well. Still, I'm exhausted, and no matter how hard I try to stay awake by constantly dangling my feet, which can't reach the floor, my mind finally gives in to what my body is begging for: sleep. My sleep is fitful.

I've carried the plane's goings-on into my dreams and dream of Molly tending to babies, with me as her assistant.

Finally, the plane takes off again, and everyone is glad to be in the air. In limbo, between heaven and earth, one of the babies chooses heaven instead of America. Molly is distressed and crying because the baby will need to be left at the Hawaiian airport. Our second day in flight, late in the evening, we arrive in Hawaii. A new level of chaos arises as we shuttle off the plane and make our way to a big building. It's January 30, 1958, according to the port of entry stamp in my U.S. passport.

We line up in a big building. It will be a long process because everyone has to clear immigration and get a medical checkup. A lot of what's happening is going over my head, so I follow directions. When we leave the people checking us in, we are fed and given a chance to freshen up. I put on my new dress—my finest ware since I want to look my very best for this last leg of the trip to San Francisco, California, where my new family awaits. With all that is going on, still a child, I'm fascinated by the entire journey. I'm looking out the window of the *pangy* (plane), wondering what the white fluffy stuff outside could be. The multi-stop itinerary, which is not in our original plan, has made everyone tired and crabby. I want to ask questions, but I don't. As we approach San Francisco, an indescribable feeling overwhelms me. My life is about to change. To what? Gripping fear rises when I try to face the reality that *hal-abeoji* and Molly will be leaving me, just like Sonyeon had done. Tears prickle my eyes. I want to cry, but Sonyeon's face looms.

"You need to be brave." I can hear him saying this in my head. So, I don't cry and do nothing to make my new parents apprehensive. Back at the orphanage, Molly told me how much this family is looking forward to meeting me, and she'd even made me feel special by saying out of all the children the couple had seen, they'd chosen me. I tuck in my quivering lips and let my anticipation take over the scared girl who's looking backward at loss and forward to receiving her new doll, a new coat, and new parents.

Seventy-two hours after we leave Korea, the plane touches down in San Francisco. I'm wearing my pretty white-and-green floral dress, which has been made for me by my new father's sister. My wavy, shoulder-length hair is neatly combed. I proudly straighten my shoulders as I get ready to leave the plane after the long ride to freedom. My white shoes are way too big. Fortunately, with my socks and them snugly knotted and tied to my feet, I don't wobble as I descend the ramp. I feel my toes gripping the big, ugly, high-top shoes, but they don't come off. I go down the stairway that's been pushed up to the plane's open door. By the time I reach the bottom and step onto the vast concrete ground, I'm ready to look forward to a new life and to step into my destiny.

A gaggle of people are here to meet the Holt flight, many photographers and reporters among the adoptive parents from all over the U.S. David Kim's book, *Who Will Answer* best sums up our arrival.

> *The scene at the airport—the families waiting at the end of the gangway as me and Holt brought children out of the plane and called out the names of the adoptive parents [was amazing]. Something unprecedented in the history of human kinship was occurring—parents were meeting children for the first time who were at once strangers and family—and no one was sure what to expect. I was astounded to see women running forward when their names were called, crying, "My baby. My baby!" Each time a child was handed over to his or her new parents, everyone watching clapped and shouted for joy.*

I surely don't know what to expect. There is massive news coverage about our arrival. In the mob of clamoring people, reporters are flashing away at new parents and their new children. I crane my neck to see all that's going on as one of the caregivers goes off to find the dead baby's expectant parents to break the bad news. I scan the crowd of strange people of all shades and hues and sizes. I've never seen anything like this. I begin looking for the woman and the man in the photo. Mr. Kim is calling out the new parents' names, but Molly seems to know the exact location to hand me over. When she grabs ahold of my hand, I feel secure and fall in step next to her. If only things could stay as they are at the moment, I'd be content. I pray to God that if I can still have Molly by my side, even with a new, loving family a few steps away waiting to welcome me with a coat and doll, I'd be the best girl ever.

Seeing my adoptive parent, Molly stops, and we come face-to-face with the stranger. With Molly's hand being the symbolic baton, she extends my hand and places it into the hand of the lady who looks exactly like her photo. My heart begins racing, and the secure feeling I felt moments before seeps out and disappear into thin air. This exchange is God's will for my life; I remind myself as I rest my hand in the stranger's hand. The man in the photo is not there, but there is a young boy with the lady. "Mrs. Clemmie Henderson," Molly says, smiling. "I recognize you from your picture." Molly begins chatting away with the well-dressed woman, and they are exchanging pleasantries, some of which she speaks to me in Korean so I can understand. I'm scared as I listen to the conversation between my caregivers. My almond-shaped eyes well up with tears that do not fall as I imagine the gist of the conversation. The truth is I, too, am inbetween worlds.

"So, Ms. Henderson, here's the special delivery you've been waiting for." Molly looks down at me.

I'm frightened and sure my large brown pupils are a dead giveaway. Mrs. Henderson has a firm hold on my hand as she bends and greets me with a beautiful smile.

"Bang Sun," Molly says, "this is your mommy."

"Well, hello, Saundra. This is your new name. I'm your mother, and this is your brother, Virgil."

*Who is Saundra?* I'm wondering. Molly, noticing my confusion, explains I have a new name, but I'm still Bang Sun. I've barely landed and, in addition to new parents and a new brother, I have a new name, too? The boy is no Sonyeon. Virgil, tall and lanky, has the same complexion as the woman. He seems to be in his teens. He smiles and waves at me, and I smile and wave back at him. Maybe I'll find a little bit of Sonyeon in him.

Looking at the heavy-set, dark-skinned woman sizing her up and down, my insecurity is setting in. I'm scared of the unknown, wondering what lies ahead for me. Molly, who was speaking both Korean and English before, now switches to speaking only English. I no longer know what's being said to my new mother. I resort to translating the conversation through their body language. I keep looking back and forth from one to the other.

The woman hands the young boy a bag and lets go of my hand. She follows Molly over to a corner where she signs some papers. Afterward, she is handed an envelope with my documents. My attention is focused on the bag in the boy's hand. I'm excited and curious to know what's in it. I'm looking at the skinny boy, and he's staring at me, too. Is it my coat? My doll? Once finished with the business at hand, Molly comes over to me, bends, and looks me in the eyes. She is speaking Korean again.

"Bang Sun," she says softly, "you are going to be loved and grow up to have a wonderful life. We will always love you. Make us proud." She hugs me in tight embrace to say farewell for the last time. I'm clinging to her, and this time tears are streaming down my face. I can't hold them back no matter how hard I try because I know what it feels like when doors close between people I once knew and loved—I don't ever see them again. I'm truly sad. I'm crying for Sonyeon. I'm crying for Molly and *hal-abeoji*. I'm crying for Korea. And, though I don't yet know it, I'm crying for the little girl in a strange land who only days before at the Holt Orphanage is a Korean girl romping freely on its vast grounds beneath the mountains of the morning calm. Now, she's an American walking hand-in-hand with a new mother into a destiny unknown.

Despite all I have endured in my short life, I know I will miss the land of my birth. One thing I feel sure about is that I'll probably be well dressed since the woman walking next to me is impeccable. My old home far away, my new home on the other side of the door that looms before me, I tighten my grip on the woman's hand, straighten my spine and begin the walk into my life in Compton, California.

# CHAPTER FOUR

## Straight into Compton

When Molly leaves, we head outside, me looking backward. Mama lets go of my hand to grab the red bag Virgil is holding. From it, she pulls out a gray wool coat and instructs me to put it on. I slip my arms into the sleeves, noticing the coolness of the lining. Mama seems to know that this will distract me from the despair of leaving Molly behind and is her way of keeping me from looking backward. Squarely, she is bringing me into her world. I look up at Mama and smile. It isn't hard for me to do because I'm visualizing Molly telling me my new mommy would have a coat for me, and she was right.

I smile again at Mama, who is saying something, but I don't understand her words. She reaches into the red bag again, and I'm drawn into the excitement of the moment. Her distraction has worked. What will be next? Mama is swishing around inside the bag, which is annoying. After what feels like an eternity, she pulls out a white doll with reddish-brown hair and brown eyes. The doll has on a red velvet top and a shiny black, red and white plaid skirt. It has on nylon ankle socks like mine and black shoes. My eyes light up. I'm wondering if she will hand me the doll or if I need to reach for it. I reach out just as she lowers the doll into my hands. It's love at first sight. I name my new doll Molly. Holding it close to my chest, I let the indescribable feeling welling up wash over me. For the first time in my life, I own things that are all mine—a doll and a coat. It feels good. Everything Molly had told me is coming to pass, so instead of fearing the unknown, I'm now eager to find out what lies ahead. The future indeed could well be an adventure.

All I notice when I step outside the airport is the jaw-dropping San Francisco landscape. I've never seen anything like this in Korea. It's not one of shattered structures, dirt roads, and swirling dust, but one of new buildings jutting into the sky. My head is spinning, trying to take it all in. As with my upgrade from Mah San Orphanage to Holt Orphanage, I give this place five stars, and once again, I feel chosen to be in America. Proudly, I walk alongside Mama and Virgil as we climb into the vehicle that will take us from the San Francisco airport to the San Jose train station. There are no ox-drawn carts, but there are many auto-motors like the ones the soldiers drove zipping along on long stretches of the paved roads of San Francisco.

By the time we arrive at the train station, I'm in awe. The station is vast. The floor and walls are marble. Mama goes over to the ticket counter while Virgil and I sit in the waiting area. I'm overwhelmed, not just by the high-back seats, but by the pristine look of everything, so my head keeps turning in all directions taking in everything I can. Mama joins us after buying our tickets, and we wait. I hear the train before I see it. My legs are double time dangling with anticipation. This train has a longer *woot woot* sound than those in Korea, and I'm ready to see it. We gather our belongings and exit the pretty building.

On the platform, ready to board the train, I'm even more mesmerized by the long shiny object approaching. It looks like it has a face! This train is modern, nothing like the rickety one in Korea. One of the things I did back home with Sonyeon was to count train cars while patting my hand rhythmically. One pat for each car. This train is so long I can't see the end and, worse, I can't count past twenty. All aboard, Mama sits by the window and pats the space next to her for me to sit. I take a seat, but I'm not happy. I want to sit by the window as I had done on my first train and plane ride. I want to continue my window watching of the changing scenery. On the seat next to me is the red bag with my doll, but I don't want to play with it. I want to sit by the window.

The train begins moving. I soon figure out that if I stand up, I can see the scenery from either side of the windows. I'm now stepping all over Mama trying to see, and she soon gets the hint to trade seats. I begin to relax and enjoy the window view. This train is so much smoother than the one in Korea. I clearly remember that rickety train ride to Seoul, where my brain had literally rattled. The new landscape we're passing has some similarities to Korea—mossy mountains and frothy ocean waves. This is comforting. Along the way, we pass many cows heartily chewing away. They are far fatter than any I've ever seen. I wonder if they are chewing gum.

When Mama gets up for any reason, she tells Virgil, sitting opposite us, to keep an eye on me. I finally take stock of the boy in front of me because he's looking at me, and I'm looking at him, too. He is the color of chocolate milk, tall, skinny, and handsome. His wavy hair is cut in a style exposing his protruding ears. His nose is not broad like Mama's, but it's very pointy with flaring nostrils. I blurt out something, and it isn't in English. When our eyes meet, he gives an awkward teenage shrug. I interpret what he is saying as "I don't know what you're saying. I'm just trying to be nice here." He then looks away and goes off into his own world. I don't try to say anything else. Instead, I awaken my sleeping doll. She, like Molly, understands me, and she's who I'll converse with from now on.

"Are you hungry?" Mama asks, acting out the question. I inhale the aroma, feeling for the first time the low rumble in my belly. I nod. We trundle off to the dining car, and Mama pulls out the notes Molly has given her. My favorite part of the train is the diner car. The wonderful smell of something delicious is wafting through to our car, making us hungrier. Mama scans the note before giving the brown-skinned man in a white apron our order. He is very friendly as he makes notes on his pad. When I'm hungry and waiting, time moves so slowly. Mama fills it by trying to connect with me. She is speaking slowly. Pointing to herself, she says, "Mama," and pointing to the boy across from her, she says, "Virgil." She touches her lips, indicating I should say what she'd just said. I quickly oblige, parroting with ease what she'd said. This exercise is my first English lesson. I'm used to hearing English words like *Jesus* and *God* from *hal-abeoji* and Molly, but I know very little about other English words. Still, I'm a pretty bright kid with a talent for observation, mimicking, and processing information.

Finally, the brown man with the white apron returns with our food. Mama heaps a spoonful and starts blowing on the spoon. I want her to hurry up because I'm starving and because I've been patient my whole short life. Now I'm impatient to taste something new. Mama finally puts the spoon in my mouth.

*No, she didn't. This cannot be porridge that she's put in my mouth! Does she not realize how I got these scars on my hands?*

In utter disgust, I spit porridge all over her fancy dress, some spewing on my beautiful dress. *That'll fix her,* I think. *I never want to eat porridge in this life ever again.* Virgil laughs at the face I'm making while Mama is quickly trying to wipe up the sticky poridge. Virgil obviously can relate. Unexpectedly, I see Sonyeon in Virgil when he breaks off a little bit of his sandwich and puts it in my mouth. I decide then and there I like Virgil, and I like what he is eating. Munching on the more delicious food Virgil shares confirms for Mama I am *really* ready to eat.

Mama orders again. This time she orders what Virgil is eating, and I get my first taste of an all-American hamburger with French fries and a Coke. It's yummy. I love the contrast of the warm beef next to the cool lettuce, tomato, and pickle. Then there is the distinct taste from creamy sauces, one white, one red, and one yellow on each side of the bun. Now, I'm feeling like someone really special, and I'm feeling very American. I'm satisfied as we make our way back to our compartment. My full belly, the warmth from the sunlight pouring through the window, and the rhythmic sound of the train finally lull me to sleep. When Mama wakes me, my head is lying on her soft, thick thigh. It's the best pillow I'd ever had. I also realize the train is no longer moving. Mama tells Virgil to collect my red bag and other stuff as she puts her purse over her shoulder. Grabbing my hand, we make our way to leave.

A man is at the door helping people off the train. When he gets to us, he winks at Mama, smiles, and proceeds to pick me up. He holds me in an embrace a few seconds longer than I think necessary. I get the feeling he is a loving man like *hal-abeoji.* Being in his arms is okay with me, but I'm concerned when he doesn't put me down after a while longer. The elevation of my heartbeat reflects my anxiety, and all of a sudden, I'm wondering what is happening. Then I hear him say, "My baby, my baby." As he hurriedly moves away from the train, his hat falls off, and I can now see he is the man in the picture Molly had shown me who would become my *Abeoji.*

*This is my daddy.*

At the moment of realization, I put my arms around his neck. Daddy's enthusiastic greeting and his outward display of affection feel like a royal welcome to America. Was he doting on little ole me? Is this for real? It feels so different from Mama's calm and controlled welcome. With mutual adoration, I seal and approve the day the new father meets his new daughter with a kiss to his cheek. I had thought because Daddy was helping people off the train that he was a porter, but Daddy is not a train porter at all; he's a mail and baggage handler at Union Station. It turns out he's made a special request to his boss to be there to meet his little girl. Because Daddy is, apparently being a consistent and hard worker for the station, his boss is only too happy to grant his wish for him to meet us and even gives him the rest of the day off to take us home.

We load into Daddy's green four-door car at the Los Angeles Union Station and begin our journey over bumpy train tracks to my new home. About thirty minutes later, the car slows and stops in front of a light yellowish house nestled between two tall pine trees. It has a big picture window and a well-kept lawn. We've arrived at 1409 Piru Street, Compton, California—my new home.

Daddy unloads the car as Mama and I climb the two porch steps leading to the door. There are two women and a little girl in the living room when we enter—my dad's sister, Aunt Francis (the one who made my arrival dress), her daughter Faye and Faye's daughter Ronda. They're here from Dallas, Texas, to welcome me and to stay for several weeks to experience the excitement of Mama and Daddy getting a little girl. They greet me enthusiastically, and I notice they have a different accent from my new mother. Their slower drawl is more pronounced. None of it matters since I can't understand them anyway. They say something, and I say something, but we are at a loss. What I do understand is their universal language of love—warm smiles, eyes that crinkle with laughter, and affectionate touches.

My new family seems to like to laugh a lot. When they laugh, their bellies move up and down, and this, in turn, makes me laugh. The one thing everyone seems to have in common is they're not skinny people. No one appears starved or withered like us Koreans. It's close to dinnertime by the time we get home, and the visiting family has prepared a meal for our arrival. Mama helps me to wash up before we sit down to dinner. Aunt Francis and Faye have made fried fish, which they serve with bread and a salad. My taste buds are excited all over again. So much food! So far, it's all been great—the burger that is. From what I tasted on the train, American food is more seasoned and flavorful than anything I've had in Korea. I'm hoping this cornmeal-breaded fish lives up to my expectation. I don't recall eating much fried food at home except the grasshoppers, and they were sautéed. With so many mouths to feed at the orphanage, bulk cooking, which often entailed dumping cans upon cans of food into a pot and heating them, was the norm. I'm by no means complaining because that food saved my life, and the loving caretakers were doing their best with the resources available. The fish does not disappoint. Now I'm sure of two things about living in Compton: I will be well dressed and will not go hungry. The warm fellowship in the kitchen over dinner makes me feel welcomed.

I'm tired from the long trip, but curiosity about my new surroundings won't allow my body to give in to it, and I'm not a nap taker to begin with, so I'll wait until bedtime to sleep. Ronda, Faye's daughter, wants to play. She is as tall as I am at five, even though she's two years younger. I let her play with my doll Molly while I check out the house. It surprises me I think the house is small, but understandably so as the Holt Orphanage is humongous in comparison. I realize the difference is that the twelve hundred square foot, three-bedroom, one-bath home is spacious for seven people to move around, but chock full of heavy furniture, it's hard to navigate. At Mah San, where it was about floor space, not bed space, this place could sleep way more people and in ultra-luxurious style too since the floors are carpeted. That night, I will share a bed with Ronda, but the carpeted floor would have been just fine with me. I give this place a five-star rating.

I still can't believe it's been only a few days since I've left Seoul. There, at this time of the year, I would've been bundled up from the freezing temperatures and piled up snow while playing, speaking to people whose language I understood—and they, likewise, understood me. Now I'm, six thousand miles away in a place called Compton in seventy-degree weather with six people who have no idea who I am or what I'm saying. For some reason, they find my language amusing and mock or mimic my intonations. While funny at times to them, it is never funny to me. I soon learn out of necessity to be understood. I begin communicating with my new family by playing charades.

My first successful communiqué is a bathroom happening. I'm in the bathroom doing a necessity. When I'm finished and look in the toilet, I see something moving. All the adults are in the kitchen, so I rush in and begin what amounts to making grunting noises to get their attention. I need my family to understand what I'm trying to say, so I act out what just happened in the bathroom. When they realize I'm purposely making these horrid straining noises, they begin to focus on what I'm doing. I stand, touch my behind, then squat again, again making a god-awful straining noise. I get up from the squat, then turn and point to the imaginary toilet from which I'd just risen. I then take my right index finger and make it parallel to the kitchen table, repeatedly bending and straightening it. I wiggle my finger around, continuing to bend and straighten it as it travels along the table. A light goes on, and I believe they get it. Mama hoists herself up and goes to the bathroom to confirm.

Then and there, on my first attempt, I've successfully communicated that I've passed a worm. I'd passed worms many times before, but I had never seen them wiggle around in a toilet, and I always tell someone if I do. Mama doesn't seem fazed by it, so I guess they know about worms in America too. She simply administers a laxative called Black Draught, which must have worked because I don't have to perform the worm scene ever again. Later, when she made my appointment for the doctor to check the shadows on my lungs, she mentions I passed a worm. The doctor, too, thinks I'm fine.

My second attempt at communicating is another bathroom incident. Standing on my tippy toes trying to reach the sink to wash my hands, I notice a glass on the ledge filled with water. It has something in it that startles and frightens me. I run to the kitchen, the usual congregation spot in the house. Since the grunting noise worked the last time, I do it again. Everyone stops and is now trying to understand my new gyrations. Laughing, they seem entertained by my superb acting skills, and I take center stage. I like commanding this attention. I point to the glass on the table, then point to my teeth, then back to the glass. This time it's not as easy for them to decipher my charade. I keep pointing to the glass, pretending to pull my teeth out of my mouth. It is then that I hear laughter. It's my dad's sister, Aunt Francis, who is chuckling away, having solved the mystery no one else seems able to. Aunt Francis disappears into the bathroom, and when she returns, she is holding the glass jar. The evidence is right there for all to see.

Everyone laughs so hard, Aunt Francis heartier than the rest. I see her sunken top lip and evidence of her missing teeth. The teeth in the glass are there to be cleaned.

I've done it again.

I begin to appreciate the power of nonverbal communication, which becomes the meeting point of understanding between the East (me) and the West (family). I'm now feeling emboldened about making my thoughts known through action. Since my arrival, my mother has forever been calling me Saundra or Sandy, and I don't like it one bit. One day I adamantly tell her, "*Nae ileum-eun Saundra anibnida. Je ileum-eun Chang Bang Sun, ibnida!*" *(I am NOT Saundra; I am Chang Bang Sun!)* It seems I've inherited the dogged stoicism and proud heritage of my five-thousand-year-old culture and make it known; I'm proud of my name. Under Mama's persistence, my bravado quickly fades, however. She eventually wins the battle of names, so *Chang Bang Sun* becomes Saundra Henderson.

After our Texas company leaves, Mama focuses on helping me learn my new language. One of the things I learn by mixing with other adoptees who are also learning English is that everybody in the adoption community knows the story of Harry and Bertha Holt. Mama says I'm in America because of wonderful people like the Holts who are changing so many destinies because of the values they hold and their humanity. Mama hadn't met the Holts except for Molly when I arrived in San Francisco. Still, she'd come to know of their cause through the network of Christian humanitarians of which Dr. Hampton Hawes, Sr., a minister of the Westminster Presbyterian Church in Los Angeles, is one. Probably a sympathizer, as his son served in the U.S. Army from 1952 to 1954, he spearheaded the identification of many Black adoptive parents in California, even with his personal crisis brewing the same year I arrived. His son, the legendary "great" jazz pianist of California, Hampton Hawes, Jr., had been arrested in something called a sting operation that targeted him as a heroin addict who might squeal on his sources. Later pardoned by President John F. Kennedy, he never gave the names of the dealers they were after.

Along with Reverend Hawes, *hal-abeoji* Holt became a beacon in the lives of Black mixed-raced orphans, so duly noted in a pictorial spread in *Sepia* magazine (circa February 1959) about the new Black parents and their adoptees. I am one of the kids featured in this article. Several months of concentrated lessons with Mama, and I *am* learning English. I'm also picking up the language from day-to-day experiential learning. Unintentionally, I seem to provide daily comic relief for the family as I learn to speak the language of the West. Most of my learning is rote by repeating phrases and sentences after Mama.

"Saundra," Mama would say, "when you meet someone, say Hello, Ms. So-in-so." I, in turn, would repeat verbatim what she said, so when I'd meet Ms. Davis, I'd say, "Hello, Ms. So-in-so." I'm thoroughly confused about whether to say hello to Ms. Davis or Ms. So-in-so and would soon find out once my ears got more attuned to English that Mama was saying Ms. So-and-So as a fill in the blank with the real name.

In September 1958, the same year I arrive from Korea, I begin my public-school education. I enter El Segundo Elementary School as a kindergartener in Ms. Mary's class. Mama thinks school is too far (a mile away) for me to walk, so she takes me there in her car. Little does she know Sonyeon and I would walk ten times that much in a day. When late, Virgil would cop a ride with us to Willowbrook Junior High, which was nearly a mile and a half away, but usually Virgil preferred to walk to school with his friend Ronnie who lived down the street. Most of the kids at my school are brown like me. There are a few Hispanics and Whites, but they all speak English.

Able to understand a little more after Mama's language drills, I'm still feeling insecure as I don't understand all the words the teacher and the kids are saying. I listen intently and observe everything around me in hopes of becoming more proficient and functional in English. Because I struggle to understand, I'm often distracted and am fascinated by the kids who get to sit in the corner facing the wall. The corner seems novel since only a few kids get chosen for this special space. Like Holt, I want to be chosen, so I observe and listen to everything they do and say. One boy in the class keeps jumping up and down from his seat—a lot. He gets sent to sit in the corner. I decide to jump up and down and move around in the classroom, mimicking his actions. Finally, my teacher says, "Saundra" and points to the corner. I feel accomplished, but that afternoon, she calls my mother to tell her about my behavior in class. My mother tells her I'm still learning English, so I get leniency. From this point on, however, both my teacher and Mama begin drumming into my head the corner is not a reward but punishment for bad behavior. They tell me the children who get banished to the corner will likely get spankings when they get home. I no longer jump up and down. Little by little, I'm truly becoming bilingual. I'm absorbing English at lightning speed. I also still speak fluent Korean, and it's a good thing.

Because of this, my parents often get calls from a lady connected with the Holt Orphanage asking if I might be allowed to go to the Los Angeles Airport to meet newly arriving orphans. Children, no doubt, who are as scared as I was when I arrived. They are about to meet strangers who will become their parents, and I can ease their burdens. I love doing this as it's a good way to connect with my past. Reflecting on the feelings I had when I first arrived, I often get sad. I speak Korean to the new kids and sometimes sing songs we sang at Holt. At the sound of our familiar language and culture, their eyes become less terrified. Being a welcome ambassador, providing a little comfort to the frightened children in a foreign land, emotionally lifts me.

Though I try not to dwell on my melancholy, the truth is there are days when I'm overcome by incredible sadness, even with my new family. Days when I'm longing for my homeland and the people I left behind. I don't know how to explain my feelings or what to do with them, and I certainly don't want to be ungrateful or complain to Mama, so I tamper them down.

Rainy days especially for some unknown reason, seem to make me more down than usual, and I go to my bedroom, sit on the twin bed facing the front window, and watch the rainfall. Almost immediately, I find myself singing the Korean rain song *biya biya ojimara*, the equivalent of the English nursery rhyme "Rain, Rain Go Away." For whatever reason, the rain triggers pent-up feelings, and a faucet of unresolved emotions flood my mind. I need closure, but I don't know how to open up. Was it because Sonyeon and I might have skipped to the rain's pitter-patter on the ocean? Was it Korea or Molly that I missed, or was it the fear that my memory is fading? With each passing day, even Sonyeon is fading. I can no longer see his face or remember his real name. To my family's credit—one I wholeheartedly appreciate is—their readiness to acknowledge my melancholy. Graciously, they allow me the alone time I need for resolve. Outside, I would often hear them saying, "She's having one of her moments. She'll be alright later." I'm glad for the airport invitations because I need these connections as much as the new adoptees need me, and it may be one way to help my healing.

After about two years, my sad spells lessen, maybe because my parents allow me to participate in the Korean Adoptee reunion picnics held in Compton at Cressey Park. I take to calling Mama the Black Moses because, like Harriet Tubman, she has a pipeline to Ms. M, the White lady who lives in Paramount and who is responsible for connecting many of the parents with Holt adoptees. These picnics celebrate us as adoptees and how well we're doing, demonstrates the fruits of our parents' labor. Seeing happy children with parents who love them is its own reward. All the mixed Korean children (mostly Black Koreans) in Los Angeles and their new families get together. While our parents fellowship, we children play, sing songs like *Nabiya,* speak in our language, and look forward to eating Korean food when we later come together for a meal. Our potluck includes American fare such as hot dogs, hamburgers, chips, and fried chicken, but most of the kids wait for the traditional Korean food provided. We have *kimchi; japchae,* my favorite noodle dish; *bulgogi; kalbi;* and of course, lots of rice. One of the foods we have in common with our Black families is potato salad, which is similar to the one we eat in Korea. I'm becoming less isolated because I have a chance to play with Brenda, Sheila, Charlotte, Pam, Robert, and many others whom Mama keeps in touch with through their parents.

Most of the adoptees who'd come as babies were young enough to be fully Americanized, though the rest of us Koreans can't relate. At one of the picnics, I see my bunk bed torturer from Holt, and even though she would have been a better link to my past, I avoid her. She doesn't say anything to me, either. The last reunion I attend is very special because we have a surprise guest: *hal-abeoji* Holt in person! He's come to our reunion to see his children—us—and wants to know how we've adjusted. He is pleased with what he sees. When the children finally realize *hal-abeoji* is in our midst, like a knee-jerk reaction, we all run to him, screaming, pulling, and grabbing at him as we did at the orphanage. "*Hal-abeoji* Holt is here!" we merrily chant.

So happy to see him, I rush over and hug him tightly. Once the orphan welcome wagon has settled, our parents organize us for a photo op with *hal-aboeji.* It's like seeing Santa. After the group picture, we line up for one-on-one photo with our beloved *hal-abeoji.* As always, wherever *hal-abeoji* goes, there is press, and our group photo makes the local paper. To my delight, my visit with *hal-abeoji* dosen't end at the park because later, he visits with me and another boy, RJ, at our homes in Compton. As I would do back at the orphanage, I sit in *hal-abeoji*'s lap, joyful to be in his presence once again. Now that I know a lot of English, I can proudly answer the questions he asks.

"Bang Sun, how are you feeling?"

My real name is music to my ears. "I'm fine," I tell him.

He already knows Mama didn't have to send me to the Denver sanitarium because of the tuberculosis exposure. Mama tells him she'd written evangelist Oral Roberts to pray for my healing, which is confirmed when the doctor says I have a clean bill of health. He and Mama echo how great God is.

"So, what do you like about America the most?" *hal-abeoji* asks me.

"The food and school," I tell him, and he laughs and hugs me. It is such a special moment. With the continuity from my old life, I feel content, and it reassures me that people don't have to be gone forever. I'm a little less sad after seeing him. I feel a connection to my home, and I'm chatting nonstop about Korea. That, however, will be the last time I see my *hal-abeoji.* Mama clips the newspaper picture and places it in the photo album. She also orders a book from the Holts, *The Seed from the East*, from which I learn more about them from *Halmeoni (Grandma)* Holt, who shares their story.

> *The Holts were successful farmers from Creswell, Oregon, a rural town of 700 people, some thirteen miles south of Eugene. Harry and Bertha Holt, along with their five daughters and one son, were living the American dream. Unbeknownst to them as they sat in a Eugene High School gymnasium one fall evening to watch a Korean War documentary was that thereafter, their life would drastically change. When the lights dimmed and the screen lit up with the World Vision film, the horrific images of the plight of the children of war would haunt them. So moved, the Holts, grateful for how blessed they were, immediately took action to support the less fortunate. The family collectively committed to financially sponsoring thirteen orphans. They began sending monthly monetary contributions to the orphanages, in addition to writing pen pal letters to kids and assembling care packages. Devout Christians giving money was certainly a Christianly thing to do, but the Holts felt they could do much more. For days and weeks, they pondered just how else they could be of service to God's work. Harry prayed*

*for an answer. Their answer; they could adopt eight of Korea's untouchables—mixed-raced children.*

*So, in 1955, the Holts petitioned the U.S. government for an exception to existing Refugee Relief Act rules that limited adoption to two children per family. While waiting out the "red tape," Harry journeyed to war-torn Korea in search of eight children who could become Holts. Finally, after what seemed forever, word came down that by a special act of Congress, the Holt Bill had been successfully passed, amending the Refugee Relief Act. Joyous as they were to fulfill their mission of becoming parents to now fourteen children, Harry could not shake the grief he felt for the children he'd seen, many whom, because of their circumstances, had succumbed to death. Having witnessed the atrocities, Harry pondered what could be done for the thousands more he'd left behind.*

*As fate would have it, there was national coverage of the Holts compassionate acts for the children of war. The publicity sparked nationwide interest, and requests began flooding in from families all over the U.S. who wanted to adopt Korean war children. This was the moment when Harry and Bertha realized their real purpose, to find homes for the impoverished children with other American Christian families. The Holts' lifelong passion and compassion eventually morphed into them becoming the pioneers of international adoption. To house the children waiting for adoption, the Holts built Hyo Chang Park, the first Holt Orphanage in Korea. The entire family was involved in orphan life, but it was Molly Holt, one of their daughters, who moved to Korea after graduating from nursing school to eventually become the lifelong caretaker of the orphanage that seeded miracles in the lives of abandoned children. It was then that the Holts honed the motto of their Christian fundamentalist mission, "Every Child Deserves a Home."*

*Existing orphanages in Korea before the war were for Korean orphans. The Holt Adoption Program focused on mixed-race children, though later, there were full-blooded Korean orphans at Hyo Chang Park. For* hal-abeoji *(Grandfather Holt), suffering was suffering. Though President Truman's order to integrate the armed services came down in 1948, partly because of the Tuskegee Airmen's success and admiration, it was largely ignored. Racism was very much prevalent in the Korean War, and the inescapable, rampant prejudice against people of color in America spilled over to Korea's battlefields. Its effect would come to rain down disproportionately on children born to black fathers.*

*Many families in the Holts' immediate pipeline were White, and race relations in the U.S. in 1958, tenuous. Relying on proxy adoptions, the Holts' only requirements for adoptive parents were that they were Christians and could pay the children's airfare. However, White families who would adopt "white mixed G.I. babies" were reluctant to consider black-Korean adoptees. The Holts then began looking and praying for ways to spur interest in the adoption of black "G.I." children.*

*Creating a faith-based specialty program, Harry and Bertha began working with a network of Black Christian families across the nation. Holts' organization relied heavily on the Black clergy to get the word out about the hard-to-place children. Communiques such as the Adoption Resource Exchanges and letters proved effective in spreading the word. Additionally, they published a monthly listing of the "hard-to-place" children that was circulated to the congregations.*

*Weathering the constant criticism from naysayers like the policy-making Welfare League of America for what they called the Holts' willy-nilly adoption practices proved a challenge. In 1960, the Holt organization was forced to comply with standard adoption procedures, making it harder, if not impossible, for children of color to find loving homes.*

After *halabeoji*'s visit, now fluent in English, I want to share Korea's memories with Mama. I tell her about the beautiful mountains and the frothy sea; about eating sea snails and grasshoppers with a boy I called Soneyon—my protector by the sea; about the lady with red lipstick and about all the dung in the streets, which I hated. When Mama and I go to the store, I point to eggplants like the ones I'd seen in the village market in Korea. I ask her to buy them, but she doesn't.

"Saundra," Mama always says when she's serious with me, "you can't possibly remember this stuff. You were too young."

The day of reckoning comes when my mother goes to a gathering of mothers who'd gone to Korea to pick up their adopted children. They'd made a film about their experience, and they were showing it at the local community center. The film corroborated many of the stories I've told Mama about life in Korea, just the way I'd described it, so she stops telling me I was too young to remember. Sharing and talking about my memories is my way of not forgetting something I want to hold on to forever. Soon, however, our picnic outings stop. Months later, I find that my language and some of my memories' details are indeed fading.

Then something miraculous happens in 1960. It becomes a big, bright spot in my life when my parents adopt another little girl from Korea. I now have an American brother and a sister who, like me, is Korean. My brother, Virgil, eight years older than me, is fifteen, so the age gap doesn't make him playmate friendly. My new sister is two years younger, so I get to be a big sister. However, for some unknown reason, Mama changes her age to be four years behind me, so instead of being five, Mama makes her three. Far more mature than her new age suggests, this move would prove a detriment to her because she'd long learned to be sassy. Supposedly, as Mama tells it, the doctor, after looking at her teeth, said she is of a younger age. I'll bet the real reason is that Mama wants to have someone to keep her company at home, especially since I went right into school when I came to America. Mama wants a baby, baby.

My new sister's name is *Mi Kyung*. Just as Mama had renamed me, together, we rename my little sister Loretta. Why? Because we'd watched an episode of *The Loretta Young Show* in which she and actor Dean Jagger portrayed the life of Harry and Bertha Holt. I affectionately nicknamed her Lolo. I, in turn, want to be called LaLa. Somehow that doesn't stick, but Lolo does. Lolo and I are close from the beginning, each other's shadow. Where I go, so does she, even to the bathroom. When I sit on the toilet, she sits on the tub in front of me and vice versa. We just plug our noses if there is a reason. With Lolo's arrival, I'm beginning to feel confident I'll never have to give up on the place of my birth or my language. Something will always connect me. We find comfort in each other, sharing a bond no one else at home can fill—Korea. Any time we're together, you can hear us singing familiar Korean songs. We are continually playing Lolo's Korean leg game, which turns out to be as peppery as Lolo's personality. It is a game where seated on the floor our legs are interlaced; hers then mine, then hers then mine. We sing a familiar Korean song and tap each other's thigh. However, whoever's leg the last beat of the music lands on gets a stingingly slap on the thigh.

When Lolo is adopted, Mama's attention to me is usurped by the spirited Lolo, who has no filters whatsoever. What comes out of her mouth startles and challenges Mama, so to keep us in line and make us know who is the boss, she doles out chores around the house to all us children, but Lolo and I, especially, become handy ladies to Mama. I've concluded that we are handy maids because I'm learning about indentured servants at school and realize I'm one to Mama. Somehow my mind works in cause and effect, so I reason I must have a debt to pay from a previous life because I truly serve my family in every way. From the very beginning, I've become Mama's arms and legs, retrieving anything she needs, be it food or her purse, which is often at arm's distance from her. With Lolo, Mama now has two helpers. When she wants to bribe us, she often says, "I'll give you a nickel if you get so and so for me." Of course, she would never pay us those nickels, which makes Lolo mad initially. In private, my sister and I frequently laugh at Mama's bribes, which we accept as a joke.

As Lolo and I become attuned to American culture and folklore, we begin to include American style games and music in our playtime—handclapping, jump rope, partner dancing, etc. Popular music like The Supremes', *Come See About Me*, is one of our favorites. Lolo and I belt out the lyrics at the top of our lungs. What makes us cute to Mama is not our loud, strained voices but the made-up lyrics we sing with enthusiasm to the songs. "No pizza, I find 'til you come back and be mine." Mama laughs at us, and when her friends come over, she makes us put on a showcase for them. We are obviously comic relief because when Lolo and I sing, they fall out laughing. Another favorite is when we'd hold hands and rhythmically move back and forth as we sway our hips to nonsense lyrics like *This away, Valerie, Valerie, Valerie, this away, Valerie all day long. Oh, strut Ms. Suzy, Suzy, Suzy, strut, Ms. Suzy, all day long.*

As a religious family, we are active in our church. Lolo and I get speeches from Mama that she wants us to perform at the Easter Sunday church service. I quickly memorize mine, but Lolo hasn't practiced.

"Lolo, have you memorized your Easter speech yet?"

"No, Mama." Lolo shakes her head.

"I see." Then Mama says, "Sandy and Lolo, can you do the *This away, Valerie song for me*?"

We jump up and get in position because we love doing our showcase. When we got to the part, *Oh, strut, Ms. Suzy, Suzy, Suzy*, we release our hands, and Lolo puts her hands on her hips, steps forward with her left foot, and begins exaggerating her hip movements. Swaying her hips to the left and right, she looks like a hula girl. As soon as

Lolo struts in front of Mama, Mama starts whipping her butt. "You can strut Ms. Suzy, but you can't learn your Easter speech!" It is all a setup. Guess who finally learns their Easter speech?

Lolo's blessing and curse is her bluntness. It seems Mama is whipping Lolo almost daily. Since I am the obedient one, I escape all the whippings. When asked for your opinion, giving it is one thing, but unsolicited advice or off-the-cuff comments can cause regrettable consequences, pain, and hurt in our household. Lolo is forever the opinionated one. Through this, I find out Mama is the sensitive kind and believes children must be children—seen and not heard. One day when Lolo has been in the United States for several months, we all go grocery shopping. Virgil, who is sporting his signature Quo Vadis haircut as I now come to know it—the one that makes his ears stand out—hoists Lolo into the grocery cart seat and pushes her down the aisles behind Mama. Mama stops in the baking goods aisle looking for flour. Next to the flour is the pancake mix. Lolo loudly exclaims, pointing to the Aunt Jemima box, "Mama."

Mama spins around and gives Lolo a look of displeasure. She doesn't appreciate being likened to a slave or a maid who wore rags on her head. Of course, this is an innocent blunder on Lolo's part, and thank goodness Mama forgives her as she is still relatively new to the U.S. Technically, however, there is a resemblance between Aunt Jemima and Mama—face, size, and color. Though forgiven, I get the feeling Mama won't ever forget her sassy child's comment. As Lolo becomes Americanized and verbal, it's evident that bluntness and outspokenness are just a part of her character.

Lolo especially loves watching cartoons and kid TV shows. One afternoon, we are watching TV when Mama wakes up from a nap. Making her way to the restroom, she passes by our room. Lolo, noticing Mama's hair is standing straight out on the side of her head from sleeping, belts out, "Mama, you look like Bozo the clown." I cannot hold my laughter because, indeed, Mama's hairstyle looks like Bozo's exaggerated style. When Mama comes out of the bathroom, she is fuming.

"You two, come here," Mama demands.

One by one, we lay over her lap as she uses her heavy hand to wallop our behinds. Lolo is crying, but I don't cry. I'm angry for getting whipped just for laughing at something that is funny and is the truth. It is my one and only whipping. To be sure we understand that discipline is love, both Mama and Daddy often say before a whipping, "This is gonna hurt me more than it hurts you." Daddy rarely beats anyone, but when he does, it's usually Virgil who ocassionally bucks the house rules, but Mama whips Lolo daily. After her corporal punishment, Mama always says to her, "Now show me some teeth." Lolo would flash her best phony smile. After Lolo's smile, she's required to hug Mama. For me, this is duplicitous and the worst part of the discipline. I'm not sure what message I'm supposed to be getting from this. We both hate the phoniness of it, and I often make snide comments under my breath, which gets under Mama's skin. If we were upset with something Mama had said or done to us, she would ask, "You mad? If so, you better scratch your ass and get glad!" This would make us laugh and break the tension.

Since the day I arrived at Piru Street, I've been shouldering many responsibilities as Mama's little helper. By the time Lolo arrives in 1960, I get some help because she, too, becomes Mama's helper, but I can't stand her fakeness anymore. Lolo is forever back talking and being brazen; One day, I say out loud, "I'll be glad when I have kids to be my slaves." That day Mama begins referring to Lolo as "brazen heifer" and me as "sneaky heifer." She laughs at her clever nicknames and makes it into lighthearted banter. All in all, Mama's control over us is firm, and the older we get, the more useful we become for household chores. She, for sure, has no buyer's remorse with us.

Regardless, our family is a blessing to Lolo and me. No matter how hard I'm finding it to turn the page of my adoption, I know my parents have given me a chance for a better life. Still, it's hard to put shattered glass back together. Breaking the bond of attachment to the land of my birth, I will find to be more challenging than I ever imagined though I've now been in America for seven years. At twelve, teenagerhood, never easy for anyone, is lurking. It's a time of cleaving umbilical cords, a time of identity and values solidification, and a time of incubation before adulthood. Will I be able to finally cleave the umbilical cord to the country of my birth?

# CHAPTER FIVE

## Identity Crisis: *Korea* Is a Bad Word

As I get older, our ties to other Korean families are practically nonexistent. Mama maintains some level of communication with the adopted families, but only now and then do we connect and share experiences. One day, out of the blue, when I'm about nine years old and Lolo is five or seven, Mama abruptly announces, "Don't ever speak of Korea again—think of it as a bad word." Lolo and I gasp and look at each other in disbelief. I'm to now fully become Saundra Henderson—Bang Sun relegated to a dusty memory. From this point on, there is a constant grinding away at my ethnicity and identity. Everything I've worked so hard to hold on to over the years must be forgotten. I can't get over how cruel this seems and how confusing for Mama to tell us to erase the truth of our existence without giving an explanation as to why. It's as though Mama is intentionally shattering our glass menagerie, which, once shattered, can never be put back together.

By the time I'm twelve, Korea is moving farther and farther away, and I'm fighting to hold on. I don't know what about my birth country that has disowned me I've held on to all these years, but Mama's edict hurt a lot. I know, irrational or not, that I felt betrayed and broken and tried even harder if silently to hold on to my dual identity. Perhaps Mama feels Lolo and I were too young to understand her reason, but I never accept this because we weren't too young. In all honesty,

I have never been too young to understand hardship. I often ponder if Mama feels left out when Lolo and I bond around our country of birth. I wonder, too, if someone in the Korean parent group offended her. And I wonder if she is simply protecting us from the added burden of racial upheaval sweeping the land.

My angst over changing my name and rejecting my country is not just one of racial identity, but a deep need to preserve my full cultural identity and heritage. Somehow in my mind, discarding my name and forgetting my country seems a betrayal, and I want to keep both. What if my biological mother did name me after the indigenous flower Bong Soong-Ah? How would she ever find me? My Korean name, Bang Sun, dubious as it might be, represents hope and is a tribute to my unknown birthright and parents. In my heart, I want it to live on and on forever. I'm perplexed when I'm told to delete one culture in preference to another. How do I do that when I'm both of those cultures? I need to find my way.

By twelve, I'm appreciating the racial struggle of America. I'm learning history in school, and assimilation is a real part of the American story. The byproduct of mixing cultures forces people to fit into the dominant culture. Though it's likely a natural occurrence, people, though outwardly assimilated, deeply value their culture. The fact that America is considered the melting pot of cultures—in New York City alone, more than 168 languages are spoken—it makes assimilation even more disturbing as America is still resolving deep-seated issues of equality and cultural respect. Back in the day, if one arrived at Ellis Island with an ethnic name, very often, they'd change it to sound more American. In New York alone, sixty-six percent of Jews arriving at Ellis Island changed their names to avoid drawing attention to their heritage, allowing them to sidestep anti-Semitism in order to find work. Assimilation is very present in our house, and Mama has bought into it lock, stock, and barrel through her dress, processed hairstyles, manner of speaking, and skin preference—passing the paper bag test is fully baked in "Whiteness." Maybe the simple answer is Mama is trying to protect us because, as a Black person in America, especially one living in Compton in the virulent civil rights era, institutionalized discrimination is a part of one's everyday orbit. Intellectually, it made sense, but emotionally it hurt. Who indeed needs to be two minorities? When we later question Mama about why she banned Korea or anything else she does that often makes no sense whatsoever, she simply shrugs and defaults to her standard explanation: "Little girls are to be seen and not heard."

In protest, I'd taken to becoming silent, reserved, and withdrawn from my family. Just about now, I have truly become the middle child since Lolo is Daddy's favorite and Virgil is Mama's. I'm left alone to fit in wherever or whenever I want, but I pretty much clam up. Fortunately, I've long learned how to enjoy my own company. Besides, I've inherited the Korean people's inner drive by virtue of my birth and circumstance. I suspect hope and faith for a better life is at play in my resolve, as both halves of me are fortified—my spiritual belief learned from Holt Orphanage and my intrinsic determination to succeed.

Mama instills that my love for education is a sure way to better my life, but my motivation to be my best self comes from God's love and abiding presence, which has never failed me. His love has seen me through so much already, and I genuinely believe it will continue to see me through any and everything. Somehow, He will orchestrate my life, shape my perspective, and nurture the desires I hold dear despite any setbacks. I have faith, too, that eventually, Mama will change her mind about wanting us to forget about Korea. In the three years since she lay down the law, that has not come to pass. There is always hope.

When Mama declared Korea a bad word was not the first time my faith is shaken. I clearly remember when a kid at school crushed my magical world. A staunch believer in Santa Claus, I'm devastated when, as a fifth-grader, a real killjoy blurts out, he isn't real. I survived. I will survive Mama's unreasonable and maddening request to forget my homeland.

I'm now learning to appreciate that the impermanence of everything doesn't have to shake my faith. Spending a lot of time with myself,

I mull over who I am and who I want to become—Saundra Henderson, Bang Sun, or both? With resolute inner strength, I'm determined to find and shape *my* belief of who I am. I've always been a good student, but now my desire for education is in overdrive, and I'm pushing myself to achieve beyond expectation. My relationship with my spiritual self also grows. True Faith Baptist Church is where you can find me every Sunday. Reverend Wilbert and Berneatha Wade, the pastor and his wife, are my godparents. I call my beloved godmother Nanny. Mama and Nanny are best friends and both sing in the choir. Nanny plays the piano while Mama leads in a few songs. One of the songs she leads and maybe improvises her own lyrics is called, "He'll be There."

> *When mother is gone, I know, He'll be there, and father too, I know He'll be there*
>
> *He'll be there if you pray an earnest prayer*
>
> *Oh, look to Jesus your strength He'll renew, and He will always watch on over you*
>
> *In times of trouble, just call Jesus, and He'll be right there.*

My mama's song reminds me that earthly things—be it Santa, Mama, and Daddy, my biological mother, father, Sonyeon, and even the Holts—don't last forever. At some point, by circumstance or design, they will leave you, but you can always count on God/Jesus to never leave you if you believe in Him, have faith, and pray. My mind connects this message with my time at the orphanages, where as a child, I'm doggedly petitioning someone for help. The answer came in the form of angels like *hal-abeoji* and Molly. Prayers protected me then, and now my faith is bolstered when I read the scripture of Hebrews 11:1. This passage becomes the bedrock of my life: *Now faith is the substance of things hoped for, the evidence of things not seen.* I'm a true believer.

Mother, regardless of her quirks, is our daily bedrock. She sets an unshakable foundation under our feet from which we can build a great life. We are physically well taken care of, educated, imbued with solid morals, always fed, always dapper, and always on time. But Mama isn't the affectionate type, and she is extremely sensitive and jealous. No matter how deserving I am, Mama just can't find it in her being to compliment or encourage me. We go through the charade of hugging and kissing, but it always feels like an obligation of duty rather than love—real love—and I feel wounded. I know Mama is doing the best she can, and I truly appreciate her, but I can't help feeling the way I do. Nanny, on the other hand, is loving, warm, affectionate, and offers the support I need to weather my challenges. She is always encouraging me and gives me the attention I don't get at home. Nanny becomes my primary emotional rock. Mama becomes very jealous of our relationship and begins to control the amount of time I can spend with Nanny. When Nanny takes up for me in any situation, Mama says to her, "Do you think the sun rises and sets with Sandy?" I can't fathom why Mama can't let me be.

The fact is, I, too, am envious of Mama's relationship with some of the young women at church and with Virgil's girlfriends, who all seem closer to her than me. She spends hours on the phone with them laughing, listening, and giving them advice. I often wonder if Mama will ever listen to me, try to get to know the real me, or if we'll ever enjoy just talking to each other as people? As if the code of silence about Korea isn't enough alienation, Mama delivers yet another blow by curtailing my time with Nanny. Whenever I mention the "K" word out loud, it is to Lolo or Nanny, and that too would get under Mama's skin if she found out. Nanny's teenage son, Wilbert, is a linguist who speaks Spanish and Japanese and is a real supporter of me. The Korean words and songs I remember are because of Wilbert, who always encourages me to talk to him in Korean and advises me never to let go of my language. Nanny and Wilbert understand the conflict and frustration this causes me and support me the best they can. Just what else does Mama need to take away from me?

My life pretty much becomes the same routine every day—school, homework, cooking, and tending to other chores needed around the house. Because I came into a nice, neat home in 1958, I know Mama is a good homemaker, but now she's delegating whatever needs to be done around the house to us kids, mostly me. Her new job is dishing out duties. Virgil, Lolo, and I take turns vacuuming and sometimes buffing the hardwood floors. While we girls do most of the house chores, Virgil is out doing odd jobs in the neighborhood or for family friends. He is a real hotshot, and Mama is always coaching him on what to say and do to sweet talk the girls who are constantly hanging around him. It works because Virgil always has many girlfriends.

Virgil's job is also to be our big brother protector, like the time when Mama sends him with Lolo and me trick-or-treating. To stave off his boredom, he brings one of his doting females. One Halloween night, when a boy snatches my goody bag and runs, Virgil takes off after him, catches him, and roughs him up a bit. I get my candy bag back, and Virgil earns brownie points from his young lady and me. Above all, Virgil is a great athlete and is becoming one of California's fastest track stars. Mama arranges Virgil's cheering section: Papa, mama's father, Lolo, and me. We pick up Papa, who lives with his lady friend, and drive over to the school. Mama parks the car in front of the school's fence, and she and Papa sit in the car while Lolo and I get out and scream in delight, seeing Virgil leaving dust on the faces of the boys behind him on his way to stardom. More than ever now, Mama continues schooling Virgil on the art of being a Romeo or Casanova.

My main chore becomes more defined. When Mama cooked earlier on, I became her sous chef in the preparation of meals. When I'm in sixth grade, Mama has to go to the hospital for some type of checkup. It's around Thanksgiving, and that's when I officially take over most of the cooking for the entire family. With all the cooking I do, Mama is steadily gaining weight with each passing day. No longer as mobile, from her seated throne, she directs everything we need to do, including fulfilling her community obligations of preparing and distributing needy baskets for the school and the Salvation Army.

In the midst of my teenagerhood, Lolo gets sick. She is nine—or maybe eleven if Mama hadn't changed her age—when she contracts rheumatic fever that leads to rheumatic heart disease from an untreated strep infection. It is a sad and lonely time for me as she's in the hospital for several months, and life is never the same. I miss our sisterly bond. I draw even further into myself. Daily, we travel to the Children's Hospital rehabilitation center to see her. From her medication and having to stay put from inactivity, she has gained a lot of weight, making her irritable and difficult to be around. After three months, she finally comes home, but life has changed because she is limited in what she can do and eat.

During this period, my duties also ramp up because money, now funneled to medical bills, stretches our purse strings and is tight. Daddy is taking any overtime and double time opportunity to keep the family afloat. Wanting to lighten Mama's load and to become more self-sufficient, I learn to sew for myself and the family. In junior high school, I observe someone doing my parents' taxes and blurt out, "I can do it." Thus begins Sandy's yearly free tax services, along with my mechanic's skills, when I have to get under the car hood at school to jump-start the car, which dies several times on Mama. This is really embarrassing.

Life in Compton is very different from my life at Holt, and Daddy and Mama are very different from *hal-abeoji* and Molly. While the Holts concern was for every child to have a 'home,' Daddy's big concern is about our home's environment and that we are keeping good company. The truth is Compton is fast becoming a place of notoriety that is not one for growing up in the best of good company. Daddy said Compton was different back in the day, and he didn't like how it's changing. Bookworm me who loves history, and to be honest, who is just the curious kind trying to understand the why of things, starts investigating why Compton became Compton. The World Book encyclopedia has all the answers.

*California is often seen as a progressive state, probably because of its "open-mindedness" and historically diverse exposure. But it has its own dark history. Back in the seventeen hundreds, Los Angeles was a Spanish colony consisting of forty-four pioneers, twenty-two adults, and twenty-two children with ethnicities hailing from Spanish, Mexican, American Indian, and African descent. In 1850 California becomes the thirty-first state of the U.S.A., and the diversity of the population shapes the Golden State. By the 1940s, when the Second World War opened up wartime jobs to Blacks, the great migration brought many Blacks to California, and the African-American population of Los Angeles doubled. By the second half of the nineteenth century, too, there is a rapid influx of Anglos from the Midwest. Impressed with the favorable weather conditions, they are dead bent on settling into and selling the "California Dream" of sunshine, healthy living, and wealth. With the arrival of more and more Whites, there is a racial shift, and of course, with it comes tensions between old and new inhabitants. But even before then, by the 1930s, Los Angeles, though not a slave state, had not escaped the influence of racism and had already been developing a troubling racial history. The result was the establishment of sundown communities where blacks were not allowed to live. The Golden Age of Hollywood ushered in a second practice known as "redlining." As part of the New Deal, it was meant to bolster the housing market and further segregate the city. Redlining, which assessed and ranked the value of land and their risks according to a neighborhood's economic and racial makeup, made it difficult for people of color to secure home loans in protected communities or move out of their "designated" neighborhoods. The Fair Housing Act of 1948 began imposing strict rules against these blatantly discriminatory practices. With the influx of African Americans and dire housing shortage, Blacks began settling into Compton's middle-class neighborhood. Compton, The Hub City in the middle of South Central (the umbrella term for Black Los Angeles), is surrounded by Paramount, Lynwood, Long Beach, Carson, Gardena, Los Angeles, and Watts. Predominantly a white middle-class suburb, Compton experienced massive "White flight with the lifting of restrictive covenants." By the 1940s, neighboring Watts has already been fully transformed into a primarily working-class African-American neighborhood, and by the 1960s, it has developed a reputation as a low-income, high-crime area infiltrated by street gangs. The violence would spill over into Compton, which later became the fourth most violent city in Los Angeles.*

Though Daddy is continually monitoring that we live in a safe enough neighborhood, in reality, Compton is fast becoming a dangerous place to live.

# CHAPTER SIX

## My Family

My perception growing up is Daddy is a good man who works hard to provide for his family. Daddy grew up at a time when young, able-bodied members of a household had to work to help make ends meet, so he left grade school to become a breadwinner for his family. With limitations in his educational opportunities as a kid, he is illiterate but no fool. Daddy often tells us when he married Mama in the 1940s, he'd found a partner who could manage him and his household. His trust and faith in Mama are complete as he brings home his paycheck to her every week, knowing she'll take care of the rest. Unlike many households, we never experienced hunger or have our utilities cut off because Daddy is a great provider, and Mama manages the household money very well.

Years after our arrival, Daddy is still sacrificing for his family. He gets up at 4:00 a.m. to get ready to take the bus to work because we're not a two-car family, and Mama needs the car for daily chores—like going to the store and taking us to school when we're late. Not outwardly demonstrative, Daddy's silent love is felt in our hearts in many, many ways and is undeniable. Now and then, he wakes us up very early to cook us breakfast before leaving for work. Sharing this time with us is how he shows his love, and we love it. Our groggy, want-to-go-back-to-sleep-at-4:00 a.m. moment is rewarded with the best over-easy eggs on buttered toast in the world.

Daddy's favorite treat is his delicious greasy hamburgers. He learned how to make them in the Army when he worked in the mess hall. Those hamburgers are a real treat for us, and the days he'd cook them, equally special for him. Unfortunately, with Daddy, Saturday morning sleepin is never an option. He doesn't believe in kids lying around in bed on weekends and makes us get up bright and early so he can teach us how to make up our beds, military-style. Like little squads, we fold the edge of the sheet at an angle before tightly tucking it under the mattress. Making our beds every day is a discipline he instills.

We have a black-and-white television, but eventually, Daddy buys a colored one. Even with Lolo as his favorite, Sundays after church is Daddy's and my bonding day. We watch the L.A. football games on TV, and Daddy is always in awe that I understand the game and the football lingo. With Daddy, I create lots of fond memories. My only angst with him is he isn't the type of father to attend school functions like PTA meetings, school promotions, and awards programs. Though that's fine with me most of the time, I sometimes want him to show up for events where I'm participating or presenting. I feel sad when he doesn't because Daddy more than Mama would have shown how proud he was of me. Only later do I realize Daddy might have felt uncomfortable about not being an educated man. I always give him a pass, considering how hard he works for us.

Mama, a stay-at-home mom, is truly large and in charge of our household. A staunch disciplinarian, she bustles her heavy frame around with authority. Mama had a year of college at Prairie View A&M University, and it's evident. She is very smart, well-spoken, and can work out math problems incredibly fast in her head. Without paper or pencil, she tackles a problem, all the time whispering to herself, "Add this to that plus this. Naught plus one times that equals..." I admire Mama's brain and wonder what she could've become given the opportunity. Lolo and I know better than to utter any slang around the house, for Mama insisted we learn "proper English" because she can't abide splitting verbs and people speaking in Ebonics.

Mama, as I said, grew up in the era where assimilating to look and be whiter was the right thing to do to get ahead. In her family's case, it might have helped, as much of Mama's family is middle to upper-class Blacks from the Dallas, Texas area. Her cousins who live in Los Angeles are definitely well-to-do. They live in the upper-middle-class Black areas of L.A. and own properties such as apartment complexes. On the phone, they sound very posh—that is until they break out into Tut, a form of English invented by slaves. Lolo and I love listening to Mama talk on the phone with her cousins. When Mama doesn't want us to know what she's saying, she speaks Tut.

I'm pleasantly surprised when I read Maya Angelou's book, *I Know Why the Caged Bird Sings,* to see that in it, she and her best friend learn and speak Tut. Like me, Angelou has heard her elders use this language game so children wouldn't understand what is meant for grown-up ears. Mama has one cousin who understands Tut well, and they would prattle on endlessly. I can always tell when she is on the phone with her other Tut-challenged cousin, as she will spell super slow or repeat words until she gets frustrated. When that happens, Mama just blurts out what she is trying to say in real English. Lolo's and my ears would perk up so we could be in the know. Good Tut requires one to be an excellent speller, and Mama's other cousin isn't so sharp. When Mama says, "Sush Hush I Tut," we already know she is spelling *shit,* but not her cousin. Knowing we'd catch on fast, she begins calling me in Tut by saying quickly, "Sush Ay Nun Dud Yuk" meaning Sandy. This is fun and underscores Mama's smartness and wittiness.

One of the only outside activities my parents allow me to participate in is Girl Scouts. On that day, I don my green uniform with its yellow tie and green beret and proudly bolt out the door to get a ride to the Spencers', whose house is just around the corner. It's my first social activity outside of school and church. I'm pumped to meet new friends and gain experience. In Girl Scouts, I get to explore, discover, and learn more about the outdoors, science, and myself. When I do well, I earn badges for various activities, and with all the cooking I do, you can best believe my first badge is for making a white sauce. One of the hardest things for my parents to do is to let me out of their sight beyond school.

Our troop is going camping in the mountains, miles away from Compton. Mama is so anxious; she mulls over the idea for days but finally decides I can go. I'm so excited to go on my very first trip because our family doesn't take trips other than in the summertime when we go to pick peaches, pears, and grapes for making preserves. To be able to go camping with my Girl Scout troop evokes, for the first time, a feeling of, "I can't wait." Traveling with the Girls Scouts will be my first time on a bus in America. The bus ride is long and bumpy. Well into our journey, it's evident the luggage rack above our heads is not secure. We can see where it is detaching. Our Scout leader, Ms. Spencer, points this out to the bus driver, who happens to be a White man. He seems to brush it off as nothing to worry about, seemingly not caring about our safety. Ms. Spencer insists it's a priority, and this is my first time hearing and seeing racism in action. He calls us "complaining niggas." Ms. Spencer demands that he stop the bus immediately so she can make a call to report the bus situation and request another bus. The bus driver, mad as he is, unequivocally states how he feels about us Negroes. Ms. Spencer could care less. Another bus with a new driver finally gets us to camp. It is all I imagine and more. Special for me is that we learn lots of songs to sing around a campfire each night. Being a Girl Scout awakens the dormant aspirations of this quiet litte girl, who is now earning badges representing her accomplishments. An opportunity to learn, do, and be rewarded for accomplishing and gaining new experiences sits well with me.

My budding self-esteem shows when I begin selling Girl Scout cookies. To be successful, I must take the initiative to go up to someone, look them in the eye, and persuade them to buy my product. I know how to do this. I did it at Mah San when *hal-abeoji* came calling. I hone my pitch as I go selling door to door, at church, at school, and at the Safeway grocery store. In Girl Scouts, I'm learning new leadership skills that I hope will one day benefit my future. More immediate, though, is that I put the skills to good use right in our neighborhood. When neighbors suffer a death or have a need, I collect money for flowers for the homegoing service or to donate to the family. As a teen, I see commercials about helping crippled and very sick children, which reminds me of Molly and how hard she worked to save sick babies' lives. Ever since experiencing the kindness of strangers in Korea, I've been filled with empathy and sympathy when situations are sad or heartbreaking. My philanthropic activities grow to include being a student leader with the March of Dimes, an organization for premature babies, and with St. Jude's Children's Research Hospital. Like Molly, I'm always sad when some of the poster children inevitably pass away.

After two years in Girl Scouts, Mama calls it quits. The only socializing I do now is with my neighbors Marshon and Karla. Marshon is a year older. She is quiet and reserved like me. She is good company in the kitchen as I do food prep like peeling and cutting potatoes for dinner or making family favorites; tacos and homemade rolls, and Mama's favorite, German chocolate cake. Neither of us are yappers or gossipers, so most of the time, we simply enjoy each other's company in silence, which isn't awkward in the least bit. When we do talk, it's about school, boys, music, and her cousin who is a fanatic about the British Invasion music groups the Beatles, Rolling Stones, and Gerry and the Pacemakers. Quiet as it's kept, I'm a closet fan of the Beatles, Stones, and Elton John. What is interesting about Marshon's cousin is that she is the exception to the rule of crossover music. You don't see Black teens on the TV screaming and fainting over the Brits, but if there were one to do it, it would be her. Her cousin's ultimate fantasy is to go to England and marry a Brit.

As a teen, I have a fantasy of my own: Smokey Robinson and the Miracles! They are my favorite singing group, but I also like many of the Motown acts. Karla, totally different from Marshon and me, lives down the street. I mean, she is *totally* different! Where we are quiet and retiring, she is boisterous and outgoing. Karla and I were in a few classes together in grade school before Karla's mother pulled her out of public school because she felt Karla was getting too fast and was hanging with the wrong crowd. Karla started going to Regina Caeli Catholic School, but we still hung out in the kitchen. I love Karla, and even though we are the same age, I'm nowhere near as mature. When she comes over to visit, she plays along with the fantasies I believe in like Santa Claus, Mother Goose, and Fairy Godmother. Recognizing how gullible I am, she insists that my goodness will allow these fictitious characters to bestow *their* goodness on me. When I tell Marshon about my adventures and escapades with Karla, she is always an attentive listener.

When Karla and I are in seventh grade, we declare our love for Smokey Robinson. We find out he's going to be one block up the street at Dooto Music Center and beg our parents to let us go. Our parents say yes and allow us to walk up to the theater. We're wearing the coolest dresses that any teen during the late 'sixties would die to wear, compliments of Karla's mother who bought them. At Dooto, singer Tammi Terrell in the flesh opens the show! The place is so intimate I get a chance to speak to her, and I spend a lot of time talking with her aunt who has accompanied her. Her aunt tells me about Tammi's constant and terrible headaches and that she had rested up for the concert that night. Rumor has it, Tammi was hit in the head by soul singer David Ruffin. I'm pinching myself. Little ole unknown me is talking with a Motown star and her family. Unfortunately, Tammi Terrell dies a few years later from a brain tumor.

The best is yet to happen. Karla has hazel eyes like Smokey and a big personality. I'm her shadow. The next thing I know, she pushes open a door, and we're standing in a room with Smokey Robinson and the Miracles. Smokey notices us. He is so welcoming when it seems to me we deserve to be chastised as no one had invited us into their dressing room. I'd ordered fan pictures from Motown a while back, but now, here I am, looking at the face of each of the Miracles. I can't believe I'm standing in front of the real McCoy! Our little Instamatic camera that won't flash memorializes the moment. Karla stands next to Smokey, and I click the camera. I stand next to Smokey, and she clicks the camera. Smokey gives both of us a hug and kisses me on the cheek. I'm in a trance for the rest of the evening. When I get home and tell Mama and Daddy what happened, Daddy laughingly says, "Oh Lord, she ain't never gonna wash her face again." And indeed, I avoid washing the area where Smokey pecked me on the cheeks for a long time.

Unfortunately, our pictures don't come out, but Karla and I have several more adventures going to the Forum to see other Motown artists like the Temptations and Supremes. We are pros at getting backstage as we would have a camera around our necks and a pad and pen saying we were writers for our school paper's entertainment section. We saw Smokey two more times, and he knew us. He obliged us with his autograph: *To Karla with a K and Sandy with a Y*, he wrote verbalizing our names. Talk about going to heaven. We finally got pictures to prove we had met Smokey Robinson.

Marshon takes in everything I'm recounting about my backstage adventures with Karla, nodding and smiling. My sporadic experiences with the outside world spur my desire to explore a world beyond Compton. I'm beginning to appreciate how constrictive it is and realize I need to get some distance from it. If I don't, my life will revolve around fulfilling my family's constant needs, aiding and abetting their dependencies while neglecting my own life. In a few years, I'll be college-bound. Maybe this will be my chance to spread my wings. Like most things, I shelve the thought.

Our house is like Grand Central Station, at a minimum a revolving door of people in and out. We always seem to have too many people around. Many of my parents' relatives from Texas show up on our doorstep with suitcases to stay for a while. Our home becomes theirs while they get on their feet for a new start in California. I'm never quite sure whose side of the family the people coming through our revolving door belong to—if they were even related at all. Out of respect, we call every adult Aunt So-and-so. Most of them forgettable except Sonny Boy, daddy's nephew who gets plenty of action with the girls thanks to hanging out with Virgil. But there are also two ladies whose presence is unforgettable; Aunt Veotris and Aunt Maude. Aunt Veotris, cantankerous to the core, is forever mad about something. Not long after she arrives from Texas, she gets a job as a maid in Encino, California, where the movie stars live. One day, Aunt Veotris comes home earlier than she usually does. She walks through the door fuming, fussing, and cussing, all at the same time, telling Mama what she wasn't going to do or take from anybody. The next day, a fancy car drives up and stops at our house. An elegant White lady and two girls are in the car. We can see them from the living room window. Aunt Veotris can see them, too, from the front bedroom and begins shouting for them to hear, "Tell 'em I'm not here."

Mama scoffs at her. "They know you're in here, so go on outside and talk with them!"

In front of our stucco house is singer/actress Julie London, whom I've seen on TV. Her daughters from her previous husband, Jack Webb, aka Sargent Joe Friday of *Dragnet,* which Daddy and I watched regularly, are with her. My eyes widen because I'd hardly seen a White person in these parts, much less a real Hollywood star. When Aunt Veotris finally goes out to speak with her, I'm being seen and not heard, standing on the porch. I'm staring at them as I did at the White soldiers with yellow hair I'd seen in Korea. I can hear Ms. London pleading with Aunt Veotris to please come back.

"Who is she? Can I play with her?" the younger girl in the car says, staring back at me. Aunt Veotris turns to the girl. Her face has now softened like I imagine the slavery time mammies who care for and love their little White babies did as she answers her, "That's Sandy." Ms. London seizes the opportunity.

"Why don't we pick you and Sandy up tomorrow morning?" And that was that!

Ms. London is currently married to Bobby Troup, also an actor and singer. The following day, he comes driving up in his shiny red car to pick up Aunt Veotris and me. My jaw drops when I walk into the massive house that could probably fit two Hyo Chang Park orphanages or maybe ten of my houses in Compton. Even the baby grand piano and their two dogs have their own space. I've never seen anything like it, nor had I ever seen dogs in someone's house before. Every time I visit Lisa, Ms. London's daughter, it is a new adventure. Dangling my feet into their crystal blue pool is great but nothing like the sudsy water of the Korean sea that offered edible morsels. Whenever there is a party at Lisa's house, I see many people whose faces I recognize from TV. My visits soon stop because Aunt Veotris refuses to stay much longer and soon moves back to Texas. It's a memorable time of being with the rich and famous, and I cherish the beautiful pleated knit skirt with shoulder straps Ms. London gave me. It commemorates a little girl named Lisa who just wanted to play with another little girl named Sandy.

Lolo is more streetwise than I am. She is the one who tells the socially naive me where babies come from when I have no idea about such things. So, when the mysterious Aunt Maude appears, her curiosity piques. Aunt Maude is a nice-looking woman with a lean stature. All we know about her is that she has two sons, Tommy, and her favorite son, Jack, whose picture sitting in the cockpit of a fighter jet she totes around. I wonder if he is a Tuskegee Airman from World War II because they are the only Blacks I know of in the sixties who were pilots. Aunt Maude is forever disappearing into the bathroom, and after what seems like eons, she emerges as this utterly gorgeous, statuesque woman. One day, while she's in the bathroom, Lolo and I walk through the den where Aunt Maude stays. There, laid out on the bed, are her enhancer breasts, a big firm-looking butt with hips attached to panties or a girdle and stockings that have calf enhancements. Lolo covers her mouth, trying not to bust out laughing. I'm still wide-eyed, trying to put two and two together. Tiptoeing back to our room, Lolo whispers, "I knew those curves were all falsies when I saw that Frederick's of Hollywood catalog."

"Was that her butt lying on the bed?"

"Yes," Lolo says, "and her titties and her legs too."

My hand covers my mouth to stifle the laughter. That explains it all. After that day, you could find Lolo and me giggling when we looked at Aunt Maude's pointy and rounded body parts, knowing it all comes off every night.

In 1965, when I'm twelve, I witness history being made. Our house at 1409 Piru Street has a new reason for its revolving door. It's the polling station for our neighborhood after the Voting Rights Act passes. Mama and I watch with pride as the flag is hoisted on our front porch, and our garage is set up with rows of voting booths. As a result of Bloody Sunday in Selma, Alabama, on March 7th, Lyndon B. Johnson immediately passed the Voting Rights Act on August 5th, 1965. The 15th Amendment, giving all citizens the right to vote, had been adopted into the U.S. constitution in 1870 but was denied to blacks through illegal barriers such as poll tax and literacy tests. Its reinforcement, through the Voting Rights Act, was the first time in the history of America that no Black person could be denied the right to vote.

Our house was jampacked on election day, and the victory was palpable. "I am a citizen, and this is my right!" engendered a pride even Californians, who'd long had the right to vote, embraced. Mama and a few voter-coordinating ladies, plus a couple from the neighborhood, assist with the voting process checking people in and handing out ballots all day long. Later that evening, as I go past the dining room, I see our table piled high with paper ballots and crammed with women who would be working fervently into the wee hours tabulating votes. I'm fascinated watching the women working in unison. Mama lets me know the significance of the moment, and I promise myself never to take for granted or miss any voting opportunity. What I'm witnessing is the result of the sacrifices of the indomitable men and women who'd been whipped mercilessly, attacked by dogs, hosed in the streets, gunned down point-blank, burnt at stakes, lynched, and used as guinea pigs but who'd never stop striving for freedom. These champions of liberty who made Black voting rights a reality deserved the reverence I observed. I'm proud of Mama's leadership and progressiveness.

Two years earlier, Black and White America had mourned the death of John F. Kennedy, the thirty-fifth president of the United States who'd been gunned down in Texas. Mama and Daddy were very sad when he died because they thought all hope for Black progress was lost with his death. Caught in the cross-current of a nation in flux, Kennedy had supported the civil rights movement out of which the voting act had found the light of day. My first bicycle, gold-rimmed, forever wears the Kennedy bumper sticker.

Voting rights history made our house the place to be, but the very next day finds Mama and Daddy arguing over some food that had been eaten that Daddy swears he didn't eat even though I saw him do it. Reality is, the households I see in my neighborhood are entirely dysfunctional, and nothing like the minor altercations I see on TV shows like the Nelsons from *Ozzie and Harriet* or the Cleavers from *Leave It to Beaver*. I don't see families on those shows hiding incestuous family members or where adult neighbors display extreme mental illness, like our neighbor whose mother wears a wool coat in ninety-degree weather. When I ask her how she's doing on any given day, her response is always, "I don't know. I haven't taken inventory today."

In comparison to our neighborhood's dysfunctionality, Mama and Daddy, who argue almost daily, are no big news. They aren't in-your-face, Annie-go-get-your-gun types, so I never worry about them hurting each other because they are lazy, docile bickerers whose weapons are words. Mama, sitting down because she is too corpulent to move, hurls words at Daddy, who is also sitting down. The war seems to start for no reason or because of something stupid or minor. During heated exchanges, I side with and feel sympathy for Daddy. He is a quiet man by nature and Mama always wins the war of words by cursing louder. Her favorite cussing phrase for Daddy is, "You'd betta kiss a fat frog's ass." When later exposed to hard-core language, I appreciate my parents' tamer language to the neighborhood "F" or "B" words, which I hate. Serious bickering, yes, but unlike some of the people I know, domestic violence is no part of our lives.

Papa, who lived off and on with Mama and Daddy before our arrival, claims he's the reason why Mama was tamed. Mama confirms this to be true.

"Indeed," she says, "Papa is the one who stopped my acts of physical violence against your father years before you guys were on the scene." Mama tells the story of the violent quarrels, most of which she initiated, which would end with her getting the frying pan to hit Daddy over the head.

Papa apparently said, "Your husband is a good man, and you'd better stop this nonsense before you hurt him or lose him for good."

That, she said, was the turning point for her.

I love Papa. He is funny, sassy, and a most consistent person. Though he is known for his hotheadiness, dry whistle, and wry humor, I find solace in him. I love to listen to his stories. We bond in the kitchen over coffee—his, since I'm too young to drink coffee. I love smelling his morning coffee and seeing the beautiful caramel color he creates when he mixes evaporated milk into it before adding a teaspoon of sugar. I love the sound of the spoon skimming around Mama's china cup.

"Papa, give me some of that." I'm forever asking for a taste.

"You taste this, and it's goin' turn you black," he says. One day he finally gives me a taste, and I've loved coffee ever since.

Papa couldn't care less about being scolded for using the back-porch washtub as a urinal. He's getting on in age, and at night when he gets confused about the bathroom's location, he goes anywhere he finds an area to urinate, usually the back porch. His mind is far sharper when he's regaling us with his stories of the Negro league, telling us about his time playing with them and about his time picking cotton.

When entertaining us with the past, he seems completely lucid. Papa lives life to the fullest, and I admire that. Dressing in his dapper hats, Papa walks miles to see his elderly lady friend, Mama Sadie, whom he lived with before experiencing medical problems and had to move in with us. Mama Sadie isn't like a grandmother to us, but we enjoy a few perks being around her. When we give Papa a ride to her house, Lolo and I like going into her backyard to pick her sweet, gooey figs, which she uses for preserves to put on her homemade tea cakes. Those tea cakes are the best, hard as a rock like scones. And hard enough that you could knock someone out if you hit them on the head with them. We happen to like their crunchy taste.

One day, Virgil, Lolo, and I are sitting on Mama Sadie's porch, joaning. Virgil tells Lolo she can never fall because of her wide Fred Flintstone feet. Joaning is a common occurrence in our urban town, but this is the first time someone in our family is doing it. Lolo joins Virgil, and they both joan me about my big Bugs Bunny front teeth. We, in turn, tell Virgil his ears could help him fly away. This day, our age gap floats away like fog, and we are simply siblings. Bursting into laughter, we head home, leaving Papa behind. Papa's visits to Mama Sadie's house are often short. After an hour or two, Mama Sadie calls for us to come and pick him up because they are fussing. Still trying to bed her, Papa wants her to "give him some," and she insists they're too old for all that.

Papa believes he is as virile and fearless as any young man. One time, Virgil gets jumped by a gang in Watts for going into the neighborhood with a girl he's walking home. The hoodlums hit him with brass knuckles, breaking his nose. A lady who'd seen Virgil struggling with the boys who'd quickly run away brought him home. Until that day, our lives in the 'hood have been uneventful. We're all taken aback and frightened at the blood and bruises on Virgil. Papa immediately checks his pocket and pulls out the knife he carries around to cut, peel, and I guess on this day, stab somebody. He storms out of the house, walking briskly to find the gang of boys who'd hurt Virgil. Mama is calling on Jesus as we load into the car to get Papa. So quick, he's already on Parmelee Street. Mama is shouting, "Papa, get in the car. God will handle this."

"Aye, God shit! *I'm* gonna handle it. I'm gonna get who did this to Bubba [grandpa's nickname for Virgil]," Papa says.

Mama raises her voice to Papa, pleading that the priority is to get Virgil to the hospital. He finally gets in the car, and we go to get medical attention to re-set Virgil's nose. That incident prevents Virgil from running in the CIF state track meet and probably any future track accolades that were to come in the near future.

Back home, Papa is back to what keeps him busy most days—swatting flies. "Don't let that fly come in here. I hate flies worse than God hate sin!" Lolo and I pounce on the flies, repeatedly swatting until they are lifeless. The only grandparent I have is Papa because my other grandparents passed before I came along. I know only too well that we wouldn't have him one day, so I savor every moment with him. When Papa is up late at night listening to the Dodgers on the radio, though I should be in bed, sharing this time with him is a gift I give myself. When I reflect on things that give me peace during periods of angst at home, it's being in the kitchen—my sanctuary alone or with Papa.

From Papa, I come to appreciate how hard life was for people of color back in the day when he was growing up. I think of my birth father and how he, too, probably had to face unrelenting discrimination, and I think of Mama pioneering voting day and realize they've paved a better road for me.

# CHAPTER SEVEN

## Young, Gifted, and Black-ish

If I'm clueless about the meaning of the Voting Rights Act of 1965 and Black history in general, the late sixties becomes pivotal to my social, political, and cultural consciousness. Culturally, until then, even in Compton, the soundtrack of my life could be recorded by shows like *American Bandstand* and *The Ed Sullivan Show* and my favorite, *Dr. Kildare*. So much so that Dad thinks I'm going to marry a White man. I'm not hardly thinking about any of this because I'm a teen, and all I want to do is go to SeaWorld, which has now been open for nearly a year. With some nudging, Daddy finally suggests we take a train ride to San Diego.

For weeks on end, I'd been counting down the days to August 12, 1965. To think Daddy would accompany my friend Karla and me to SeaWorld felt special. I'm really looking forward to our father-daughter date and spending time with him. But this doesn't come to pass as on August 11, 1965, five days after the Voting Rights Act is enacted, the very day before my special date with Daddy, I'm watching Watts burn. The virulent sixties that are spewing White vitriol all over Black people aren't easy to ignore as the revolution is being televised. During this unprecedented time of mobilization for Black social, political, and economic justice, to say long-standing resentment against racial injustice boils over is an understatement. Magnificent Montague's radio mantra becomes "Burn, Baby Burn!" when the Watts riots break out, and the city is indeed burning. Black, Jewish and Asian Merchants, pleading for mercy against looting or burning their establishments, put up window signs that read "Soul Brother."

Amid the sirens, fires, and looting, the only solace I find is in playing 45 rpm records on repeat: the Supremes' *Stop in the Name of Love*, the Temptations' *My Girl,* James Brown's *I Got You (I Feel Good),* The Four Tops' *I Can't Help Myself (Sugar Pie, Honey Bunch),* and my favorite, Smokey Robinson and the Miracles' *The Tracks of My Tears.* Mama is just about ready to go crazy over my nonstop, on repeat music as the conflict lasts for six days. The Watts rebellion devastates the city, resulting in thirty-four deaths, 1,032 injuries, and thirty-five hundred arrests. By the end of it, more than 34,000 people had been involved, one thousand buildings, totaling forty million dollars in damages, have been destroyed, and it would take 14,000 National Guard to get the city under control. Armed guards surround our entire neighborhood, and we are prisoners in our own homes, watching as blazes light up the sky.

Through all the trauma, I learn one thing. There was no turning back from the cry for freedom. If White folks didn't know before, in the late 1960s, everyone would come to know the Black story, and if you happen to be Black, it is a time of kinetic excitement and change. Those who might have "passed" in the past are now proudly wearing afros. Western garbs are jettisoned and replaced by colorful African dashikis. Music of the revolution, protest, and Black pride fill the airwaves in our neighborhood. Nina Simone's sultry voice belts out the anthem *To Be Young, Gifted and Black,* while James Brown's *Say it Loud—I'm Black, and I'm Proud* has the dance floor stomping to a new kind of shuffle. Tears filled people's eyes when in 1964, Sam Cooke appears on *The Johnny Carson Show* and sings *A*

*Change Is Gonna Come.* And, while Aretha Franklin rocked *Respect* people like her father, the Reverend C.L. Franklin, freedom fighters, and the unforgettable father of the Civil Rights Movement, Martin Luther King, Jr., led the charge for Black freedom. Political leaders such as Andrew Young and John Lewis, entertainers such as Harry Belafonte and Sidney Poitier and activists such as A. Phillip Randolph and Bayard Rustin are leading the charge for racial equality. President Lyndon B. Johnson announces in his televised address to the nation, that he is signing into law the Civil Rights Act of 1964, legislation supporting racial equality in America as proposed by his predecessor John F. Kennedy.

Closer to home, the revolutionary Black Panther Party for Self-Defense, on the heels of Watts' disquietude, is gaining steam. Founded by Bobby Seale and Huey P. Newton from Oakland, California, they put the politicos on notice. The party is registering and empowering five thousand Black men and women to take a stance and action, if necessary, against racism. As a person of color in America during the sixties and seventies, I fully come to understand and see the parallels in the discrimination that lead to my abandonment and expulsion from Korea. The effects of discrimination on my life seeded at birth continue to be a heavy load.

But life goes on. So off I go to junior high. Vanguard Junior High helps me adjust in unexpected ways. Academically, it is a breeze. Of all the things to get excited about, even after a couple of years, I still get a kick out of running back and forth to my locker to stash or retrieve books for classes. It represents independence and responsibility, and I like managing my own time. Vanguard is also where I find my social gene. When I say I have become social, I mean it. I join clubs like the Brotherhood Workshop, choir, the Varangians, an honor society and even run for the student body office as Commissioner of Athletics, which I won. *Ha-ha,* me an athlete? A joke. The Brotherhood Workshop sponsors talent shows.

Though I'm a mediocre singer, I decide to enter the competition. I sing *To Sir With Love* by Lulu since I'm now a ninth grader about to go to high school (in the sixties, ninth grade was middle school), and the song seems appropriate for thanking and saying farewell to my favorite teachers. My performance is a hit, and unlike most, I did not lip-sync. The next act is Gary's. The Gary I've had a crush on forever who's super popular, super handsome, and lives around the corner from me. His parents and my parents are friends—in fact, they were the couple helping Mama with the voting poll. Gary and his friends slide onto the stage and suavely perform a Smokey Robinson and the Miracles song, *The Love I Saw in You Was Just a Mirage*. They lip-sync the entire song, but their choreography is on point! Since I love Smokey, my secret crush on Gary is now at swoon proportion. His group takes the top spot and wins the talent show, I'm convinced, because of the loudness of the screams and the length of the cheers.

I usually walk the mile and a half trek to school, but Mama gives me a ride when I'm late. It's almost guaranteed we'll see Gary running to school because he's always notoriously late. Mama stops to pick him up. Now, however, I'm super conscious of my crush, and I clam up even more. My heart is doing the mambo when he gets into the car, and even though we are sitting close, I can't find words. We rarely have conversations other than a basic greeting, or when I answer a question he asks, so it's okay.

After my performance, Gary, a talented, self-taught jazz pianist, invites me to join his group as a vocalist. It's a pretty big group—a pianist, flutist, bassist, drummer, and conga player, along with three other female vocalists and me. I'm honored. During band practice, we rehearse *Wade in the Water* and *Mas Que Nada,* a Brazilian song that I'm to lead. I'd belted out *To Sir With Love* in the talent show, but for some reason, in front of Gary, I freeze, and the quiet, shy girl takes over. Instead of lead, I opt to be a background singer.

My final crowning glory in junior high bolsters my confidence. I'm named Ms. Vanity Fair of the month. It's a contest where all the homerooms girls are judged for their most lady-like qualities—appropriate dress length, manicured fingernails, overall neatness, and even trendy attire. Surprisingly, I'm selected and blush all day as the school-wide broadcast blares on the AM and PM announcements: "We congratulate Saundra Henderson for being selected as this month's Ms. Vanity Fair." I send a silent thank you to Daddy, who, before Lolo got sick, would take us shopping at a boutique near Beverly Hills. He always insisted we stand out from the other girls, so off we'd go to school wearing silk dresses or rocking a fashionable leather skirt.

Virgil has gotten married, and just as soon as he ties the knot, the marriage is annulled. He joins the Navy. Before taking up the post, he's already involved with another girl whose mother is Black and father is from India. She gets pregnant and can't go to her family's house, so she lives with us while Virgil is gone. Even though we know she is half east Indian and not American Indian, we teasingly said we'd call her baby Pocahontas if it was a girl. When her beautiful baby arrives, it's a boy, and we jokingly call him Pokey. Because his mom works every day, and it's the summer before going to tenth grade, I'm honored to babysit Pokey. I'm loving every moment of being with this precious new life and enjoy him rewarding me with his winning smile.

One day, while I'm holding Pokey out in the front yard, some unknown guys start driving up and down our street. Stopping in front of our house, they come on to me strongly and are being incredibly fresh. Pokey, probably sensing my anxiety, becomes unusually fussy, so I take him inside, trying to calm him down. That evening, I follow the same routine his mom taught me: change him, feed him, burp him, rock him to sleep, and lay him down in the crib on his stomach. When Pokey's mom comes home from work at 3:00 a.m., she's concerned because he doesn't wake up for his usual feeding. She picks him up, and he is lifeless. She screams, and we all rush to see what's happening. She is holding her lifeless baby. Immediately, I'm wondering if I did something wrong. Was he feeling sick when he started crying outside? I'm bawling inconsolably because Pokey was my baby. He'd seen me more than anyone in his little two-month-old life. I now know how Molly felt when she'd lost so many babies. Virgil didn't even get a chance to know his son.

We later find out that Pokey died from 'crib death,' but I still feel it is my fault. Virgil's relationship with Pokey's mother doesn't last much longer. She goes her way, and the Navy sends him to Japan, the Philippines, and later to Vietnam. His debonair charm seems to work as well overseas as it does at home because Mama soon gets a letter from a woman in the Philippines telling her that Virgil has fathered a little girl whom she's named Little Clemmie, after Mama.

Junior high ends way too soon. It's now the fall of 1968, and I'll be attending Centennial High School, home of the Apaches. It's the same high school from which Virgil graduated as a top track athlete. A few months before school start, I'll try out for the prestigious Centennial Centennettes team—revered as the classiest dance team in Compton. With their red corduroy out fits, white-bordered fringe loincloth aprons, white gloves, knee-high or ankle leather moccasins, Indian headdresses, plumed with bright red and white feathers, they indeed put on a show. I'd dreamed of being on the team from the first time I saw them perform. I make the Centennettes! Because I am under five feet, one of the shortest girls on the squad (and in the school), I'm chosen to lead the line of our Indian Warpath drumming during our pep rallies. Students and the football team alike scream as we enter the gymnasium, ready to pump up our school spirit for an evening or weekend football game.

My social life is even better in high school, and Mama seems to take great pride in this. What I learn about Mama is that her children's popularity gives her bragging rights. As early as sixth grade, Mama had allowed me to go to house parties. Her only rule: She had to call the host's parents to verify adult chaperones were on hand. I'm even allowed to give parties in our garage. I wouldn't say my parties were the talk of the town because Daddy would pop up way too often to check on things, and at precisely 11:00 p.m., he would raise the garage door and say, "Okay, it's over. Good night."

For teenagers, a good party is when the lights are dimmed or off and boys and girls are slow dancing to what seems like never-ending songs like The Dells' *Stay in My Corner.* For those coupled up, it's known as grind time against the wall, and for the rest of us wallflowers or red cup holders, we awkwardly wait for the end of the very long song. Seeing Gary and Karla coupled up against the wall makes me realize I'm still very much a nerd and that my dancing ability is mediocre at best. Probably the reason Gary doesn't like me back.

Trust Mama to come to my rescue. Always talking about how good a dancer she was back in the day, Mama takes me under her wing. From her seat, using her legs and feet, she dances to upbeat music. Mama shows me a swing dance the kids call the hop. During our lessons, Daddy plays at dancing by rolling his belly to make us laugh. Thanks to Mama, I start to hold my own on the dance floor.

At sixteen, when I get my driver's license, my parents give me free access to the car, which I mostly use to run errands, like picking up cigarettes for Daddy and Big Macs for Mama. On late days, I drive to school. On more than one occasion, I've forgotten that I've driven and do the craziest thing after school—walk home. It's only when I get home and don't see the car in the driveway that I realize I've left it at school.

Besides being a Centennette, my most ardent desire in high school is to be a member of the Tomahawks, the school's classy social club known to make things happen at school and in the community. Mr. Lawrence Freeman, a reading teacher who everyone agrees runs the school instead of the principal, is someone to be admired. He demands and expects excellence, encourages sophistication, and inspires a work ethic of success. I not only become a Tomahawk but its president in my senior year as Mr. Freeman's right and left hand. The Tomahawks are involved in the arts and entertainment with the reputation of bringing class acts like the Young Holt Trio, Doug and Jean Carn, and Lou Rawls. I'm also part of the political activism program, charged with organizing protests when needed and making phone calls to the community to remind them to vote.

Through Mr. Freeman, I meet his neighbor, jazz singer Nancy Wilson, whom we bring to our school to perform. I have the honor of presenting her with our timeless Tomahawks tweed uniform. Nancy Wilson becomes my mentor, even showing up unannounced to eat lunch with me proudly wearing her Tomahawk uniform. At one of her concerts, she invites me to join her backstage. To my utter delight and awe, Bill Cosby, the most popular black actor and comedian in the TV series *I Spy,* walks through the door. When Ms. Wilson introduces me, I gush and compliment him on being a great actor.

"I know it," he says flippantly, neither making eye contact nor acknowledging my presence. About thirty minutes after Bill Cosby leaves, Muhammad Ali walks through the door with a bouquet of roses for Ms. Wilson. Now, I'm pinching myself. Mr. Ali extends his hand, smiles, looks me in the eyes, and says, "Hello." Based on what I've seen on TV, I'm expecting him to strut around all cocky and arrogant chanting, "I'm the greatest," but he's very polite and warm. I learn that day not to judge and not to assume.

Another accomplishment as a Tomahawk is renting the Masonic Hall every weekend to have a safe hangout for teens to dance and socialize. Being a member of the Tomahawks even introduces me to the fact that the word *gay* has more than one meaning. At our weekly

Masonic Hall dance party, I become a listening ear for one of the regulars, Fran. Over the weeks, Fran shares with me that she's recently been released from a juvenile camp for girls. As I'm listening to her, I feel a lot of sympathy for what she's had to experience. She is going on and on about the women she meets at her juvenile home. Finally, realizing I'm clueless in reading between the lines of her story, she asks me, "Are you gay?"

I answer, "Yes. I'm very happy."

She breaks out laughing. As Mama says many times, I have book sense, but zero mother wit or street smarts.

Regardless of how much of a misfit I feel on the inside, I seem to be putting the past behind me. Then I meet a girl at school named Jackie. She is light-skinned with tight Asian eyes and thick black hair. She takes one look at me and asks, "Are you from Holt?" I nod. For the first time in a long time, I acknowledge my past. With Mama's ban on all things Korean still in play, I'm excited to meet Jackie. I feel an immediate kinship with her because we are of the same African-American and *Korean* mixed heritage, and we are both from Holt. We begin to refer to each other as cousins. Our parents become friends, too, and I'm hoping that Korea won't be a bad word anymore. Of course, that never happens, and the ban on Korea continues. Spoken or not, between Jackie and me, there is an acknowledgment of our shared history. Jackie, however, has a Black advantage since she'd come to America at the age of three. Embracing the Black experience and being a part of Black culture is all she knows.

In high school, the era of Black identity is in full swing. I'm still struggling with my identity. Reverend Jesse Jackson, a prominent civil rights activist, comes to our school to emphasize how proud we should be of our Blackness. Sporting his giant afro and African dashiki, he mesmerizes us with his rousing speech. By the end of it, we are all chanting, "I AM SOMEBODY." Everyone in the late sixties is wearing huge afros with picks signifying Black pride.

The Afro pick can't hold up in my hair. I'm becoming more and more aware I'm not pure anything. Not pure Korean and not pure Black. What I am is ethnically Korean, ethnically Black, but not totally culturally Black or Korean.

I want to fit in, want to blend in, but to be honest, it is hard for me to fit in anywhere. I'm beginning to feel the effects of my cross-cultural adoption and the cross-generational perception of what being Black means. My parents are hold-your-head-down-and-work-hard types and weren't keen on the Black Power Movement, touting confrontation and accountability. There are subliminal messages everywhere of who I should be, and the fact is, as a Black Korean in America, I am Black. The one-drop rule coined by White America says so, but for me, it is a period of my invisibility. I could be neither too Black nor too Korean. I'm having a full-on identity crisis though you'd never know it, and I'm beginning to think Mama is right after all that maybe *Korea* is a bad word.

Seeing up close and personal the atrocities leveled at Black folks and realizing this is the same kind of hatred that brought me to America in the first place, I feel total solidarity with Black Americans. I'm learning about African-American history in school, and I'm living it in the neighborhood. My choice is leaning heavily toward fully claiming myself as a Black woman. Why, indeed, should I care about a country that abandoned me? Left me tied to a tree? One that created the doubt, the loneliness, grief, and pain of a forever mourning abandoned child? One that didn't even try to fight for my freedom? I'm Black because I'm my biological father's child. But I'm also Korean because I'm my birth mother's child. As confused as I feel, what I do know is how grateful I am to my Black mama and daddy from Compton for raising me! Who would I be, and where would I be in Korea today?

By senior year, I have a new crush, Reggie. This time, Reggie likes me back, and we become sweethearts. I'm drawn to his quiet calm, yet I'm not blind to his aggressive tendencies. A top athlete on the football field, Reggie doesn't mind letting his "thug" come out when confronted. I find this quality in him attractive. But Reggie is also involved with another girl. His friends tell me that it's because I am a "good girl," and that's his way of respecting me. I did not feel any consolation from that rationale. Though Reggie and I end up going to the prom together and both realize there'll always be a special place in our hearts for each other, we go our separate ways. Where I'm heading to or what I'll be doing is still unknown, but I know I have to leave Compton to explore a new reality.

Mama gets a call from my counselor in early January of my senior year. I'm tied with two other students to be the valedictorian of our school. I can't wrap my head around getting up in front of the entire graduating class to give a speech. One-on-one and in small groups, I'm okay but outgoing and uninhibited, I'm not. I purposely start letting my schoolwork slip by not turning in my English class assignments and once even cut school with my friend and fellow Tomahawk officer, Lynda.

I can't believe three years have rolled by, and now it's time to think about college. Focusing on my education has paid off since I'm a top student and have pretty much been accepted to every school to which I have appled applied. Set on going to UCLA, having long forgotten my Girl Scout promise to leave the city, I let some of the pressure on my shoulders drop. My UCLA decision changes the day I plop down in front of the TV on New Year's to watch the Rose Bowl with my father. Ohio State is again playing against some team. I'm impressed because they make it to the Rose Bowl every year, which has to mean one thing: They have a great school. Now I want to apply there, not only because it *might* be a good school but also because it is far away from Compton. Going there will fulfill my desire to see and experience another place, and honestly, as provincial as I am, I want to see if there's really a place called Ohio.

Since arriving in Compton, I've never been outside of California. I know there are forty-nine other states in the union from my geography class, and I've seen none. Going to other states is always a sore point, especially since my father works for the railroad. Why has he never thought to use his benefits to allow us to travel? By the end of the game, Ohio is looking good as a first choice.

I share this new excitement with my counselor, whom I like a lot. He is proud of my academic accomplishments and encourages me to reach for the stars. One day in his office, he hands me an application and suggests I apply to a school called Stanford University. I know nothing about Stanford, its location, nor its prestige. But Stanford is prestigious. Founded in 1885 and established in 1891, Stanford is a world-class teaching and research institution to which admission is coveted. I apply. Stanford responds affirmatively, and along with my letter of acceptance, I'm offered a full four-year scholarship.

I don't know how excited I'm supposed to be, but my counselor is ecstatic. He insists I immediately accept the offer, and I do. Located in Palo Alto, like Ohio, Stanford ticks my two imperative boxes: It'll allow me to be away from home, far enough to gain my independence. It's a drawback, though, that it's still in California. Again, my naivete doesn't register, this is a big deal. I'm not sure my parents understand it's a big deal either because Daddy and Mama are having mixed feelings about me going nearly four hundred miles away to school. Since my adoption, I've been my mother's arms and legs, doing everything for her and my family. I wonder if Mama wants me close so that she won't lose her arms and legs. Whether or not Mama understands the significance of my acceptance to Stanford, deep down, I know she's proud—proud of the standard I've set as an outstanding student and proud it gives her bragging rights.

The truth is Mama deserves a great deal of credit for my interest in being a good student. Since second grade, she's been active in my school life when she'd bought me the reading text *Fun with Dick and Jane* before entering second grade. My teacher was very opposed to this and felt it gave me an unfair advantage over my classmates. Mama simply shrugged it off. After all, what's done is done. I already had the book, and I had read it. When I made a B in high school, Mama marched herself to school to find out why. It was the teacher's policy not to give A's. Mama challenged her on such practices, reminding her they can demotivate. Thank God for Mama's forward-thinking and her access to resources; I will be off to Stanford. I feel eternally grateful to her. I can't help but laugh when I think back to primary school. When Mama is lonely, she'd always feel free to say, "Saundra, why don't you stay home with me today, and we'll watch our stories and eat Velveeta cheese and matzo crackers?" This Velveeta and matzo cracker eating habit she'd picked up from the Jewish family years earlier, where she'd worked for them temporarily as a domestic. Now more than ever, I'm convinced that's why she changed Lolo's birthday so that she could have someone home with her for two years.

"Mama, you know I can't do that. I have to get my education," I always replied.

"Alright," she'd relent, knowing how much I loved school and didn't want to miss it for the world.

Despite my shenanigans of skipping classes and not turning in my homework to tarnish my record just a bit, not only do I graduate with honors, but I'm tied for third and still have to give a speech. I half-expect Daddy to come to my high school graduation because this is such an honor for our household, but he doesn't. Years of not having school expectations of him, I find it easy to give him a pass. Mama is there, and I am glad for her presence.

The summer before heading off to college goes by quickly. We go shopping for things I'll need on campus. As it gets closer to me leaving for northern California, Mama seems sad. I know she'd prefer that I am closer to home. But it's time, and I'm packed and ready to go. Mama tries her best to go along with making sure I have a happy sendoff though I can see in her eyes she's sad. I, too, am sad. Standing in the dining room, I'm thinking how much my life has changed in the thirteen years since I've arrived in America. I'm remembering birthdays in the soft green dining room with furniture too large for the space where I would devour Mama's famous marshmallow, coconut, lemon-filled double-layer cake. Where children gathered for my birthday party chanting, "Make a wish, make a wish" before breaking into birthday songs. That soft green dining room is also where I would study and do my homework and special projects until past midnight. I'm now fondly remembering that between the dining room and the front door was a Singer sewing machine on which Mama would make my see-through nylon dresses, and self-taught, I, in turn, would make fashionable clothes for the family.

Feeling nostalgic, I walk the entire house. Next to the dining room is the green-carpeted living room boasting a fancy couch covered in heavy plastic. The cold, sticky plastic finally comes off for good when my teenage male suitors start coming by to court me. Luckily, they avoid the stick-to-your-bottom plastic but not Daddy's point-blank stare and questions. I'm imagining, too, my mother's scrunched face grimacing in protest to my continuous playing of the component system in front of the picture window spinning Smokey Robinson and Carol King songs over and over.

The three-bedroom home on Piru Street holds so many memories and secrets. At times, our family would swap rooms for a while, sampling each other's space for comfort. The so-called master bedroom, nearly the same size as Lolo's and mine, has an extra closet and is my favorite. Upon my arrival from Korea, that closet held forty outfits Mama and my godmother had bought to dress me like a doll-baby every day. The other closet in that room was my secret prayer closet, fortifying my relationship with God. The room where Daddy controls the evening programs. Sitting in front of the TV as he inhales, the burning ash from his Marlboro illuminates the dimly lit room. He's watching his cowboy shoot-em-ups with squinty-eyed Clint Eastwood as Rowdy Yates on *Rawhide*. It would also be the first room I shared and bonded with my sister who'd christened the bed with pee. My family had a good belly laugh when I announced Lolo had been sweating all night and the sheets were wet. It would also be the room where I got my first and only whipping because of Lolo, who got a whipping daily.

The front bedroom is where Daddy rescued me from my constant nightmares, telling me he'd fart very loudly on the monsters that dared to frighten me. Laughing, he'd take away the edge of fear, bringing the joy of laughter back to my frightened eyes. This room is solemnly where as a rising tenth grader, I lay Virgil's son (my two-month-old nephew) down for bed, and he died of crib death. This fateful room, too, is where I gave Papa mouth-to-mouth resuscitation when I was about fourteen years old. Getting the much-needed oxygen to his brain, he lived several more years.

The bedroom/den near the kitchen is the room where Mama controls our black-and-white TV during daytime soap operas. While snacking on Velveeta cheese and matzo crackers, she's crying crocodile tears watching actors fake their pitiful dilemmas on *As the World Turns*. It still holds the couch bed that almost smothered me. Once when Virgil and I were playing, he folded me up in it. I got stuck and began screaming, "I can't breathe." For thirty minutes, Virgil worked to get me out of that sofa and begged me not to tell. The den is also where I became a teenage political junky, sneaking to stay up late into the night to follow Bobby Kennedy's presidential campaign only to see him assassinated before my eyes on TV, only five years after his brother.

The bathroom—oh, that bathroom. The inspiration for my first communication, Lolo's and my special place, and where Mama, not trying to listen to Daddy go on and on about the water bill, would save up rainwater to wash my hair every blue moon, and where Daddy would insist on scheduling the family's wash-ups to conserve on the water bill. Lolo, who always had a sense of humor, would obstruct Daddy's exit by weaving a web out of thread while he was in the bathroom. Feeling the cord wrapping around his legs as he exited, he'd start cursing, "Got dammit, Lolo," he'd say, amused but trying not to show it. It was where Daddy would take Virgil as a teenager to give him a whooping. I would cringe from the sound every strike of his belt made. It's also the place where Daddy handed me my first sanitary napkin when I started menstruating a few weeks before my tenth birthday.

In the hallway, we would fear blowing up the house every time one of us had to turn on the furnace and light the pilot with a match. Once lit, the warm glow of the fiery metal heater is where we'd huddle on cool mornings, warming up next to it. The luxury it gave was not without events because that furnace would brand us with burn marks for being too close.

I walk to my favorite place in the house, the pinkish kitchen, my sanctuary. It's where I spent the most time during my entire stay on Piru Street. It is a proving ground for my culinary skills where I'm Mama's sous chef—getting spices, stirring custard, turning over frying chicken, washing dishes, scaling and cutting fish to fry, and making tacos. It became my social hangout spot with my neighbors Marshon and Karla. It's where I got introduced to coffee by Papa, and it's where Virgil would taunt LoLo and me by bringing home the best ice cream sundaes, which he wouldn't share. It was where he'd make the best sandwiches, purposely adding ingredients he knew we wouldn't like so we would stop begging him to share.

The laundry room with its washtub and wringer washing machine is where Papa would smell up the area by urinating in the washtub. It also was the spot for our caged parakeets. Singing, making a mess, and dying too soon, we were always replacing those birds. The spacious backyard with a seven-foot-high three-prong clothes-line provided exercise time. Since I'm vertically challenged, it would force me to jump fifty times to reach fifty pins to hang twenty-five wet items. In the backyard was the swing set and seesaw Lolo and I played on. We always loved it because in our memory of our time in Korea, is the seesaw at Holt. The tetherball and pole that I'm very good at is where we chain our dog, Trouble. In my mind, it was a cruel thing to do as he only had a fifteen-foot romping range. Blackberries, strawberries, peaches, and apricots from which we made homemade jelly/jam grew abundantly in the backyard. The backyard was also home to Virgil's pigeon coop. Debbie and our famous father pigeon, Webster Web Foot, rule their roost. When neighborhood thieves stole Webster, they clipped his wings so he couldn't fly. So, what did Webster do? He walked nearly a mile, finding his way back home. Talk about a homing pigeon.

I walk back to where my family is waiting. Outside, Daddy has packed my belongings into the Chevy. He hands me my twenty dollar airline ticket, which he's bought for my journey. In a gesture of love, Mama rolls seventy dollars in cash into a handkerchief and ties it to my left bra strap. It creates an obvious bulge on my ninety-five-pound frame. With every fiber of my being, I know how much Mama loves me, whether she can show it or not. My eyes well with tears, and my heart swells with gratitude for the life she has afforded me. We do our cheek kiss and hug, and I climb into the car alongside Daddy, heading to the airport for my very first plane ride since leaving Seoul. I'm leaving Los Angeles aware that my life is about to change. So far, it has been determined by two wars, the Korean War and the War for Black Freedom.

I glance over at Daddy who is driving me toward the next destination in my life. I wonder what he is feeling? He's worked so hard, double-time and overtime when he could get it to make sure we had what we needed. I wonder, too, if my birth father could imagine his little orphan girl on her way to college—Stanford at that. From experiencing life in America, I understand the uphill battle Black men must endure for a chance to get ahead. Daddy works so hard for so little. I know how much I have to be grateful for and look over at Daddy, wanting to say thank you. Thank you, Daddy, for a good life, but I say nothing. I also know why I'm unable to; I haven't reconciled my pain. All these years, I've been internalizing the loss and pain of being an orphan, trying hard to be thankful by denying the fact that adoption in itself is a trauma. I truly am grateful, but the reality is, when one is adopted can one ever stop being an orphan? In the stillness of night, at some unconscious level, I've remained an orphan all these years.

# CHAPTER EIGHT

## Taking the Reins

I wave good-bye to Daddy and walk through the glass doors of the airport. With trepidation, I take the reins of independence, wondering what the future holds for me. On the one hand, the unknown intrigues me, yet, on the other, from years of conditioning, it frightens me. Mama always finds fear in any situation. It is her default reaction. I feel fear begin to creep in and have to get a grip. The solution, as I see it, is to put my faith into action by trusting in God. Taking the reins with Him at the helm means He will guide me through the ups and downs of life's journey as He has done so far. By the time I'm on the other side of the airport door walking toward the gate, I've let go and let God because I know, without a shadow of a doubt, I'm in good hands come what may. I board the flight to San Francisco, resolved. I do trust God, but a lot is going on in America, and my immediate anxiety is the rash of plane hijackings that have been headlining the news.

I take my window seat. Looking out, I see the plane's massive wingspan and even a bird's-eye view of an entire plane docked at the next gate. I'm mesmerized that the plane I'm sitting in, which weighs tons, will be airborne soon, floating around like a feather. How incredible! A man sits next to me. I give him a once-over thinking he or any of the passengers on the plane can be a hijacker. Boarding with a lethal weapon would be as easy as walking on board with a cup of coffee.

The stewardess begins the safety demonstration, but it does nothing to calm my nerves. Seeing I'm visibly nervous, clasping my hands and rubbing my thumbs together, my row mate strikes up a conversation. I share with him this is my first flight and my first time away from home and that I'm on my way to college. I see no point in telling him about my very first "Babylift" flight, as it is a fading memory anyway.

Sensing my nervousness and probably testing my vulnerability, he says, "I know how to help you to relax and enjoy your flight." Clueless and gullible, I look at him, perplexed. He takes my silence as an invitation to tell me how satisfying he is to women and that he can relax me. To add insult to injury, he adds even more details. Disgusted, I put the armrest down between us. With no chance for him to misinterpret my action, I turn my rigid body ninety degrees toward the window. The clod isn't a hijacker but far worse, a pervert. Because I'm used to being invisible, it doesn't dawn on me I can tell the flight attendant about this man's despicable behavior. What's the point anyway? It'll probably end up being dismissed the same way it was when as a tween, I told Mama about the doctor who'd been touching me inappropriately. Mama's stance was to consider his status and see it as a compliment as a woman's cry for help will yield nothing but advice to grin and bear it anyway.

I'm drawing closer to the window when the plane suddenly takes to the sky. My weirdo seatmate's innuendos have overshadowed my experiencing the plane's impressive takeoff to which I was so looking forward. As the aircraft climbs higher and higher, I wonder if my life will be a crapshoot of randomness like today. Certain I'll be faced with the good, the bad, and the ugly of people like the man next to me; I commit then and there to be ready for life's randomness. I keep my back turned on the ugly man the entire flight. Focused on the goings-on outside the window, in a surreal moment of complete *déjà vu*, I see this fluffy white stuff floating above the plane. It's the same as the ones I'd seen on my maiden voyage from Korea! Though I hadn't thought of this since the age of five, the memory of being puzzled is vivid. Here I am, thirteen years later, looking out of the window of the *pan*gy and silently chuckling. I'm only now realizing the white stuff that had my little mind in a quandary were clouds. *Duh*, Sandy. Clouds! I chuckle, happy to finally and unexpectedly resolve an unsolved childhood mystery. Absorbed by the clouds, I ignore my seatmate who is a mixed bag of scary.

Forty-five minutes later, the stewardess announces we should secure our seat belts for landing. Ignoring Mr. Disgusting, I exit the plane and follow the signs to baggage claim. Having experienced the lows of flying with a weirdo and the highs from solving my clouds mystery, I'm hearing in my head, "Sandy, just get on with your life." I collect my bags and head over to the Stanford welcoming committee of upperclassmen holding identifying signs. It's mid-September 1971, and as a bright-eyed and bushy tailed "adult," I'm about to enter college.

It's a beautiful mild and sunny day in the Bay area. When my suitcase and footlocker trunk are loaded onto the shuttle bus, along with other bright-eyed, bushy tail students, I board the bus headed to Palo Alto. As we go through East Palo Alto, I see Black people in what appears to be a typical Black California neighborhood with a barbecue joint called Day and Night. When we cross the railroad tracks, it becomes clear why the barbecue place has its name because suddenly, all the houses that lead to Stanford are white stucco with manicured lawns and all the people I see in them are White. Someone says it's where the professors live. My eyes light up with excitement when I see the signs that let me know my destination is near. The bus slows to a crawl, and I take in the magnificence of the campus buildings with their Spanish rooftops and signature archways. The foliage is verdant, and the splendor of the natural beauty of the campus grounds captivates me. I've never seen a school like this ever. I'm dropped off at Stern Hall, which houses my dorm, Lassen House. When I find my way there, I'm greeted by our house associate, Nancy, and advisors, Billy and Suzy. I give my name at the reception desk and receive a name badge, a welcome packet, and a key to Room 5 on the first floor. Besides a two-night camping trip with the Girl Scouts, this is my second experience being away from home overnight and my first time being away from Compton.

As said before, when I got accepted to Stanford, I knew nothing about it—had never even heard it mentioned. But everyone here seems to know about the venerable university because they are making a big deal of being here. My discernment of all the to-do and hoopla and the beautiful grounds is that I'll be in the lap of luxury, mingling with the wealthy and privileged. I imagine my accommodations to be like the posh hotels I've seen on TV. When I open the door to Room 5, all I see is a metal twin bed topped with what looks like a thin hospital mattress. On the opposite wall is a wooden dresser with a mirror too high for me to see myself. The bathroom and shower are a community affair. I'm depressed. My pity party is interrupted when the door bursts open and in walks this cute brown-skin girl who is about the same height as me. This is unusual as most people and even some children are taller than me.

When I signed up for housing, I had the option of selecting my ethnic preference for a roommate or I could live in the all-Black dorm, Roble. Coming from a predominantly Black setting for most of my life, I wanted a mixed dorm but a Black roommate.

"Hello. I'm Sandy." I stare at the cheerful girl.

"Hello. I'm Melonie."

"Where are you from?" I ask.

"Ohio."

"Oh, wow," I stupidly say. "You mean there really is an Ohio?"

She chuckles at my provinciality. That moment begins a forever friendship. The other three Black students in Stern Hall hadn't selected Black roommates, nor did they associate with us.

Stern Hall, built just after World War II in 1948, was originally a men's dorm, and now things began to make sense about the place. Stern Hall has two buildings, Lassen and Larkin, which house 104 students, of which ten are Black. Of the ten, I bond with four of the six girls and two of the four boys. The two boys (Arba from Berkeley, California, and Caryl from San Diego, California) live upstairs from Melonie and me. From Larkin, I bond with Bev from Claremont, California; Darlene from St. Louis, Missouri; and my Compton homey, Paris with the perfect Afro whom I'd met in ninth grade. The Black male students who live on the other side of campus begin calling us five girls the Sistas of Stern. Since Stanford has no Black Greek organizations and the Sistas of Stern is made up of the academic cream of the crop from our respective high schools, we do represent a sisterhood of sorts and become our own sorority. The boys' Sistas of Stern name sticks, and we adopt the initials SOS as our pseudo Sorority.

I'd never seen myself as poor or rated my family in any kind of class line-up. Since leaving Korea, my gauge for a successful life was that I no longer felt the pangs of daily hunger, I wasn't dirty or wearing rags, and I had a roof over my head with uninterrupted utilities. The day I appreciate Black wealth disparity comes when the SOS members go to the bank to set up our accounts. Sighing, while filling out the deposit ticket, Darlene says, "I wish I had more to deposit."

Remember that seventy dollars Mama tied to my bra? Well, that's my whopping deposit! In my world, it's a lot, so already feeling the "I got your back" pledge of sisterhood, I chime in earnestly, "I have seventy dollars. I can give you some of mine."

Rather than snicker or embarrass me, Darlene says, "Oh, that's okay, Sandy. I'll make do with what I have." Of the five of us, I deposit a number in the tens—seven of them to be exact—another one deposits hundreds, and the others deposit in the thousands. Hilarious!

It's not long before I realize I'm truly on my own. I'm experiencing freedom as never before. It's scary, but it's great. I'm now making critical decisions and exercising choices about my own life that could make or break me, but I'm up to the challenge. Fully engaged with scheduling my classes, prioritizing my time, balancing my studies and my social life, and continuing with my spiritual growth and fellowship, I'm immersed in life. My four freshman dorm mates add a great deal of value and stimulation to my life through their rapid-fire intellectual prowess and worldliness. The sheer fun and laughter of being with them feels special to me. All of us have similar studying habits. We hit the books hard during the week hunkered down at either the library or in our dorm rooms. By the weekend, however, we are down for the activities happening around campus; football/basketball games and even parties.

One of the weekend activities our dorm sponsors is a talent show. Our showcase was a dance choreographed by none other than Paris and me to *Ball of Confusion* by The Temptations. The piece was intended to emphasize race relations and the state of our country and world. With lyrics like *People movin' out, people movin' in, why, because of the color of their skin* and supple body movements, we deliver our intended message and shine in our performance. But Roble Hall's weekend Black Party is the place to be. So famous, it draws students from neighboring San Jose State and the University of San Francisco. Frequenting the parties are my one-sided high school crush Gary W., and my school mates Karla, Pam, and Linda W. Yes indeed, jamming to Aretha Franklin's *Rock Steady* and Sly and the Family Stone's *Family Affair,* Compton is well represented in the house.

Rest assured, though, on Sundays and definitely by Monday, SOS members are re-focused on their studies. Melonie and Bev are pre-med, Darlene is majoring in economics, Paris in communication, and me in computer science. Ambitious, we all schedule more than the standard number of classes each quarter hoping to graduate a year early. We might have entered college as bright-eyed, bushy-tailed freshmen, but we are changing fast. The influences, cliques, controversies on campus, and the generally charged 'seventies atmosphere is shaping our opinions and beliefs. College is molding us into conscious beings, and we are eager to apply what we are learning to the real world.

I go home one weekend to Compton to find that Papa and our dog Trouble are not doing well. Trouble has constipation problems. I administer a suppository and stay with him in the garage, but nothing changes. The next morning, Daddy tells me that Trouble is gone. I love Trouble and relied on his unconditional love. Papa, such a stronghold in our family, has been suffering frequent mini-strokes and is blacking out. Papa is strong and always seems to recover from his many ailments, and that's just what I expect him to do, recover. I go back to school and can't believe it when I receive the call in my dorm, February 7, 1972, I'm expecting to say, "Happy ninety-second Birthday, Papa," but it's Mama crying, telling me that my beloved Papa is gone. I am well aware of the circle of life by now, but death is an arc of the circle I wish I never have to face. I am glad I went home.

On campus, I'm navigating through the volatile early 'seventies. Like the rest of the country, Stanford students are protesting the Vietnam War. Trained to be ethnically invisible, I silently protest because my Asian side knows all about war and its devastating effect, plus my brother is fighting in that war. Thank goodness he is discharged from the navy soon after I get to college, and he is not a casualty of war. Like the Korean War, I wonder how many children will be left behind like me as the forgotten mistakes of war.

I'm an equal opportunity silent protestor on my Black side, too. The Black Student Union (BSU) is protesting and demanding the release of the incarcerated Black Panther Bobby Seale, accused of murder, and Angela Davis, the party's radical, fierce feminist activist and member of the communist party accused of purchasing the firearms used to kidnap and kill a Marin County, California, judge. Bobby Seale is revered as one of the Black Panther Party's founders and coiner of the enormously popular slogan, "All Power to the People," which becomes an anthem for Blacks. As a BSU member, Mama and Daddy's conservative influence makes me a covert supporter, donating when I can to help pay for student protesters who go to the courthouse to support Seale and Davis. Other times, I contribute to their defense fund. It is truly a time of radical change. Native American students who had been protesting the school's use of the Indian mascot of Stanford's athletic teams for years, finally win their petition. The Indian symbol is officially dropped in 1972 after over a thirty-year tradition. The Stanford Indians become the Stanford Cardinal.

Another hot-button controversy on campus that makes national news is incited by Dr. William Shockley, Nobel Prize winner in physics for the creation of the transistor and professor of electrical engineering at Stanford University. I'd not heard of Shockley's shocking claim until one day when the members of SOS and I go to the dining hall for lunch. Sitting nearby are some upperclassmen, graduate, and law students engaged in fierce conversation. Our ears perk up when an African student, his strong, heavily accented and commanding voice is becoming more and more indignant with each word he says; "Unbelievable, that man. How could he be here?" Shockley had told him to drop his course since he had no chance of being successful.

It turns out that Shockley is a radical White man and a proponent of Eugenics, which blatantly promotes a theory that Blacks are intellectually and genetically inferior. I'm incensed. It's one thing to espouse your views, but it's another to apply them to discouraging Black students from taking your class. Such behavior should have no place at Stanford, period. The gall of a man to even suggest that Blacks should voluntarily submit to sterilization to control the breeding of an inferior race of people. To ensure his race and genes continue, he donates his sperm to the Repository for Germinal Choice in the so-called Nobel Prize Sperm Bank.

I enroll in a course from Dr. Cedric (Clark) X, who, in counter to Dr. Shockley, discriminates against White students in his class by telling them his class is only designed for Black students. An enraged student threatens a lawsuit. The dean asks Dr. Cedric X his reasoning behind such an action. His response is he's conducting an experiment of reverse prejudice to Shockley's preposterous actions against Black students. The BSU, fueled by the professors at odds, wants to set up a debate between them. Along with The BSU's insistence on a debate, some Asian student sympathizers interrupt Shockley's class demanding he debate Dr. Cedric X. To get them to leave his classroom, Shockley agrees; however, they are later charged with violating campus disruption policy. I'd been approached by a fellow student who is also half Asian, trying to persuade me to join a group called the Mixed Bloods Society. I ignore the offer and continue my code of ethnic silence by avoiding being a part of any group. But honestly, I'm proud of the Asian students' solidarity and secretly admire Dr. Cedric X's rebuttal.

The debate finally happens on January 23, 1973, in Memorial Church, and it is at capacity. Having no interest in fighting the crowd, I listen to the four-hour live debate on our campus radio station KZSU from my dorm room. The day after the debate, I hear through the proverbial grapevine and confirm when I read it in *The Stanford Daily* that Dr. Shockley wants mixed-race students to submit to blood tests to assess the amount of Caucasian or non-Black blood in their ancestry to see how it contributes to their higher IQ. I'm glad I declined membership in the Mixed Bloods Society because no part of me—Black or Asian—will contribute any data to this racist man's unsubstantiated claim.

All this Eugenics buzz is finally silenced when the show *Tony Brown's Journal* brings the prominent Black psychiatrist Dr. Frances Cress Welsing and Dr. William Shockley face-to-face on his show. Dr. Welsing elegantly rebuts and overpowers Dr. Shockley's argument, suggesting the superiority of the Black genetic code since life started in Ethiopia is the reason for the White supremacy culture in the first place. Supremacy is nothing, she contends, but White fear of their race being annihilated by melanin. Eventually, because of continuous mainstream coverage of Dr. Shockley's shocking and preposterous claims putting the spotlight on Stanford, he is alienated from the academic community and retires from Stanford. His work in the transistor's development, which had ignited the digital rise of Silicon Valley, is now tarnished, as is his Nobel accomplishments.

Through all of this, there is a standout student, the one instrumental in organizing and monitoring the Dr. Shockley debate, the Free Angela Campaign, and who writes many articles in *The Stanford Daily*. He is a young man from Merced, California, named Charles Ogletree. It is evident he's going to have a bright future. A born leader, he is the chairman of the BSU and a member of the Associated Students of Stanford University Council of Presidents who inspires social consciousness and spearheads political and community activism on campus. Charles is at the forefront of any concerns that involve the advancement of the Black students and the Black community. Braids, like afros, are popularly worn by Black guys and girls at this time, and I become one of the hair braiders on campus. I also crochet red, black, and green liberation hats, which Charles and other conscious brothers and sisters sport. Charles becomes even more potent when he begins dating a fellow Compton sister, Pam, whose quiet spirit is the wind beneath his wings. Though he is a serious brother, articulate, and all about business, he knows how to party like the rest of us at Roble Hall, where he lives. My admiration for Charles is real. I love his focus and commitment.

Growing worldly or not, I have to concentrate on my classes and grades because I'm on a full scholarship and must maintain good academic standing. My initial major is computer science, which suits my analytical mind. I'm enjoying the beginning courses of my major. To complete my programming assignments, I ride my bike to the computer lab, which is quite a distance from my dorm. Often, I don't leave the lab until past midnight, and going through some of the desolate areas to get back to my dorm is a little scary. While visiting my parents during a school break, news of a female student attacked while jogging on campus is startling enough, but as it happens, the news is full of stories anew about the Zodiac serial killer who has been killing in the Bay Area for years. It has been eerily quiet for a while, but now he is out there killing again. So far, he's targeted four men and three women between the ages of sixteen and twenty-nine and claims to have killed as many as thirty-seven victims in taunting letters and cards he's sent to the local Bay Area press. Could he have been behind this recent attack? This news wreaks havoc on my mind and nerves.

Alarmed and thinking of the many bike rides I make alone at night to and from the lab, when I return to school, out of fear, I make a decision that might not serve me well in the long run to drop my computer major. I then declare psychology as my major instead. Deciding on my major is one thing; expanding my social circle is another. It is well known all over campus that freshmen are looked upon as "fresh meat" by upperclassmen. Nancy, our resident associate, gives us straight talk and firm advice. "Guys," she tells us, "will come sniffing around, but you must keep your senses about you." As it turns out, one of Nancy's senior friends is Gary C., to whom she introduces our crew from Compton. In fact, Gary C. had been Centennial's student body president, so I'd met him when I was a ninth grader. I'd even attended a March of Dimes event with him. Gary C. becomes our big brother and sets the standard of what being a good guy should look like when deciding to date. Paris's cousin Linda also attends Stanford. On weekends we all ride back home as often as we can. Through Linda, I meet Charlie Mac, our star football player, and his friend Lenard and through them, I meet Al.

Al is an upperclassman who seems to be friends with just about everyone. He starts coming around quite a bit to our dorm, but he's different from the other guys who only drop by because he hangs out with us in our dorm room. At night when we're ravished, he drives us to Round Table Pizza. I soon find instead of the group, it's become Al and me going to get pizza. Then it's Al and me at the movies, and the next thing I know, he's my first long-term relationship. By the spring quarter of 1972, we're going steady. I don't know that I've chosen this relationship as much as drifted into it. I suspect one of the reasons is because of Mama. Before I left for college, a flame rekindles with Mario, a boy from my earlier high school days. The problem: our timing and our goals. I, of course, was going away to college, and he wasn't. As charming as he was, I know getting involved with him could derail my dreams. But the thing that turned me off the most was not the fact he just became a father, but *my* mother. Mama didn't care if this guy was a horrible person or how many children he'd already fathered because he was light-skinned, had green eyes, and "good" straight hair. As such, he could do no wrong in her eyes. Everything was about his looks and not his character. For that reason, I rebelled against what Mama would approve of, and Al was just the opposite of Mario in looks.

Tall, dark, and handsome in his own way, Al is a man of God, which is super attractive to me. He and a faithful group of Stanford friends attend Mountain View Baptist Church. Al is with me at church every Sunday. Everyone is now assuming that like Charlie Mac (our football player friend whom we support every home game weekend) and his girlfriend, who has transferred to Stanford to get married, Al and I had the makings for a great future together. Unfortunately, our relationship soon develops into an unhealthy one when Al becomes controlling for no discernible reason. When things go from verbal to physical abuse, I begin to put the brakes on our relationship, but I don't leave. At first, I try to understand, but I have no clue why Al is turning into this kind of person. He sometimes seems troubled, but he never talks about what's bothering him. Because I know he's experiencing something psychologically, I try to be understanding. Being with Al makes me able to relate to women who find themselves trapped in abusive relationships with people wrestling deep psychological and sociological issues. I'm beginning to know firsthand the dire implications of staying in an abusive relationship for my own psychological reasons, not all I fully understand. Self-esteem is hard-won for so many, including myself.

Fortunately, despite my relationship's slow erosion, I keep my sanity and stay ahead of my academic demands. I'm taking twenty-plus credits each quarter. During this period, I find social outlets by volunteering to tutor at a school in East Palo Alto with the Black Student Volunteer Center. I'm also taking African dance classes and performing in plays. My work-study job for the renowned Dr. St. Clair Drake, founder of the African and African-American Studies program at Stanford University, fills up the rest of my time. In contrast to his vast academic stature, the giant of a man is physically short in person. He's personable, down to earth, and his authentic demeanor surprises me. I'm blown away when in conversations, he seeks my opinion and respects my thoughts and perspectives. To me, he is taller than the tallest mountain. Around Dr. Drake, my confidence soars, and I'm learning so much about life in the Black Diaspora. I'm learning so much about the real history of African-American contributions to America's success, including that of my birth father. Dr. Drake is an objector of World War II due to the way Blacks were treated. I try to imagine what it must have been like for my father and the Black soldiers of the Korean War's 24th Infantry facing discrimination on both continents. The six hundred thousand Black soldiers minus five thousand by the end of the war who had given their lives for a country that despised them. It must have been demoralizing. What, I wonder, had gone through the minds of stalwart, heroic Korean War soldiers such as PFC William Thompson, Sargent Cornelius Charlton, and Ensign Jesse L. Brown as they lay dying on the battlefield for someone else's freedom, their own freedoms at home unattained?

If my birth father is alive, would he feel vindicated by the progress of the 'sixities and 'seventiess? Would he have been a freedom rider to put an end to the decades-long struggle to end sanctioned racism, discrimination, and segregation of the Jim Crow Era? Would he have cheered on the forty-two-year-old Rosa Parks from Montgomery, Alabama, who sat in the front instead of the back of the bus, and when asked to move, refused? Pleased to see his people's solidarity as they stage the Montgomery bus boycott, and what would be considered the first rebellion of the civil rights movement? History brings clarity, and Dr. St. Clair Drake is blowing my mind. I don't know that I thought so deeply about anything before. But I do know I'll side with rebellion against discrimination in any form—be it from inequality stemming from Korea's mijok, Japan's Kegare class, China's Hukou, India's Dalits, England's feudal system, or French Bastille prolétariats. Inequality in any form would be my enemy.

By the middle of my third year, I have enough credits to graduate, so I take a lot of fun courses to finish out the school year. Part of that time, I spend in a primate research lab testing Rhesus monkeys' intelligence. At the end of this project, I'm asked to consider working at Moffett Airfield to continue my research. After seeing chimpanzees injected with radiation to observe its effect, my fascination with research ends. I'm at war with any inhumane act.

Many of the elective course I've taken throughout my years at Stanford are a return to my first love: languages. I begin learning Spanish in earnest, thanks to my nanny's son, Wilbert, who'd inspired my affinity for the language. I enjoyed these classes and hoped they'd help as I intend to spend my fourth year at a study abroad program in Spain. Unfortunately, Stanford has no study program set up in Spain, so with no other option, I graduate a year early, in June 1974.

Daddy, who never attended any of my high school events, surprises me and shows up for my graduation. He rents an RV and drives the entire family up to Palo Alto. I'm elated, too, that Nanny and her family are also here to celebrate this milestone with me. The school makes dorm rooms available for our families and friends to stay. The day before graduation, the school hosts a reception for our families at Tressider Union, a student affairs building where we gather to eat. Dr. St. Clair Drake makes it a point of meeting Mama, telling her how proud she should be of me. The next day, I have to attend two ceremonies; the general graduation with all the graduates and the departmental one to receive my diploma.

On graduation day, I look out from the stage, and there's Daddy with a movie camera recording the historic moment. Everyone is there except Mama, who has stayed behind at the dorm. I'm beyond disappointed and can't hide it in the pictures we take. Their whole trip is about this moment, so why had Mama not shown up? Mama claims she didn't feel well. I don't believe it because I've seen Mama take the wind out of sails many times before, and I wonder if she'd done this intentionally. How could she dash this high point of my life? Mama is a hypochondriac and likes to be the center of attention. I believe her absence is because the attention is on me, and no one was doting over her. I'm upset and stay that way for a while. You'd think by now I would've learned how to handle disappointment or take it in stride, but I'm truly hurt. I want to forgive her, but I've yet to learn how to forgive people who don't know they have done something for which they should be forgiven.

The trip home is a crazy eight-hour ride in the RV. Daddy is continually nagging Virgil about his driving while Mama and Lolo are snipping and snapping at each other. I'm sitting with a blackened, swollen big toe from the Dr. Pepper bottle Lolo accidentally dropped on my foot. As I observe and listen to what I'm moving back home to, I'm a bit disheartened. Three years away and a head filled with the knowledge of a world larger than Compton is making me see things differently. I'll miss my intellectual friends from Stanford, but this is my family, and I love them. I console myself. God makes no mistake. For some reason, He'd chosen them to be my family, they'd chose me to be theirs, and in the larger scheme of things, I'd somehow chosen them.

My plan once home is to take some time to figure out my next steps, but the day I get back to Compton, my high school mentor, Mr. Freeman, calls. He advises me to apply to the University of Southern California (USC) for the Masters in Education Teacher Corps Program. Uncertain, I listen because so far, life has somehow seemed to orchestrate my every move, guiding me to even greater heights. I do just that, apply to USC. Within a few weeks, my acceptance arrives. I'm to begin the program in August 1974. My next move then keeps me in Los Angeles.

# CHAPTER NINE

## The Joker's Wild

During my first year at USC, I continue to carry over baggage from Stanford in the form of my tumultuous relationship with Al. He's been accepted to law school, so we both end up in the Los Angeles area. My inability to walk away from Al may seem like I'm a glutton for punishment, but that should come as no surprise since emotionally, I have the profile of one who might look for love in all the wrong places. After all, I'm an orphan, a war child prone to settling for anything that looks like love and connection.

Rationalizing our unhealthy relationship as one that can be viable probably stems from seeing my parents argue all the time yet stay together. Though I've never seen physical abuse in my parents' relationship, according to Papa, it had been there. In my case, deep down, I know this relationship is wrong, but I'm still thinking of Al as my life partner. Al and I have been together for three years now, and his mother loves me, but I can't say the same about my mother's love for him. Al is polite and respectful when he meets my parents, but it's obvious from Mama's body language that he doesn't tick her boxes. I know he's being rejected based on his looks. Even if she'd known about his neurotic and abusive behavior, that wouldn't have been the reason she wouldn't like him. Being dark was just not Mama's idea of ideal. Out of rebellion, I stay longer with him than I should.

By September 1974, along with nineteen other students selected from thousands of applicants, I completed my USC orientation. I feel blessed to be going off to graduate school on a full scholarship, one with a monthly stipend to boot. The Teacher Corps Program at USC brings me back to Willowbrook Junior High School. I'm back in southern California and back at home in Compton, living with my parents. As soon as I'm back, I get a call from Al asking me to accompany him to CBS Television City in Los Angeles.

He is going to audition for the popular game show, *The Joker's Wild*. On the show, contestants have to answer a series of questions from subject categories randomly chosen by a contraption that resembles a slot machine. Al is super bright, so he'll likely do well on the show. I decide to go with him. While he's taping, I'm sitting in the waiting room when in walks a staff member who approaches me and asks if I'd consider being on the show too.

"No, thank you," I reply.

She asks, "Why not?"

I tell her. "Your show wants people to be giddy and excitable, and that's not me. I'm just here waiting on someone to finish their taping."

Persistence is the staff manager's superpower, and I finally give in. Before I realize what's happening, a "bio person" appears carrying a notecard. He takes one look at me and says, "Korean War baby." No reply or even an exchange of dialogue is possible as he quickly turns and walks off. I'm blindsided and speechless by the accuracy of his assessment. If his question did require an answer, what would I've said? Would I have been rendered mute?

I take my place behind the machine, and the announcer introduces me, "And…hereeee is Saundra Henderson from Seoul, Korea." My heart flutters, realizing the code of silence I've held for years for Mama's sake would now be public. The forbidden K-word would be exposed on national TV. I take a few breaths. *Okay,* I tell myself, *you've gotta calm down and focus.* Though I'm on national TV, the show is not live, so I figure I will implement a damage control strategy and ask the producer to edit out any reference to Korea. No action may be necessary as Mama doesn't watch *The Joker's Wild*.

Shifting gears, I'm now focused on the game show questions. Considering my knowledge base is not as worldly as Al's, I surprise myself by correctly answering many of the questions. I end up not far behind the leading contestant in money value. What will not be shown in the aired show, I'm sure, is how many times I pulled the lever to answer a question, and the darn machine didn't budge. It's now time for the final question. When my opponent pulls the lever, the luck of the draw is with him as he gets three Jokers, winning the game. Al thinks it's a hoot that I got on the show, but we don't talk much about it on the way home, and it did not lead to any incidents.

My consolation prize is a Mr. Coffee Maker and cans of Veg-All Mixed Vegetables. I wonder what Mama is going to think when they deliver them to the house. I'll have figured something out by then. No one in my family knows I'm on the show, so I pray when it airs, they don't see it. God is on my side. I dodge that bullet because Mama indeed doesn't see the show. My only worry for the next week or two is that a neighbor who might have seen the show will call Mama to chitchat about my being on TV. Miraculously no one calls her. I relax, and life goes on as before.

At Willowbrook, my mentor, Mr. Freeman, is now the principal. He basks in the benefits of getting four student teachers to enhance his school's program. A unified team when it comes to working and completing projects, we exceed his expectations. Like at Stanford, I bond with my new USC teammates (Amy, Aurelia, Michael, and Sheila). Each day, we grow closer and closer, and to me, we have the potential of becoming lifelong friends like my go-to sistas of SOS. I call us the Mod Squad since our team includes one White, a Hispanic, an Asian, a Black, and me—the mixed one. Why Mod Squad, you may ask? Because *Mod Squad* featured a diverse cast with the promo "One White, One Black and One Blonde."

Things are going pretty well in my program. I buy a new car and move away from home to an apartment in Downey with my SOS Melonie. I'm excelling in school while Al is failing law school. To make matters worse, I'm no longer dependent on him, and I think this is driving him crazy. He's now hanging out with a group of older women, partying and drinking. He tells me he is deejaying for them, and it's clear that while my star is rising, Al is falling into the abyss. He senses that we are moving farther and farther apart, and knowing how much I'd admired dogs while at Stanford, especially Irish setters, Al tries to reel me in by gifting me a cute full-bred Irish setter puppy. He is right. My heart melts for the puppy at first sight and at Al's thoughtfulness. We call our puppy, Sundance.

Along with Sundance, we move in together in Inglewood, creating a false sense of a pseudo-family. It isn't long, however, before I'm going to USC's clinic for all the bruises on my body. Having to lie to the doctor that I'd fallen off my bike or accidentally hit my head is the beginning of the end of my relationship with Al. One too many visits and I can tell even the doctor doesn't believe me anymore. I finally decide enough is enough after an altercation, which almost costs me my life. I decide to move out when Al is out of town. Nanny and her son Stanley come to help. She'd known we were having problems, so when I ask for help, all Nanny says is, "Let's go." I feel so ashamed, but not once does she judge me—or make me feel stupid for making a bad choice in Al. I debate taking our puppy, deciding to bring Sundance since Al bought it for me, plus the puppy is afraid of him. As though choreographed to the moment, as we pull away from the apartment, I hear the Temptations' song, *Don't Look Back*. I don't look back because I'm done.

My USC Mod Squad and Nanny become my support system as I navigate the gamut of unexpected emotions that come with any breakup. As they say, love is a hurting thing. Wavering on my decision to leave is not an option. I know I can do better than this. I know I'm worthy of love. The past doesn't have to determine my future because I'm no longer abandoned, orphaned, or rejected—haven't been for most of my life. Yet, my self-esteem and value haven't caught up with the system in my head, which says otherwise. Walking away from Al, I hope, means that I'm finally free of trying to rescue anyone but myself. I'm done taking the brunt of things I don't deserve. I've got to believe that I'm worthy of real love and respect.

The showdown that nails the relationship coffin shut forever happens on the day I hear my name over the school's PA system. "Saundra Henderson, Saundra Henderson, you have a visitor." It's Al. Al, who's called my regular school and found out I'm teaching at this school for the day. I'm working with students when the announcements come over the PA that he's waiting in the office. When I meet him there, he asks if I will walk with him to his car to discuss our dog. He wouldn't dare make a scene in public, so I walk with him. Was I ever wrong! Before I know it, all six-three of him and four-eleven of me are tussling on the ground. My teammates, seeing I'm in trouble, run toward us, screaming at him to stop. Al immediately stops, and I can see in his eyes he knows he's hit rock bottom. It's a pity because inside, Al is a very good person who needs help. That day, Al finally realizes our time together is truly over.

I move to a new apartment near USC and cut off all contact with him. I'm overjoyed learning my SOS Paris, who is a comfort, lives around the corner from me. Through it all—the doubt, the fears, the stark realizations, the identity crisis—I soldier on. I double down on my studies and take refuge in my education. I'm a good student and stay on course. I graduate with my master's from USC in June 1976. This time, my college graduation is old hat, and Mama is the only one who comes. She attends the general ceremony but again misses the departmental ceremony where I received my diploma. This time it's because Mama didn't realize she has to change locations to see me accept my diploma, so she sat waiting in the general graduation area. At this point in my life, I'm just glad she's physically here with me.

Three of us from the USC Teacher Corps program are recruited to teach in Las Vegas, Nevada. The Clark County School District personnel manager, who is eager to seal the deal, invites me to come and check out the city. It's sometime in May 1976 when I step outside the McCarran Airport into the brutal and prostrating heat of Vegas. I thought people were kidding when they said you can fry an egg on the sidewalk of Vegas during 118-degree-daytime temperature. They were not. For sure, this heat will take some getting used to, even for a California girl.

My ride to the hotel takes me along the famous Las Vegas strip. Gaudily lit with colorful flashing lights illuminating the Stardust, Sahara, Caesar's Palace, Aladdin, and on and on, Vegas is the epitome of kitsch. My head is spinning, trying to take it all in. That evening, still ninety-five degrees minus the sun but bright with lights, I feel safe enough to walk around and take in the hype about Las Vegas. The sound of a gazillion slot machines greets me as I head into Stardust. I pull a couple of dollars from my bag and exchange them for nickels. I feed the never-satisfied machine and pull the lever some forty times. Pretty good odds as I won a few dollars. Like every good gambler, by the end, I lose the entire two dollars I played plus my winnings. That day I realize I'm no gambler, so Vegas better have something else to keep me there. The heat and chaos are already enough strikes against it. On a teacher's salary, even two dollars might put a dent in my budget. The only time I envision revisiting a casino will be to eat (as food is cheap) or to bring anyone visiting me.

The name Las Vegas, a hot, parched desert, oddly enough, means *the meadows* in Spanish. When the oasis was founded in 1905, underground artesian wells created greenery in the middle of the desert, drawing the gold rush to its surroundings. Many early settlers from all over the U.S. came to find their riches. Many were connected to the entertainment industry, so soon, Las Vegas became an international resort city known for its gambling, entertainment, and nightlife. Run by the notorious mob, it was flashy, seedy, and greedy, earning it the name Sin City for its anything-goes attitude. "What Happens in Vegas Stays in Vegas" is coined as its motto in 2003, and the green meadow of yesteryear became the green dollar signs of today. With the entertainment industry at full tilt, it should come as no surprise that Vegas's school system is an afterthought.

The next morning, I meet with the school district's personnel director, Mr. Tumbleson, who takes me on a tour of a few schools. Maybe pulsing my lack of enthusiasm, on the way back to the district office, he says, "You know what, I want to make one more stop to introduce you to someone." That stop is at Valley High School, where I meet a social studies teacher he'd recruited a year before from Los Angeles. Something in my heart likes Marilyn immediately. She is nice enough to give me her phone number to call if I have questions or decide to move there. I accept the position. It'll get me out of LA and away from Al should temptation arise. Excited to get my very first paying job, I sign my teaching contract. With the final stroke of the pen, I've gone from being a college kid to a woman who just signed her first employment contract. I'm about to get a set salary every month that's all mine! Yes, yes. Unbelievable.

My first order of business is to go apartment hunting. I settle on a one-bedroom apartment not too far from the MGM Grand hotel because they accept pets. I'm writing the deposit check when pausing, I let the situation sink in. I'm an adult making adult decisions. At USC, I'd had a taste of living independently and even living with Al, but this is different. Being in Las Vegas means I'm truly on my own with no option to dash home to Compton or run to Nanny for comfort.

Back home in Compton, I rent a U-Haul, and my brother Virgil helps me make the trek eastward. I'm still in shock. I'm managing all this on my own. Sundance, who gets car sick easily, is out cold from the tranquilizer pills the vet gave him. An hour outside of Vegas, the U-Haul, none too pleased with the blustering heat, conks out on Interstate 15. Stranded in 118°desert heat, we're hot, hungry, and thirsty. Mama's training had me pack a few chicken salad sandwiches and drinks for the trip, which tides us over as we wait on the replacement U-Haul. Transferring all my worldly possessions to another truck is no fun, and we arrive in Vegas a few shades darker than when we left L.A. Virgil and I are exhausted. He stays overnight then heads back home the following day. At 23 years old, I arrived in Las Vegas for my very first paying job.

Sundance, who thinks he's human, is finally alert and is a great companion. I don't feel so alone as he lovingly stares at me, sitting like a human, with his hind parts on the couch and hind legs touching the floor. He even gets the newspaper and brings his leash when he wants to go out. Alone, however, when I'm gone, his neurosis comes out full force. He's already shredded my furniture and chewed up a few pairs of shoes. Because of him, I invest in something I hate and never guessed I'd buy as an adult—plastic covering to protect my new furniture.

I must now establish new connections to bolster me intellectually, socially, and spiritually, so I call Marilyn after settling in. Marilyn is tall, dark, and statuesque with an itty-bitty Afro. Not only does she enthusiastically welcome me to Las Vegas, but she invites me over for lunch. She and her boyfriend live close by, but she, too, is in the unhealthy relationship club from which I'm finally liberated. As we grow closer, I begin sharing my journey, finding it hard to believe someone as serious and intelligent as Marilyn can fall into this trap. But I'm a witness that intellect has nothing to do with psycho-social imprisonment under the guise of love.

Our connection is comforting and provides mutual support. Marilyn becomes like family. We enjoy cooking; frying fish; listening to Earth, Wind, and Fire; and going to events together. Marilyn introduces me to new friends, experiences, and places. We go to events

I would have imagined out of my reach—like tickets to *the* Ebony Fashion Fair and so much more. I'm glad as a teen I taught myself to sew because now I'm using that skill to make us fashionable outfits to style in at our events.

Teacher Corps has prepared me well for my first teaching job at Jim Bridger Junior High School. I'll be teaching social studies. During my Stanford research assistant days, I'd learned the art of teaching isn't just about getting students' attention, but in keeping it. Innovative and energetic, I approach my class with openness. Though my classroom is set up in the typical rows of desk configuration, I invite students who learn differently to stretch out on the carpet in the middle of the classroom and listen to soft music to aid their learning. I'd know about this from working with a Ph.D. student who used Harmonic Induction (the title of his thesis)—music in the background while learning or studying to enhance recall.

I love teaching, but I have six classes. At the end of the day, I'm doggedly tired. When my students draft me to sponsor the drill team, tired as I am, I can't refuse as many Black girls at the school are a part of the team, and for them, this will probably be their only extra-curricular activity. I use my sewing skills to make the snazzy uniforms the girls don at parades. I'm the proud sponsor of one memorable competition when the girls glammed up in their new outfits outshine all in the competition. Their choreographed routine to the song *Flashlight* sweeps the honors, and they're hailed the fans' favorites.

My social circle expands to include three new people. Jeanie, my work colleague, is particularly interesting. She's affiliated with the Black Panther party because her daughters' father is a Panther. Her children, who become my godchildren, are named Africa and Afeni, a nod to Black Panther member Afeni Shakur. There's never a dull moment around Jeanie and her family, as with most families, I know, are dysfunctional, but I deeply admire their unwavering love and support of each other. In Vegas, too, I find my Black card when I meet Tony and Steve, brothers from Detroit.

Tony is an art teacher and his younger brother, Steve, is a student at the University of Nevada, Las Vegas. I meet Tony at a teachers union assembly. We both become involved with the Minority Caucus as the Black representatives of the teachers union. Remember Sandy, the silent protester during the Stanford years? Well, I find my voice in black-and-white print through the Minority Caucus newsletter. Tony and Steve are great young men, positive, down to earth, and optimistic despite all the bad luck that seems to follow them, car breakdowns and food scavenging being two of them. As poorly paid teachers, we all have to scavenge for food way too often. Since I have wheels, I'm their good-luck charm as I tool them around town. I earn my fairy godmother status one weekend at a teachers union gathering. As we enter, we are given raffle tickets. Within fifteen minutes of being seated, they call my number, and just like that, I win one hundred dollars. That is a whole lot of money, and always hungry, we head straight to the strip to enjoy a five-star steak, seafood, and dessert.

The only time I'm exposed to Vegas' nightlife is when I'm with Tony and Steve. They hear about a hot club, and off we head for a night out. On several occasions, our color is a barrier to our entrance. We see the bouncer's selective nod to certain guests, then wide-eyed turn to us and say, "We're at capacity," code for unwelcome guests like us. I learn firsthand. WE HAVE NOT OVERCOME!

The Las Vegas school district has many issues, one being it's been in litigation for years trying to desegregate the school system. The Black area is West Las Vegas, and as far as schools, there are six elementary schools in the area with no junior or senior high school. Black children are being bused out of their neighborhoods for most of their school years. White families are refusing to bus their children to the elementary schools in the Black areas. By the time I get to Las Vegas, the school board has reached a desegregation compromise. The six elementary schools in West Las Vegas will be converted into Sixth Grade Centers. This is the so-called desegregation option for White families to send their children for ONLY their sixth-grade year while Black children are bused out of their neighborhood all their years except the sixth grade. This action erodes Black children's sense of community for their area.

At the Minority Caucus meetings, we are complaining. In February for Black History, the one week allowed is mostly ignored or not included in school plans. The mortal sin of racism is in full tilt in undereducated Vegas and this blatant disregard for the well-being of the whole Black child incenses me. As a social studies teacher who teaches Anglo history, I'm infuriated at the widespread ignorance of African Americans' contributions to America's success. I take action. I write an article for the newsletter about the travesty of omitting the one week designated to highlight Black history and boost Black students' cultural pride. Not that any of it helped, but I am proud to have been *out* for a cause.

Las Vegas is full of adventure for many, but not me. Feeling a need to center from Vegas's indulgence, I decide to go home for Columbus Day weekend. Gone from home for almost four months—the longest period I'd ever been away from my family—to be honest, I'm homesick. I catch the Greyhound bus to Los Angeles, and Daddy meets me downtown at the station. When he pulls into the driveway, I'm excited and eager to see Mama, so I rush out of the car, run up the porch stairs, and put my key in the door. As I turn the key and open the door, I hear loud and clear, "And hereeee's Saundra Henderson from Seoul, Korea." I stop in my tracks. I can't believe my ears. I'm literally being introduced as I walk through the door. The noise coming from Mama and Daddy's bedroom is the re-run of the two-year-old *The Joker's Wild* show. I slowly approach the room, and there's Mama, sitting on the edge of the bed a few feet in front of the TV watching the show. Was this the twilight zone? How unbelievable the moment is. My anticipated happy reunion disappears; as Mama stares at me, her lips pursed. I have done the unthinkable: declared myself Korean.

Mama ignores me the entire weekend. I'm sure she feels betrayed. Not even her usual lament of "After all I've done for you" leaves her lips. Something in me changes. I realize this is an act of God—His divine intervention for all of us to stop living a lie. To stop walking on eggshells around our reality. To be honest, we are so indebted to Mama for taking us unwanted children that we could only comply when she ordered the ban on Korea. Perhaps, it dawns on me Mama needs to live in a fantasy world. I always thought her delusional when she'd scold Lolo and me, saying, "After all I've done for you, cleaning your diapers…." Lolo and I would look at each other, thinking how far and ridiculous can this charade go? We both were nearly five when she adopted us, hardly in diapers!

The weekend finally ends the charade that had begun with me acting out my worm-passing scenario. It took a game show from two years earlier for Mama to see it might have been cruel to have us deny our heritage because I'm indeed half Korean, and trying to take away that part of my heritage is wrong. This is a moment in time when Mama and I could have had a heart-to-heart talk about who we really were. But neither Mama nor I could rise to the occasion.

I love my mother very much. I've been obedient and respectful to her my entire life, from the moment we met, yet I've always wished for a real mother-daughter relationship, a closer relationship that goes beyond just the parent-child boundaries or duty. As an adult, I'd hoped that Mama would permit me to really become family and not feel beholden to the fact that I was just an acquisition. Just an orphan being offered a home. I want Mama to see me, hear me, feel me, and love me. I want to tell Mama. Let's go beyond obedience and obligation, but how? I want to tell her I desire mutual and unconditional love, but how? I want to tell her that throughout my childhood, I never truly felt I belonged that I've often wondered if I'll ever feel a true kinship with her, but this weekend has shown me that Mama has categorically shut the door on that idea. Emotionally I have to move on.

Maybe I want something that just doesn't exist and can only be gotten from a maternal parent, much like she wants something that doesn't exist, a child born of her own flesh. I would always be to Mama just a little girl she named Saundra Henderson, and she would always be the woman who took great care of me. Something in me shifts. I'm no longer willing to be a "china doll." That moment during the Columbus Day 1976 weekend becomes the most significant moment of my life. It forces me to accept that people need to believe in their delusions and illusions and that no matter how hard one tries, they need their own reality. I need mine, too. That day set me on a path to shed the guilt of being who I am. Disappointing though the realization is, it is freeing. I now have freedom from feeling obligated and beholden. I have the freedom to be me.

A few months later, I go to a restaurant and I serendipitously meet Alex Haley and Jackie Brantley, his public relations person. It is just after the phenomenal success of his book *Roots.* Haley had written *Roots* based on snippets of his grandmother's stories. I begin sharing my Korean story with them, wishing somehow it could lead to some answers for my confused mind.

"Your story is your journey," Ms. Brantley says, encouraging me to write it down. She gives me her card. That day, I learned to exhale, and I begin to release pent-up feelings through poetry and journaling of a past I didn't want to forget and a present worth remembering.

After my first year in Vegas, Marilyn moves back to L.A. to teach, and my honeymoon with Vegas is pretty much over. Before leaving, she introduces me to her friend Ann. Ann is a teacher. An athletic and top racquetball player, she spends a lot of time away from home. We end up renting a house together but somehow never get a chance to bond. I'm learning to accept people for who they were and keep it moving. I'm still trying to make it in Vegas but find it hard. Apart from the awful pay, at the end of every month's payday I have 'more month than money I'm sick of the heat and the provinciality. Marilyn resolves my money issues by sending her monthly car note to me as float. She trusted me enough to allow me to use the money as I needed and to pay her bill when it became due at the local credit union when I got paid. The second year in Vegas ends up being the last year for Jeanie, Tony, and me. Steve, unfortunately, has to stay to finish his undergraduate studies. Before leaving, it seems I need an unforgettable Las Vegas story to tell in the future. Thanks to Jeanie, I get it.

Now Jeanie is no joke. Her radical experience with the Black Panthers makes her a no-nonsense kind of woman. One weekend, a male teacher known for stretching the truth about himself invites Jeanie and me to his home for a gumbo party. When we arrive, we notice there's no one else there but us. Mr. Stretch-the-Truth proclaims once we'd entered his home, that he needs to shower and get himself together for the party, so we should make ourselves at home. In a flash, the savvy and wise Jeanie catches on to his setup. Is this guy expecting to seduce us into a threesome? Is he planning to drug our drinks?

"We're out," Jeanie says as we get ready to hightail it out of there but not before teaching the clod a lesson. I feel like Wonder Woman's sidekick. That's how baaadasss Jeanie is. While he's in the shower, Jeanie directs me to scoop all the gumbo into a carryout container. She then grabs his car keys, pockets them, and we walk out the door. Just like that. For a week, the fake isn't able to drive his car. Suspecting Jeanie has confiscated them, he comes begging and pleading for her to return his keys, which she does after he apologized for inviting us to his house under false pretenses. He knew no other guests were invited and was being shady.

By June 1978, I'm departing Vegas. Jeanie is moving to Houston to go to law school, and I decide to join her and her girls. Before going, I help Tony move back to Detroit and have the pleasure of meeting his wonderful parents (Papa Wil and Mama Lee) who, on day one take me in as the daughter they never had. With them for only a day, I understand what unconditional love feels like. They are warm and genuine. Papa Wil and Mama Lee become an emotional bedrock for me.

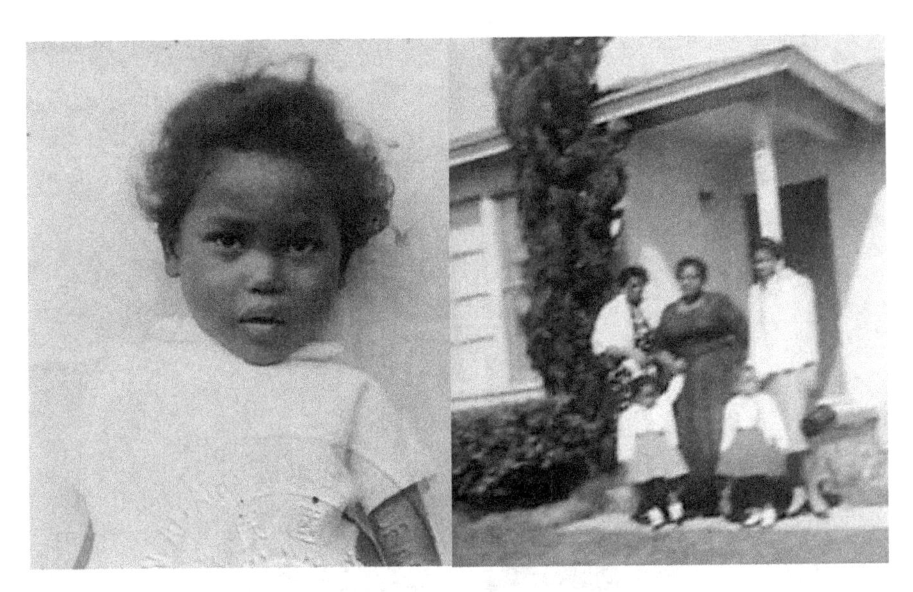

Chang Bang Sun, at Holt orphanage.

Our home at 1409 Piru Street Compton, CA

My adoptive parents James and Clemmie Henderson

Me (*right*), on my arrival in Compton, with my big head and distended belly.

The following Christmas in Compton. My body has normalized.

Me and my doll.

Loretta and me (*right*) after her adoption.

Me (*left*) at Sheila's birthday party with another adoptee.

My birthday party was filled with adoptees.

Me (*second from left*) at Girls Scouts.

Papa, my mother's father, still courting in his eighties.

REUNION—Harry Holt, Oregon farmer who has brought some 1,200 Korean-American children to this country for adoption, holds a happy reunion with some of his former charges at Free Methodist Church. Holt, with six children of his own, has adopted eight.

Halabeoji (Grandfather) Holt visited our reunion picnic.

Sepia magazine's article about Holt Adoptions which included me *(top right)* (circa February 1959).

Gary, my childhood crush.

My brother, Virgil, a track star and a Vietnam veteran.

My godmother, Nanny/Berneatha.

Nanny's son, Wilbert, his wife Cynthia and me (*right*).

1984—Our family, Daddy and Mama (center top), Virgil's wife at the time, Myrna (*in white*) and their children, Valencia (Daddy's left), Monique and Veronica (*with Virgil*), Loretta holding son Aaron, me holding Gibran, and Daddy with Ravi.

Me with Smokey Robinson.

My best friend, Karla, with Smokey Robinson.

Jackie, our homecoming queen, my mentor Mr. Freeman, and me (*right*).

Me as a Centennette. The Pride and Joy of Centennial High School.

Smokey Robinson and me.

My high school mates who formed our reunion committee: Daryl, Peter, Franchelle, Cynthia, Lynda, Ann, Jackie and me.

1971—Stanford class of'75. My Sisters of Stern (SOS) and some other dorm mates.

The SOS reunites in 2019: Darlene, me, Bev, Paris, Melonie.

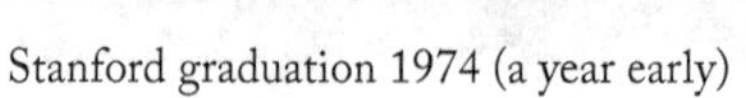

Stanford graduation 1974 (a year early)

1976—USC graduation Mama is frowning because she missed my actual diploma ceremony.

Loretta and me (*left*) as adults.

1976, Las Vegas, Nevada—My first career job, teaching social studies.

Las Vegas: My lifelong teacher friends Jeanie and her daughters, Afeni and Africa.

Marilyn, my lifelong friend and travel buddy and me.

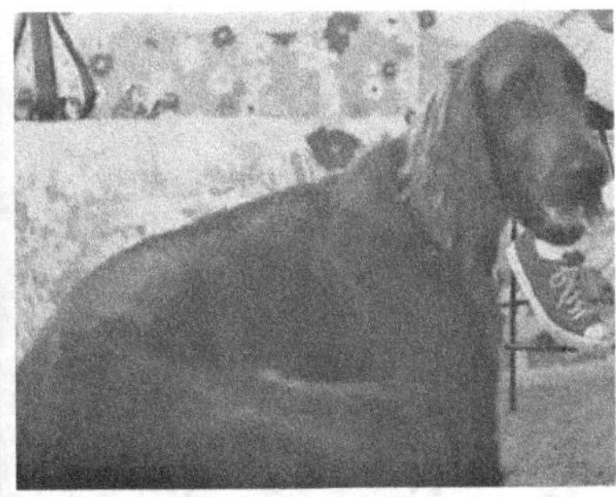

My beloved dog, Sundance.

My 1974 USC graduate school team, 'the Mod Squad' (Me, Sheila, Michael, Amy, Aurelia (deceased).

2016—Me and the Mod Squad with some of their family members.

1980s, Atlanta Georgia—The Windom Family; Sandy, Ravi, Gibran, Gary. The picture right includes Amir.

My friend, Ester, babysitting the kids.

Mr. and Mrs. Bacon's fiftieth Anniversary. Their sons, Steve (and wife, Cheryl), and Tony (and wife, Ann).

Sunday school class at Greenforest Baptist Church, Sherri, me, Deacon Mitchell, Linda, Nancy, and Eunice.

Molly Holt and me on my visit to Korea.

Me at the Korean War Memorial, in Washington, D. C.

Grandma Holt at my home in Atlanta with my kids and me.

Korea 1989—the whole family with Jake, a resident/ cook, at Il San, Korea.

The kids and me in Korea with the Yeot man.

Love Lifted Me

PART I

PART II

by Saundra Windom

My article "Love Lifted Me" for *Holt International Magazine* was later included in a book, Years of Love, for Grandma Holt.

Halabeoji Holt's grave site at Il San in Korea.

Atlanta Public School Middle School Teacher of the Year Celebration with Marilyn.

Dorothy and me as Olympic hostesses for the Equatorial Guinea representatives.

Ravi's godfather, Tony R., and me.

My children in their late teens and me.

My grandchildren, Skylure, Aiyanna, and Athan. (*Top row:*) Mackenzie and Mariah.

Gibran, known as DJ Polo and Keys to the City Creator.

Amir and Cidney's wedding with the Windom Clan.

Ravi presenting Ambassador Andrew Young an award at the Bronze Lens Awards Show. Photo credit Sue Ross.

Amir: Grammy award winning Record Executive, Film producer and Music Supervisor.

Our family at a gala where Amir served as a board member of ZT Corporate and Altus Foundation.

After forty-three years as an educator, me as principal of Crim Open Campus High School, my last stop before retirement.

Trayvon Martin's Mother, Sybrina Fulton and me.

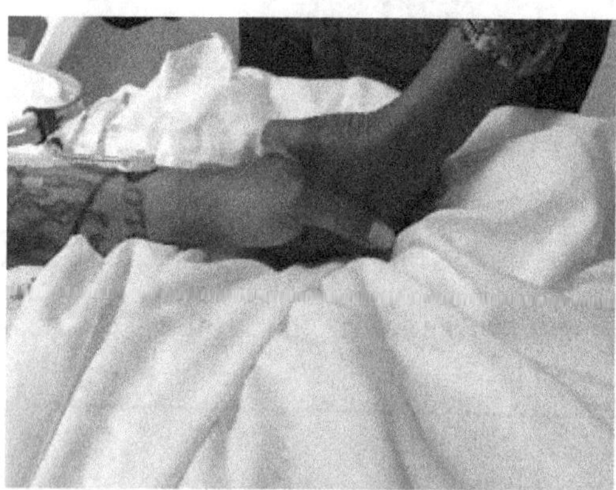

Me in hospital holding Gibran's hand the day he was admitted.

A painting of Gibran by Donice Bloodsworth, Jr.

2016: A healing Thanksgiving with our family.

Me shaking hands with President Obama.

Dr. Augustus Stephens, my ophthalmologist. His prediction came true.

The woman with the red lipstick, my mother.

My mother and her siblings. The younger boy (*to the right of my mother*) I feel is Sonyeon.

My grandparents, aunts and uncles in Korea. My mother had already left for the USA.

My new brother and sister Harrison Jr., and Yvette Woolfolk and me.

2018—the meeting of our two families, Yvette's and mine.

My mother (*top right*) is visiting her brother, father, and sister (in white) in New York.

My youngest brother, James, with his sons, Kai and Carter.

Jackie, (my high school fellow Holt adoptee), with her birth mother.

My sister, Loretta, with family members found through Ancestry DNA.

## The Letter to America

*Reprinted with Permission*
*Creswell, Oregon*

***Dear Friends,***

*In some ways we are working in the dark. We have so many applications for children of white fathers and only the Lord knows how many there are. Many of the children have died there this winter. We surely thank God for everyone who has sponsored an orphan through World Vision. Only God knows how many little lives have been saved this way. One little girl that I prayed over last summer has just died and one of the little boys is in the hospital very ill. If this is true of the few that I knew personally over there, I can only wonder how many there are throughout the country.*

*Many of you have asked what the age limit is on prospective parents. We do not know the attitude of the Korean Government about this. I suppose they will give the preference to the younger couples. We still need many homes for the half-negro babies; also, there are thousands of pure Korean children.*

*The plane fare is $259 to Portland and, I believe, $255 to Los Angeles. This can be paid in payments. Enclosed is a brief explanation of the difference between proxy and welfare adoptions.*

*I suppose most of you know that World Vision's own Dr. Bob Pierce and Billy Graham are over in the Orient now. We ask your prayers for them as they are very greatly in need of our prayer support.*

*I only wish the Lord would give me the ability to help you understand what the little ones are going through over in Korea. The little boy or girl that may be, by the grace of God, in your home by this time next year is right now lying on the floor in the cold Korean winter, huddled under whatever covers they happen to have. They are always cold and there is never enough to eat. Most of them are weak with malnutrition and sick with colds and dysentery, and many others with the beginnings of tuberculosis. We should thank God for the Christian Koreans that are sharing what little they have and doing the best they can to take care of them. We would ask all of you who are Christians to pray to God that He will give us the wisdom and the strength and the power to deliver His little children from the cold and misery and darkness of Korea into the warmth and love of your homes.*

*Many people have asked how our own children are getting along. Except for some runny noses, they are all in good health. Bobby has grown two and one half inches and all of them have grown at least one inch. They all gained weight and are all happy. They did not begin to speak much English until they had been here about six weeks. This was probably because there were so many of them, they could continue to jabber between themselves. But after that time, they began to talk, and now they are learning words rapidly. They are a God-sent blessing to our family, and we realize that we were not complete without them.*

*Yours in His service,*
***Harry Holt.***

*Holt facilities, are now in thirteen countries across the world and continue to stay true to the vision of its founders, Harry and Bertha Holt. Bertha Holt died in 2000 at the age of 96. Molly Holt, often called the Mother Teresa of Korea, died in 2019 at the age of 84. Like her father Harry Holt, who died at age 59 while on a trip to Korea, she is buried at the Ilsan Holt Center in Korea.*

FOREIGN SERVICE
UNITED STATES OF AMERICA
MEDICAL EXAMINATION OF VISA APPLICANTS

Seoul Sanitarium & Hospital [illegible]

Jan 8. 58

At the request of the American Consul at Seoul Korea

I certify that on the above date I examined Chang Eung [illegible] 4 [illegible]

I examined specifically for evidence of any of the following conditions:

CLASS A:

Tuberculosis (in any form)

Leprosy (Hansen's Disease)

Dangerous Contagious Diseases: [illegible]

Mental Conditions: [illegible]

CLASS B:

Physical Defect, Disease or Disability [illegible]

CLASS C:

Minor Conditions

[illegible]

My examination, including the X-ray and other reports below, revealed:

(1) No defect, disease or disability [illegible]

(2) [illegible]

Tuberculin test positive

Heavy hilar shadows. No evidence of any active chest pathology.

Film # 35385

Negative

Negative

George [illegible] M.D.

My medical travel clearance for my adoption.

SEOUL DISTRICT COURT
REPUBLIC OF KOREA

CERTIFICATION OF ADOPTION

1. Adopting Father:
   a. Name: James Henderson
   b. Domicile: 1400 W. Piru St., Compton 4, California, U.S.A.
   c. Date of Birth: June 12, 1910
   d. Occupation: Mail & Baggage Handling, Union Station
   e. Nationality: American
2. Adopting Mother:
   a. Name: Cimmie Henderson
   b. Domicile: 1400 W. Piru St., Compton 4, California, U.S.A.
   c. Date of Birth:
   d. Occupation: Housewife
   e. Nationality: American
3. Child to be Adopted:
   a. Name: Chang, Bang Sam
   b. Domicile: 58 3rd St., Chung Chung Ro, Suh Dae Moon Ku, Seoul
   c. Date of Birth: April 1, 1953
   d. Occupation: None
   e. Nationality: Korean

I hereby certify that in the matter of the adoption of the above-named child to be adopted by the above-named Adopting Father and Adopting Mother, all pertinent laws of the Republic of Korea have been complied with and that said adoption is in all respects legal and valid as of the date of the notification thereof to the above-named, Head of Local Administrative agency of the residence of the Adopting Father.

Dated: 31st Day of December 1957

H. H. Lim
Judge
District Court of Seoul Area
Republic of Korea

上記와如히 證明함
檀紀4290年 12月 31日
서울地方法院長 林 漢 璟

My parents' application to adopt me.

No. 161 October 18 1957

Received from James Henderson

Two Hundred Fifty-three & no/100 Dollars

Transportation Fee

$253.00 Harry Holt

No. October 19 1957

Received from James Henderson

Forty seven and no/100 Dollars

adption fee

still owe three dollars on it

$47.00 Suzanne Holt

Their receipt of $300 paid for transportation and adoption fees.

# CHAPTER TEN

## The Past Becomes the Present

My eastward trek takes me farther away from home, this time to Houston. Jeanie and her kids are renting a lovely house there, and I'm going to be sharing the residence with them. What I love most about the place is the bountiful pecan tree in the backyard, as it is a constant reminder of Mama and Nanny. Both of them love pecans so much that during harvest season, they import them from Texas. I credit my strong right grip from being an expert at cracking two shelled pecans to make each half of the nut come out perfectly.

While outside with Sundance, I often put a brown paper bag under the pecan tree and show him how to put fallen nuts into it. Sundance soon becomes the best pecan gatherer, and in no time, the bag is full. Wagging his tail and lapping up the attention he's getting as others marvel at his intelligence, he seems downright cocky. Sundance is indeed my constant companion, whether I want him to be or not.

One day, I decide to walk to the grocery store around the corner from the house. Unknowingly, I leave the gate open, and smarty-pants follows me. As I'm perusing the aisles, a frantic clerk is announcing over the intercom. "if there is a customer who owns a red dog that's going up and down the aisles, would they please come to a customer service station." Of course, I ignore it. But low and behold, I see

Sundance bouncing around the corner, trying to find me. I know my dog gets anxious when I leave him, but… I gather him, and we head home, no groceries bought.

Houston turns out to be a time of discovery, self-awareness, and growing confidence. I'm not yet licensed in the state to teach and needing to make some fast cash I get a job as an encyclopedia salesperson, which, by the way, pays much better than a Texas teaching position. It turns out to be the wildest and most eye-opening job I've had. One of the first things I notice about myself in this job is my newfound self-confidence. Because I'm an educator who believes in the value of educational resources, selling Collier's Encyclopedias turns out to be right up my alley. I'm a natural at it as I was at selling Girl Scout cookies. Growing up, I didn't have access to a library, so all my research and reports were successfully completed, thanks to Mama and Daddy's purchase of a set of World Book Encyclopedias A-Z. Another discovery is my acute ability to assess situations. The moment I knock on a prospect's door, within minutes of them answering, I can evaluate if they have the qualifications to make a purchase—a checking account. Once I get in the door of the checkbook holder, my pitch, polished to a tee, often yields good results. The caveat: If they buy today, they will have access to the new rage, something called the Information Superhighway, of which I'm clueless. To my delight, I achieve top salesperson of the world one week for closing four deals. For each set of encyclopedias I sell, I make $250, and this money is very good. Still, I know this gig has to be temporary, especially after having several harrowing experiences walking home late at night through a pack of dogs. Worse, however, is the whizzing bullet from a shotgun that goes past my head while giving a presentation. That sends me right back to teaching.

Unfortunately, Jeanie and I have to move from the house we're renting. Trying to find an apartment that takes pets turns out to be more difficult than I expect. I can't afford the extra pet fees on my salary for the ones that do. Deciding it's best to find Sundance a loving, stable family, I allow my fifth-grade class paraprofessional and her family who love Sundance to take him. Giving Sundance away is the hardest thing I've ever had to do. I discover again that I have separation anxiety. I visit Sundance a few months later and am appalled at his disheveled state. Sundance is outside with another dog who also looks neglected. His beautiful red coat is matted, and he has a large goiter under his throat. I'm riddled with guilt, and he knows it. The look he gives me makes me think of how I must have felt when I was discarded in Korea. I never get another pet.

Without Sundance, life is a little lonelier, but soon I meet a lovely man. Not at a party, a nightclub, or on a blind date. I meet Sam in the grocery store. He's a sales distributor for Pillsbury, who is checking on the store's display. Sam is quiet and easygoing. We become friends and spend a lot of time together—church on Sundays, and he even accompanies me on student field trips. I know Sam is a great and dependable person the day I'm in a near head-on collision. The accident is my fault, and it's bad enough that I'm rendered unconscious. When I open my eyes, I'm lying on the ground. A White man with shoulder-length blond hair and blue eyes is hovering over me. I think I've died and am now meeting Jesus. The man is telling me to stay still, that I'm in shock and that the ambulance is coming. It turns out the good Samaritan is a bystander, but I can't help thinking and laughing about my association with him as White Jesus. My brainwashing religious conditioning makes it a knee-jerk reaction kind of thing. Images of Martin Luther King Jr., John F. Kennedy, and White Jesus are a staple in so many Black homes.

When the hospital discharges me, Sam is who I call to pick me up. He's impressive. With a strong, muscular physique, he swoops me up, carries me to his car, takes me home, and tucks me in my bed. The movie *Superman*, currently playing in theaters, has me thinking of Sam as my personal superman. Unlike Al, there is nothing negative about Sam. Always a gentleman, as much time as we spend together, there is no pressure for intimacy. My superman is my Mr. Perfect, and I want us to continue along this road, even to intimacy. Maybe, at last, this will be a relationship of mutual love and respect.

An urgent call from home informs me that Daddy is sick. For months the doctors have been trying to make a diagnosis, and they can't determine what is wrong with him. He is withering away so rapidly that they've even tested him for AIDS. Mama is frantic, so I know I must move back home. It's been a year since I've been in Houston and since I've seen my parents. Regardless of how independent I've become, I have to be there when my parents need me. It seems a recurring theme every year or two: I'm saying goodbye to new friends I've met along the way. Parting with Sam is difficult, but we've committed to staying in touch.

When it's time to leave, it turns out Jeanie's mother, a trusted babysitter for Africa and Afeni, is in town and can look after the girls. Jeanie decides to ride back with me as far as Vegas, and from there, I'll continue to Compton. It's good to be home. Mama and Daddy are glad to see me, but I miss Sam. It seems he feels the same as we talk nearly every day. The more we talk, the more I like him, so much so that I even tell Mama about him as I think he could be the real deal.

When Sam calls and Mama answers the phone, he spends time talking to her, and she likes his attention. On the strength of his attentiveness, Mama seems to like him. Encouraged, I invite Sam to visit for a few days and pray when Mama meets him, she doesn't change her feelings or judge him for his looks, though in my eyes, he's a good-looking man. Since I'm the beholder, what should count as beauty should be my judgment anyway. On Sam's visit, we're planning to drive up the California coast for a weekend. I'm excited, and waiting for him is making me impatient. He could be the one, I think. I want to find out.

I take on a teaching job at Willowbrook Junior High School with my mentor, Mr. Freeman. I also keep busy by taking Daddy to his doctor's appointments. Though there's still no diagnosis for his illness, he's turned a corner, and so far, he's doing pretty well. Daddy helps by being a good patient who follows doctor's orders, and he's watching his diet and managing his diabetes carefully. I'm glad. Now that Daddy is feeling better, I don't have to feel guilty about looking forward to my trip with Sam. On the day Sam is arriving, I'm excited. To ensure no hitch, I head over to my friend Marilyn's house in Inglewood, which is much closer to the airport. Marilyn and I chitchat until it's time to go. I'm leaving earlier than necessary so that I can park and meet Sam at the gate. As I grab my purse, Marilyn's phone rings, and it's a call from Sam. Apparently, Mama has given him Marilyn's number since he'd called her trying to reach me.

When I answer the phone, I'm not prepared for what he tells me: Sam tells me his trip has been canceled because his long-term girlfriend, a flight attendant, tells him a trip to L.A. is off-limits to our friendship. Away often, she has apparently allowed him to have a platonic relationship with me, but when he tells her he's coming to California to visit, she orders him to end our relationship before it becomes anything other than friendship. Sam, my superman, has been living a double life as Clark Kent with someone else. Though he has never been inappropriate, we'd emotionally invested a lot in our relationship. I hang up the phone, devastated. Thank God I'm with Marilyn. I cry hard, and the ache inside is unbearable. I cry even more when I wonder what it is about me that makes me undeserving of love. Why does everyone want to control, reject, or give me up?

Jackie, the half Korean Holt adoptee and my high school friend and I have kept in touch over the years. Her kinship as mine and Lolo's "cousin" has been unshakable. Jackie so happens to call when I get back home to invite me to go with her to the class of 1969's reunion. My weekend with Sam to Carmel by the Sea now canceled means being home with Mama and Daddy. Since I have no place to confine at home solitarily, and though my inclination is to pass on Jackie's invitation as I'm already at a party—my own pity party—I say yes. Deciding that being with Jackie is better than sitting around moping, I put on my façade, woman up, and ready myself to party.

At the reunion, several guys are giving us too much attention. We get accosted in the restroom by some girls from the class of '69. "You're from the class of '71. Why in the hell are you here?" they want to know. Jackie, our 1971 homecoming queen who knows everybody, turns to them. Calling them by name to lessen the tension, she says, "Relax. You have nothing to worry about here. We've paid, so we're supporting your class. Plus, Sandy and I are on our reunion committee. We're doing research. Please support us, too, in two years, okay!" We smile and walk out, and to my disbelief and shock, I run into Gary, my secret junior high school crush who lived around the corner. He's visiting from Atlanta.

I've seen Gary on a few occasions since high school. We'd run into each other when he'd come to some of the Stanford Black Dorm parties at Roble Hall while a student at San Jose State. The last time I saw him, several years before, he was with our mutual friend Karla who also attended San Jose State. As it turned out, it would be the last time I'd see Karla. The following weekend Karla's friends from high school came up from Compton to visit her in San Jose. On their way back to Compton, they were hit by a tractor-trailer, and Karla was instantly killed. The other girls, though severely injured, survived. When I heard about the accident that had taken my dear friend's life, I refused to believe it, unable to accept that Karla was truly gone. Karla, my partner in crime who'd aided and abetted our breaking into many stars' dressing rooms, especially Smokey Robinson's; who sat with me countless times in our kitchen peeling potatoes, was really gone. I've seen a lot and learned early to cope with the finality of death, but not with her. Her death shook me to the core.

I couldn't bear my last memory of Karla being one of seeing her in a casket, wanting always to remember her alive, full of spunk and vivacity, and making others laugh. Her death is a memory that still weighs heavily on my heart, and I carry significant guilt about not attending her funeral, but God knows, I couldn't. Her mother never understood why I would make such a choice, but I couldn't and wouldn't accept

Karla's death in that way. Selfish on my part, I know, but it was what I needed to do to cope. Seeing Gary brings me to sadness.

I snap out of my trance when Gary hugs me. Jackie and Gary exchange greetings and hugs. He's in town from Atlanta, and a friend also invited him to attend the reunion of the class of '69. We chat about the last time we'd seen each other, and we talk about Karla. There is a sense of sadness beyond our shared grief for Karla. We know each other well enough to tell something debilitating is going on with each of us. It turns out he's going through a heart-wrenching situation with one of our former classmates whom he is dating. He'd given her money to purchase tickets for them to take a trip to Jamaica only to find out she used the money to go on the trip with someone else. To confront her is the main reason he's in Compton. Without words, we relate to each other's hurt, and I'm wondering if fate is bringing us together. If not, why did our paths cross again when we were both brokenhearted? Was this silver lining in our life's journey a sign that we were meant to be with each other all along—a divine plan and now a divine intervention? In some Asian cultures, it's believed that destiny is afoot if you randomly meet someone three times. Full circle for Gary and me—Compton, Stanford, Compton.

Over the next few days, Gary and I are constantly together. It has taken us getting to adulthood to finally acknowledge our mutual attraction. Before he goes back to Georgia, we commit to a monogamous relationship. After all, we're both looking for our soulmates. Since we share years of life experiences and family values, why not try to make things work between us? With this kind of familiarity, we would bring little to no baggage to a relationship. There is just one hitch: Marilyn and I have been accepted into UCLA's doctoral program. Serendipity is now putting a wrench in my plans, and I'm at a crossroads.

"Lord, what should I do?" I ask over and over.

In Atlanta, Gary works for Shirley Franklin, the commissioner of cultural affairs under Maynard Jackson. His love for music and the arts lands him in the perfect career: He is in charge of the city's annual jazz festival. I, on the other hand, have more flexibility, but I make no rash moves to join Gary in Atlanta. I need to figure out my future. The following year, during the summer of 1979, I get the opportunity to take twenty-five students from Willowbrook Junior High School in Compton to a six-week program at Talladega College in Alabama. It is a program in partnership with Auburn University. By the end of the six weeks, I'm asked to consider working on this project through Auburn's doctoral program. If I accept, it will only be a two-hour drive from Gary. It seems the stars are aligning after all for my love life and my post-graduate studies to co-exist. On the way back to L.A., I take a detour, and the trip bears more fruit as I get in a visit with Gary. Our visit gives me the push I need to end our long-distance relationship and try our hand at becoming a real couple. It's been a year since we've dated, so I decide to move to Atlanta in the fall of 1979.

Mama and Daddy are not happy. Neither is my boss and mentor, Mr. Freeman, principal of Willowbrook. Mr. Freeman's impression of Gary from his high school days is that he's only interested in organizing or going to parties. The bottom line for them both: Gary isn't good enough for me. I'm worthy of the best. I'm honored they think so highly of me, but I know, as well-meaning as they are, they also have ulterior motives. Mama and Daddy don't want me to leave them, and Mr. Freeman wants me to help him start his own school. With all love and respect for them, to their dismay, I move to Decatur, Georgia, to be with Gary and to further pursue my education at Auburn University.

Gary and I live in a small two-bedroom cottage behind the property owner, who lives in a well-kept tri-level home. The best part of the cottage is the screened-in porch. I've lived through near 120-degree dry heat in Las Vegas, but it's crystal clear why they call this place Hotlanta. Hot, humid, muggy, tornadic, thunder filled, and stormy—Atlanta is hot and sticky. The screened-in porch's cool breeze is welcomed, as is the tranquil sounds of nature.

We are diametrically opposite, Gary and me. Living with Gary reminds me of a hippie's lifestyle. He is a naturalist. We have no TV, no AC, and he is definitely not a traditional planner. I should've gotten clued about his free spirit when we took a trip to Haiti and one to Jamaica earlier in the year before I'd relocated to Georgia. Since Gary has not reserved a hotel in Jamaica, we're forced to go with the flow, which means staying with strangers we meet along the way. The experience, wonderfully memorable, however risky, is a dead giveaway that our approach to life is vastly different. Of course, I ignore the red flag. That kind of laissez-faire living isn't okay with me as a way of life. I need to find a way to negotiate a balance between his hippie lifestyle and my life, which requires clear directions to nurture my mind, heart, and spirit. This is our first difference to reconcile. Our settling period over, I turn my attention to thinking through how to manage my time with school looming. A few months before, I was unsure what I would do but decided to continue on with my original plan. Triangular traveling between Atlanta, Auburn, and Talladega will be a challenge, but I'm used to challenges. As I'm looking at a calendar, map in hand, trying to figure out the best route and days for the convoluted travel plans required to pursue my doctorate, my eyes zero in on a date on the calendar. I've missed my menstrual cycle by a few days. Anxiously I wait for my period to show up. Nothing!

Finally, I find the courage to buy a pregnancy test to stop all the wondering. If I'm pregnant, that will change everything again. It'd be my second pregnancy. Several months before, my last pregnancy ended with massive bleeding in the first few weeks after confirming the pregnancy. The doctor says a high percentage of miscarriages happen during the first trimester when something is wrong with the fetus. Because it's so early in the pregnancy, I'm spared the emotional rollercoaster of losing a child or having motherly feelings. I can't imagine what I'd have done if I'd formed an attachment to the child. I look at the stick, and it has turned colors. I'm indeed pregnant. I want to do nothing to jeopardize this pregnancy because I want to have this child more than anything in the world, if God permits. Deep down, my desire has always been to have a child—to have someone I can protect and love unconditionally. A child who will continue my unknown bloodline and become part of a family I can truly call my own. All my new plans fizzle away. I can't risk another miscarriage. It's logical what I need to do. I can't go into the Ph.D. program.

It turns out I'm the only one excited about my pregnancy. Mama isn't at all thrilled. Maybe because she feels my devotion can shift and preferred that I continue with my education. Gary isn't that excited because he isn't thinking about this level of commitment or responsibility at this point in our relationship. Though I table school, I am not about to sit around for nine months and do nothing. Because I don't have my Georgia teaching license, I decide to get a temp job at an insurance company to keep me occupied and to establish my independence. From day one, I can tell Gary is a man concerned about his money.

The personnel director to whom I've become very close encourages me to apply for the training director job that has just opened up at my job. I'm reluctant because I'm pregnant but do so anyway. The company president, who has been taking notice of my work and professionalism, offers me the job. I love it. My responsibilities include providing 250 employees with home office training, teaching insurance courses, managing their tuition assistance, setting up their wellness program access, and organizing their continuing education modules through Lunch and Learn. Perfect for a teacher.

I'm feeling well and haven't gained much weight on my ninty-eight poundframe. Perplexing, though, is that at monthly check-ups, my blood pressure is always elevated. At least this time, I'm not nervous about a miscarriage since it's my second trimester. Still, after each visit, my doctor requires me to remain prone until my blood pressure stabilizes. Usually, as I lie there, my mind wanders. On this day, I'm trying to figure out if I'm having a boy or a girl. For months, my intuition has been telling me it's a boy. I'm even dreaming of him in my womb. The baby's daily hiccups are noticeable and make me wonder what is causing them. I pray nothing goes wrong since I have to wait ninety more days before my health benefits kick in. It's the irony of all ironies: I work for an insurance company, but I don't have insurance for prenatal care. I make it through okay.

My water breaks thirty-eight weeks into my pregnancy. I call the hospital and tell them the pains are close. They tell me to try to relax in the bathtub and call them in the morning. My instinct tells me otherwise, so I insist that Gary, "Get me to Grady Hospital—now!"

Gary drops me off in front of the hospital and goes off to park and to sedate himself with the bottle of wine he's brought from home to prepare for what's ahead. I'm stressing because I feel the baby coming, so I choose the stairs in front of me versus walking the long distance to the elevator. I climb and climb and climb until finally, I see the labor and delivery signs. Registering, I gush that "I'm ready to give birth!" Having documented my earlier call and being pregnant for the first time, they think I'm just anxious. They continue to ignore my pleas until I demand to be examined. The examining mid-wife says, "Oh my, your baby *is* coming."

Gary makes it just in time to see the delivery of our four-pound, five-ounce son. We name him Gibran after Kahlil Gibran, the author of one of my favorite poetry books, *The Prophet*. There will never be words to describe the feeling of holding my first-born. I stare at his Asian features and feel his tightening hold on my little finger, as though he knows he'll have me to hold on to forever. With love, I nurse him, and my soul is at peace. I am a mother. With a four-and-a-half day stay in the hospital, I have plenty of time to ruminate on long-forgotten memories. The past again in view, I'm wondering whose womb I was in, kicking, stretching, and hiccupping on God's perfect assembly line of life. I'm also wondering about the woman with red lipstick in Korea. If affection is an indicator of love, she might not have been my mother after all, as she didn't seem to have any feelings for me. But someone I know did. And I know someone cared. I'm here today because that someone must have nursed me, perhaps even held me through my restless cries. I'm eternally grateful to whomever it was—my birth mother, I believe. In her way, she must have cared for me. Whatever action she had to take or was forced to take, I survived because of that love when so many were left to die. I might not know where my bloodline begins, but I know it continues in my beautiful baby boy.

I marry the guy next door, backward. Gary and I finally tie the knot. Living in Georgia, being married, a new parent, and having a job are drastic life changes. The funny thing is, I've pretty much looked forward to this my whole life, so I am adjusting well. Between 1981 to 1985, we have three children, Gibran, Ravi, and Amir. Me, a mother of three. With each of my beautiful and unique children, I feel a jolt of love that is indescribable. Nothing I can ever write can explain the love and attachment I feel for them. When I lay eyes on my daughter, Ravi, it's love at first sight. I look at her sweet, beautiful face and promise we'll have an unbreakable mother-daughter bond. At nine pounds, three ounces, Amir is his own person, coming into the world large and in charge. He is delivered by C-section because he's too big for my small body. Holding him, I can already see his individuality from day one. I can tell my job will be to help nurture his passions no matter how much patience I'll have to have.

As a mother who deeply loves each of her children, it becomes harder for me to understand how any mother can give up her child, but I can now see how the need to protect one's child can lead to choosing the lesser of two evils. The history of my past where no one knows my name, my age, or my birth prepares me from the moment of giving birth to record every moment of our special times together from day one. I click on the live recording in my brain and on my camera and observe their every moment. "Til death do us part" has never been more real to me. Unlike me, my children's life story will have a beginning, a middle, and an end. I wonder, too, if one day they will ask about their Asian roots. Will they even notice? I hope so, and I hope one day I'll have the courage to tell them my story.

My husband begins working for Delta, which gives our family attractive travel benefits. I'm able to take my children to see their grandparents on both sides in Compton, and we visit often. Years of disappointment become reconciled with grandchildren who are a dose of medicine for grandparents. Somehow, they bridge the communication and emotional gaps that eluded both Gary and me with our parents. For the first time in my life, I feel treated as an adult. Daddy is eager to share his version of the art of parenting. "Because you can't watch their every move, the environment in which you raise them will contribute to how they are influenced, so one of the most important things you must do as a parent is to ensure that your children are in a neighborhood where they can thrive," he says. It's great to speak with Daddy one-on-one, and I listen intently. I can tell he appreciates that I value his opinion by the look of satisfaction on his face. Mama has fully warmed up to her grandchildren—her favorite is Amir.

Though I'm building new roots in Atlanta, I try to come back to L.A. as often as I can to soften the blow of distance and to allow me to monitor my aging parents' health. Daddy's health issues began with his diabetes, diagnosed when I was in high school. He slowed his fast track to mortality for over a decade by eating healthier, stopping smoking cold turkey, and even going to church. But his health was never the same because of the mysterious illness the doctors never diagnosed. Now my father's health is beginning to deteriorate again. How uncanny that it's right after he retired in 1979. By 1984, Daddy is very sick, and the doctors still don't know what's wrong. It's hard watching him weaken. Gary's mother, who has also been ill for a while, passes away. Fortunately, Daddy is mobile enough in July 1985 to drive the kids and me to the car wash so we could use his car in the procession for Gary's mother's funeral. Little did I know that the following month, on September 6, 1985, I would receive the dreaded phone call about Daddy.

Mama is distraught. Forty-three years of marriage is over, as is life between the dashes—Daddy now has a beginning and an end date to be put on his headstone. I'm penning his obituary on the plane, tears flowing, blotting out the words as I write. I reflect on Daddy's simple life, which didn't include fancy degrees, high-ranking positions, extraordinary wealth, or status, and I'm so grateful for the man whose selflessness and heart of gold jump-started the lives of those of us who found refuge at 1409 Piru Street. Me, a little orphan girl who in 1958, is given the hope of a brighter tomorrow by a man with such a big heart. My daddy, the simple man who set the standard for *commitment,* is no longer. He showed commitment to his family by providing food, clothing, and shelter without fail. Commitment by being present in family life, bringing roaring laughter from his booming farts and signature belly-rolling dances. Commitment to two of his children, not even biologically his, yet no one would ever know. As I write through the tears, I'm glad he had the opportunity to see how well I turned out because of his commitment. I'm also happy he's met his grandchildren, and I'm glad to have so many meaningful memories to take forward. I'm indebted, and I only hope I've made him proud. My tears flow faster as it all registers. My daddy is gone, and I'm writing about him in the past tense.

Lolo, Daddy's favorite, is with him in the intensive care unit when he passes away. I'm grateful to her.

"Sandy," she keeps saying, "he looks like he is sleeping."

When reality sets in, Lolo falls apart. "Our father is gone. He will never wake up," she whispers.

Shortly after Daddy's death, Lolo moves to Kensington, England, with her husband David, who is transferred there by his investment banking firm. Having to start a new life in a new country keeps her mind occupied.

Virgil moves back in with Mama for a while.

Atlanta is growing by leaps and bounds and represents change in the South. Beginning in the eighties, I watch as it becomes the Mecca for Black progress. Aptly so as for many decades, Atlanta has been linked to the civil rights movement. In fact, it is known as the birthplace of the civil rights movement. Civil rights activists and visionaries such as Andrew Young, Jr., a close confidant of the late Martin Luther King, Jr., become a central figure in Atlanta politics. In 1982 he becomes the fifty-fifth mayor of Atlanta. Under his stewardship, Atlanta is catapulted into national prominence, earning it the name City of Dreams. The city is booming, thanks to entrepreneurial success stories such as Home Depot and CNN. It has the world's biggest and second busiest airport next to Chicago, so it is cosmopolitan. By 1988, Atlanta is an important enough city to host the Democratic National Convention. Since then, it has never looked back, growing more successful as a state, attracting the best and brightest. The city's forward-thinking approach, which includes providing scholarships for public school students, is progressive, and I find myself thinking of Atlanta more and more as home. My ties to Los Angeles are now partially gone; my home in Atlanta welcomed me back from my daddy's tragedy.

# CHAPTER ELEVEN

## Grandma Holt Is Alive?

The year following Daddy's death is a painful one for us all, but especially for Mama. I make a point of calling her frequently, and we work through our grief together. Reminiscing one day, I find myself flipping through an old family photo album to keep warm memories of Daddy alive. In one of the albums is a professionally taken picture of me I haven't seen in years. It was taken for an article in *Sepia* magazine that was about *hal-abeoji*'s (Harry Holt) proxy adoption that brought mixed Black and Korean orphans to Black families in the United States. I remember we had the magazine at home, but it magically disappeared with other Korean keepsakes when Mama censored Korea. Looking at the picture, I think about the meaning of family. My birth mother and father are family, even if absent. Sonyeon was family, even if lost, as were the Holts, especially Molly. Mama and Daddy, Lolo, and Virgil, too, are family though we all don't necessarily share a drop of common blood. How lucky am I in my life to have had four families? It's all a matter of perspective. How much more positive could the outcome be for a poor little orphan girl?

Now that I've gone down the rabbit hole, I'm wondering how to go about finding this magazine article. The magazine itself has long been defunct. The library archives make sense as a starting point, but unfortunately, their microfiche of the magazine doesn't go back to 1959. Then a bright light comes on. I can call the Holt International office in Oregon, and that's just what I do.

"Hello. I'm calling from Atlanta, Georgia. I'm one of the children from Holt. Do you have a book entitled *Seed from the East* and any copies of an article from *Sepia* magazine in 1959?" I inquire.

"We sure do," the voice on the other end responds. "By the way, do you know that Grandma and Suzanne Holt are on their way to Atlanta?"

I'm speechless—beyond euphoric—that Grandma Holt, *halmeoni* (grandma in Korean), is on her way to my city. I'm also embarrassed because I'd assumed she'd passed on. After I hang up, I'm an emotional wreck. Montages of deleted images and stories from my childhood are rapidly being retrieved. I don't remember Grandma Holt ever coming to Korea when I was there, but every one of us knew who she was—the woman fighting for us on the political front to pass legislation that would allow us to be adopted in the U.S. She raised money, collected food and clothing, and even helped to operate the orphanage from a distance. So impactful was her work that Vice President Hubert Humphrey honored her nationally as the 1966 American Mother of the Year. Unthinkable, Grandma Holt is alive and heading to Atlanta. Later the same day, I receive a phone call from Holt's office. "We told Grandma about you, and she is so excited to hear about one of the early adoptees. She wants to know if you would consider hosting her and Suzanne at your home." Now I'm choked up! What a blessing and an honor it'd be for me to meet and host Grandma and her daughter Suzanne in my home. Because of them, I have a home. I end my day in tears of joy.

Grandma and her daughter Suzanne stay with me in Decatur, Georgia. In my very presence are the heroes who directly impacted my life. It is an esteemed honor, and I try hard to make their visit memorable. We talk nonstop, and I regale them with tales of their family from the orphanage; about Grandma's daughters Molly and Barbara who cared for us around the clock; about her husband, Harry (*hal-abeoji),* who took me in his station wagon for TB follow-ups at the hospital. I talk about the long plane ride from Korea to San Francisco and about babies dying at the orphanage and on the plane ride. I even show her the faded burn scars on both of my hands from the hot porridge accident. Grandma says she purposely sent oatmeal and Cream of Wheat to us so that we could eat more than just rice and was sorry about my accident.

Grandma marvels at my memory while I marvel at her stamina. She's in her eighties and is still jogging a mile a day and touring the country. She is here to celebrate Holt's thirtieth anniversary. The next day, I will attend the anniversary celebration with her. It hits me that at thirty-three years old, I'm a living testament of what God had charged Harry and Bertha Holt to do. In 1955, Harry Holt was making his first trip to Korea to adopt eight Amerasian children. On a layover en route, he hears about the long adoption process and all the red tape that goes along with it and feels discouraged. Worse were the people who were suggesting his false motives for adopting the children. He got up in the middle of the night, praying on his knees, asking God for direction. He randomly opened the bible, and his thumb landed on Isaiah 43: 5-6 "(5) *Fear not: for I am with thee: I will bring thy seed from the east, and gather thee from the west; (6) I will say to the north, Give up; and to the south, Keep not back: bring my sons from afar, and my daughters from the ends of the earth.*" This scripture emphatically assured him he was on God's mission. What he realized after picking up his eight adoptees was how sad he felt leaving behind so many destitute children. The big picture of that scripture led to establishing the Holt Adoption Program where they believed that "Every child deserves a home." It seems life has come full circle.

I never felt the need to burden my children with my complicated past. Grandma Holt tells me I should share my story with them. "This is their story, too, Saundra, and it'll let them know how good

God is!" Up until then—my children, five, three, and two—know nothing of my Korean past. I'm so conditioned not to talk about it; I don't even give it a second thought. The truth is they don't notice their features or mine as they're still very young. Grandma Holt's visit awakens my past and a dormant desire to write a children's book about my journey to America. It further inspires me to go back to Korea to introduce my children to the unknown part of their heritage. I'm on a natural high after Grandma's visit. She, Suzanne, and I write letters to update and encourage each other to keep striving. My immediate focus is now on my mother, who's been calling nonstop because she hasn't seen or heard from my brother, Virgil, since Thanksgiving. It's now almost Christmas. I can't take another tragedy so soon after Daddy's death and honestly want no bad news. Still, hospitals and county morgues are called. His ex-wife, Myrna, goes searching in areas where the homeless hang out. Virgil has had brief disappearing acts before, but this is the longest period he's been away from the family.

Our family flies to Compton early on Christmas Day. I arrive to the good news that Myrna has found my brother in one of the places where people go to sell their blood plasma. At the time, none of it makes sense because Virgil always has a place to stay, and he doesn't seem to be on drugs. What happened to Virgil? Was he, after all, a causality of war? Left to deal with the psychological trauma of being in Vietnam? Like many Vietnam veterans, Virgil is suffering from the long-term effects of agent orange and post-traumatic stress disorder, which devastated so many emotionally and mentally.

Mama can now relax. It's Christmas 1986, and all her children are home. A few weeks earlier, she'd seen Lolo, who'd come for a visit from the United Kingdom. I happily prepare the entire Christmas dinner, including Mama's favorites, dressing and German chocolate cake. While home, my friend Marilyn plans a weekend getaway trip for us to San Diego and Tijuana. I need this break away from everything. I make arrangements for the children to stay with my sister-in-law Barbara (my husband, Gary's sister), who lives around the corner from Mama. The most surprising thing about this particular visit is Mama's attitude. Usually unhappy about me spending time with anyone other than her, she encouragingly says, "You deserve to enjoy yourself. Have a good time." I do a double-take. The only thing she's complaining about is that my baby Amir isn't going to be with her. Amir is affectionately Mama's *Medee*. She loves bouncing him on her lap and singing her made-up song, "*Goodness gracious Medee. Goodness gracious, Medee, Lawdy. Goodness gracious, Medee.*"

Marilyn picks me up the Friday after Christmas, and we take a pleasant two-hour drive to San Diego. I don't feel too bad about leaving Mama because my brother is with her, and over the weekend, his four daughters will probably be visiting also. Marilyn and I talk about the good, bad, and ugly of our lives. The joy and challenges of parenting, family, relationships, work, and growing spiritually. That night in San Diego, I dream of being in a massive warehouse with a clipboard counting and writing. It seems I'm taking inventory. The next morning, while we're having coffee, that dream lingers in my consciousness, so I share the details with Marilyn. It all seemed so real. After breakfast, we visit Marilyn's brother and sister-in-law and later walk across the border into Tijuana. In just a step, we've left the U.S. and are being welcomed by aggressive Tijuana street vendors imploring us to look at their wares. Our senses perk up at the sights, sounds, and the inviting aroma of food cooking. The rhythmic music of the mariachis and traditional ranchera fills the air. Salsa dancers, shoulders and hips snapping are dancing in the streets. We thoroughly enjoy the day of cultural immersion in Mexico.

That night at the hotel in San Diego, I dream vividly again. This time it's about my mother. She is lying in a large casket, and for some reason, my emotional state is more heightened because in my dream my brother and sister are shouting and cursing at each other.

I bolt upright, my heart beating fast. This is a disturbing dream. What is all this dreaming supposed to mean? That as a mother of three, I can finally get into a deep enough sleep state without sleeping with one ear attuned and one eye open? Is this how tired I am? Marilyn and I have coffee on Sunday morning before heading back to Compton. I share this vivid dream, but this time I'm perturbed. Why would I have this kind of dream? Needing an answer, I begin to rationalize.

A few months earlier, I'd gone to my Las Vegas/Detroit friend Steve Bacon's wedding in North Carolina. At the wedding is an extremely overweight cousin of the Bacons. I later learn he'd passed away shortly after the wedding. I remember visualizing the size of the casket they'd have to make to bury him. Was I subconsciously thinking about Mama's weight, which has ballooned past 350 pounds? Mama's weight is surely a concern. I order a take-out coffee and take a big gulp. The most upsetting part of my dream I realize is that my sister and brother were fussing and cursing at each other. Again, I breathed a sigh of relief that it's just a dream, but maybe I can get Mama to lose some weight.

Marilyn and I arrive home Sunday afternoon. Before going to Mama's, I pick up my kids. Mama is glad to see us all when we trundle in. I can't get over how different her behavior and personality are on this trip. No matter what I say, Mama is agreeable to everything, even things she usually complains about. Before going to bed, Mama asks me for some German chocolate cake and cranberry juice. I cut her a large piece of cake and say, "Mama, sit up so that you don't choke."

I decide I'll have the weight talk with her in the morning. Mama has always been a hypochondriac, so maybe I can convince her that carrying so much weight is doing her a disservice. About 5:00 a.m., Mama wakes me up. "Sandy, get me a Bufferin." I can hear the sense of urgency in her voice, so instead of looking for my glasses, I squint to sharpen my vision. Finding the pills, I give her one, and she swallows it.

Shortly after, she gets up, uses the restroom, and shuffles to the living room to sit in her favorite chair. I accompany her, as her breathing seems very labored. Even though Mama's always been on the obese side, she has been relatively healthy. But this morning, something isn't right. I feel so strongly about it that I wake my brother and ask him to call the ambulance. The attendants have come to Mama's house several times when she's fallen out of her bed and can't get up, so they're familiar with our home.

Mama is struggling to breathe. In a weak whisper, I hear her say, "Help me." I look over, and it seems she has stopped breathing. Since Mama weighs 350 pounds, and I'm less than one hundred, I can't get her out of the chair to lay her down to do mouth-to-mouth resuscitation. From the chair, I tilt her head back as far as I can and blow into her mouth. I'm desperately praying and blowing air into her while she's sitting. Virgil is outside looking for the ambulance. They finally arrive forty-five minutes later. I call Barbara, Gary's sister, to come and stay with the kids who are still sleeping. The attendants lie Mama flat on the carpet. She's still alive because her face grimaces in pain when they straighten her arthritic knees. She has pink froth coming from her mouth. A plastic mouth-to-mouth breathing tube is forced down her throat. The medics put her on a gurney and wheel her to the ambulance.

With the siren blaring, Virgil and I follow the emergency vehicle. I'm continually praying and notice I have jitters going through my body. I've been through trauma—several times as a teenager having to give Papa mouth-to-mouth and with my two-month-old nephew who died from sudden infant death syndrome—but this seems to top all of them. When we get to Martin Luther King Hospital in Watts, they've already wheeled Mama to a room. About fifteen minutes later, they tell us Mama didn't make it.

I'm in shock and can't believe Mama—my larger-than-life Mama—is gone. Lord, I'd just come home to L.A. to celebrate the holidays with my family, not for Mama to say her last words of "Help me," and I couldn't help her.

Virgil and I go into the room where she's been wheeled. They've already put her in a big, clear zip bag, but her face is exposed. I can tell she fought hard against dying because her teeth are clenched tightly over the plastic breathing tube. Maybe the medics are wrong, after all. Maybe Mama isn't dead. I'm always fascinated by the story of one of my mother's young cousins who was declared dead and sent to the morgue. Fortunately, she gasped in the morgue before she was refrigerated. Her near-death experience of hovering over her body and then seeing and feeling the wonderful light make me hopeful. Is Mama hovering? Is she, like her cousin had said, reviewing her life? Will she be told to go back because she isn't ready? None of that happened. Mama is dead. I tearily say, "Go to the light, Mama."

It has been a little over a year since Daddy's passing, and Mama will join him now. I find a smile on my face imagining Daddy in Heaven welcoming Mama with a Big Mac and a box of See's candy. Heaven, I'm sure of it, has welcomed two ordinary people with extraordinary hearts. On earth, two formally abandoned children I know have reaped the rewards of those angels in Heaven. Thank you, Mama, for twenty-seven years of caring for us. Instead of getting ready to enjoy a New Year's Eve concert featuring the Delphonics, I'm planning Mama's funeral. She dies on Monday, and by the afternoon, I'm making an overseas call to break the news to Lolo. Mama must have had a premonition herself because she took me to the bank to put my name on her accounts a few months before and had me meet her lawyer.

Now that she's gone, I don't have time to grieve. I have lots to do. Lolo makes it in by Wednesday. Thursday, I call her lawyer Mr. Caruso to let him know. He tells me he is mailing a form, and I have to take INVENTORY of everything in the house. I am freaking out now because it hasn't been a week yet that I dreamt of taking inventory. I'm running errands, taking care of the funeral expenses, and when I get home on Thursday, I hear all this noise in the living room area. Virgil and Lolo are having it out. I don't know what precipitated the argument, but I can hear about who did what for Mama and who didn't do for Mama. I'm freaking out again because here I am, trying to intervene in a shouting match that I dreamt about a few days ago. Lord, give me strength! My dream was a premonition.

# CHAPTER TWELVE

## A Family of My Own

They say death comes in threes, and indeed in a year and a half, my children lose three of their four grandparents. Just as jarring is the loss of Mama Perrin, the children's godmother who'd been a great support to our family for the past four years. It was Mama Perrin who would feed the kids and who made celebrations like birthdays, Christmas and Valentine's Day extra special for them. When Mama died, my son, Gibran, finally releases his pent-up anxiety. "Everybody's gone. What if you die? Then what's gonna happen to me?" He's crying, and I'm crying. Holding him close, I try to console him, but Gibran, who is five years old, is noticeably distraught. At the very moment of his outcry, I notice a change in him, a turning point that begins to shape him into a new person. Before, Gibran was loud, cheerful, and engaging. Since facing the harsh reality of recurring death, he is quiet, low-key, and aloof. He seems hesitant to invest any more of his emotions on unrestrained love, no doubt, to shield his heart. Gary's father steps up his involvement as the sole grandparent, but the losses are more than Gibran can bear.

Meeting Tony and Steve while living in Las Vegas has led to lifelong and cherished relationships with them and their parents. Mama Lee and Papa Wil Bacon, the only family I've met, represent the real Huxtables (a middle-class Black TV family of a two-parent household who are positively engaged with their children and community). They have become such a beacon in my life. I want Gibran to meet them. I figure, since they'd had such a positive impact on me, they will too on Gibran. Gary's travel benefits allow us to visit them often, and true to my thinking, the Bacons help to fill the grandparent void for Gibran.

While Gibran is recalibrating his outlook on life, I'm facing a layoff after eight years at my insurance job. The president who hired me has died of cancer, and my boss, the personnel director, has left. With the shakeup in leadership, the company is downsizing. I feel bittersweet about my impending layoff, but I'm still bummed. As the only Black person in management, the bitter is I know what microaggressions and slights look and feel like on a daily basis. In my eight years, I've never been welcomed into upper management as one of "them." I remember only too well at lunch how they'd talk around me, never including me in conversations they feel I couldn't possibly know a thing about, like the sports teams they talk about regularly. I could have chimed in to prove a point, but I chose not to as I have nothing to prove to this good ole boy network. If they don't want to include me, that's fine because I'm not one who is going to sing, dance, or shuffle to fit in. I consider myself pretty informed about many things in life, including current affairs, politics, and the sports team they often discuss.

The sweetness from this impending layoff is that I get to be with my kids. When my children began elementary school, it finally sinks in I'm in the deep south. I'm looking forward to spending Memorial Day with them. I'm told I have to work. When I complain about working on a national holiday, one of the managers tells me, "That's a Yankee holiday. Our holiday is Confederate Memorial Day, and it's in April." The kids, I find out, too, aren't getting Memorial Day off. I'm also mad about how the company is handling the timing of my layoff. The current president, who came aboard from a sister company, is retiring. He and I are only a few months away from being fully vested in the company's pension program, so what do they do? They allow him to stay until the fall to meet his vesting period though he has no formal responsibilities. To add insult to injury, he moves into an office away from the business floors where he putt-putt golfs all day. I, on the other hand, am let go and unable to vest after eight years of service to the company. My dander rises, and the bitterness I feel is real, but it softens when I think of being present in my children's lives in a routine and predictable way.

The truth is, I'm thinking about returning to education. It's 1988, and the school systems under Mayors Maynard Jackson and Andrew Young are striving to match the city of Atlanta's progressiveness and pursuit of excellence. I'm given the money I paid into the pension plan, which will keep me independent and afloat for a good while. Lucky for me, too, is that I'd bought a credit protection insurance policy that, if necessary, will pay off one hundred percent of my credit card debt for a year should I become unemployed and fall behind. What I wasn't prepared for is Gary's reaction to me being able to become a full-time wife and mother. He's not happy one bit that I'm going to be at home. At first, I'm confused by his reaction as my layoff adds no financial burden to our lives. My pension is enough to manage my expenses. I'm scratching my head, asking why since he doesn't have to pay any of my bills nor give me spending money. Shouldn't that have at least gotten me a pat on the back? Why wouldn't he be happy that I'm now able to spend quality time with my family as a wife and mother? This question plagues me for a while.

When moving through life at warp speed, there's so much that is missed. On the treadmill, it's hard to appreciate whether one is truly happy or not. One has to be still or listen to the echoes of the heart. Doubt and insecurity rise with Gary's annoyance. Had we really been in love? Had it only been loneliness meeting loneliness? Had we fooled ourselves into thinking it was love? Have we ever been happy? I remembered the song Gary sang in junior high school, Smokey Robinson and the Miracles, *The Love I Saw in You Was Just a Mirage*. Was everything about us just a mirage? These questions are rhetorical because I have no answers. The reality is we have three children to raise. I push back on the rising fear and step into my role as a full-time mother.

I love walking Gibran and Ravi to school every morning. We chat along the way as I push Amir in his stroller. When Amir and I get back home, I love spending one-on-one time teaching him to read and play educational games on our new home computer. I love being home with my children, and that's a fact. This hiatus provides me the opportune time to raise my kids and seed them with the values I hold dear. I visualize being a good wife even to my reluctant husband and hope he will find that spending time together is good for our relationship—he'll see me and I him.

After Grandma Holt's visit and seeing Korea host the 1988 Olympics with time on my hands, I finally plan my first return trip to Korea in over thirty years. Grandma gives me Molly's contact information, and I write to her, re-introducing myself as an adult Holt adoptee looking to come back to Korea for a visit. I also let Molly know that if a child ready for adoption needs an escort from Korea to the United States, I will volunteer. Many former adoptees when they return to Korea, do this. It's a way of giving back and giving thanks as we come full circle in our journey.

Molly immediately writes back:

> *November 28, 1988*
>
> *Ilsan, Korea*
>
> *Dear Sandy,*
>
> *I was thrilled to receive your letter and autobiography with the pictures. I recognized your first picture as you were especially thin, and I recall had a big tummy at first. I think you were a rather quiet little person who noticed everything.*

*It is amazing how well you can remember those months at that first orphanage. I vaguely remember the incident of burning your hands—so terrible you still have scars. I certainly remember that very long airplane trip! One child died, and one we left sick in Hawaii.*

*If you write to Holt International Children's Services, you can get my mother's book, "Sons from Afar," and read about that trip. The narration is an observation of my memories. Only we landed in Wake Island instead of Japan. One engine was out, and the engine had to be changed!*

*You have lovely children, and I suppose a husband too—You certainly have become a lovely and accomplished young lady. It is too bad your parents made you never mention Korea, but I am glad you can accept it now, why they did that. Sometimes parents are threatened by adopted children's memories of their previous lives. They love their children so much. Here in Korea, adoptions must be kept secret for the sake of the child, or else he gets treated like a waif or 2nd class citizen. But it sounds like they were wonderful parents.*

*Graduating from Stanford is no small feat! And you certainly accomplished a lot since then—plus raising a family! I am thrilled to hear you want to visit Korea. January would be a good time to visit as far as I am concerned. However, it is cold then, and may not be convenient. Also, you wouldn't see Korea at her loveliest. Spring and/or fall are really lovely here. Of course, you could stay here. I have rooms where people can stay at my home, or if they are occupied, we have guest rooms elsewhere.*

*When you write to the Holt Office, tell them you want to escort a child, and they will tell you if it is possible. Then let me know well in advance so I can plan to be here and can meet your plane. I will send more information later. The orphanage is in a different place now, and it is now a rehabilitation center for mostly mentally disabled children and adults. But don't let that discourage you they are lovely people and will enjoy your visit.*

*I would love to read your stories. Your number is #213, and I will look up your records here to see where you came from. Do you remember anything before you came here? You might have come from Isabell Orphanage in Pusan, but I don't know yet. I will look forward to hearing from you again. My love to you in our Lord Jesus.*

*Molly Holt*

Gary and I set our travel date for February 26, 1989. I'm glad he's coming with me. Maybe he'll appreciate my life's journey and learn a little better how to understand me. I call Molly to clear the dates and offer to bring any supplies needed. She tells me they make jelly and jams for all the residents and need lots of pectin as well as rubber baby pants and heating pads. She also lets me know there will be no children for me to escort on my return trip. I'm honored to be able to support the orphanage that saved my life in any way. I make arrangements with my friend Ester, whom I met years before at the insurance company, to keep the kids while we're away. Ester is very unorthodox about everything, but she loves my kids, and they love her. I fully expect they'll be on a steady diet of junk foods and entertained by marathons of *Miami Vice* and Disney movies.

Gary and I are up and ready early as we have to catch a flight to Portland, Oregon, where we'll connect to a flight to Gimpo International Airport. I have a window seat, of course. Gary and I don't talk much. He likes to read or nap on flights, which he does intermittently. I can't turn my mind off. I'm so emotional. I can't believe I'm heading to the land of my birth—a homeland where my accidental birth was never welcomed or recognized but, nonetheless, my landing point on this earth. I begin to calculate how much rest I will need to be fully energized when we land and for what lies ahead. The flight attendant announces our westbound crossing of the international dateline. She informs, "A minute ago was today. Now it's tomorrow, and today is now yesterday. The day known as today, which lies between yesterday and tomorrow, you won't see again until you return eastbound, and that's where you'll find it again." I ponder reality and perspective. Thirty-one years before, I don't remember this cute announcement—or at least I wasn't aware of it. Then again, we weren't exactly flying commercial, and our main stewardesses were Molly and her crew whom I'm sure had far more on their minds than meridian time zones. Emotions ranging from depression to elation begin to surface, and I can't quiet my mind. Thoughts of Mama and Daddy trigger sadness. With both gone to heaven, I suddenly miss them so much, and feelings of eternal gratitude well up in me. How blessed I am to have had them as parents. Was I betraying them returning to Korea? The feeling nags at me, especially since Mama had discouraged my memories and forbade any discussion of Korea, period.

Something outside the window snaps me out of this melancholy. I see the soft white clouds and smile, remembering my curiosity about them when I left Korea. Here they are to take me home again. As we approach our destination, I look down at the vast terrain thinking somewhere down there is my birth mother and Sonyeon. Somewhere down there, somebody knows I exist. I think of *hal-abeoji*, Molly, Barbara, and *Halmeoni*. What a blessing that God touched their hearts with compassion for kids like me. I'm wondering what God has in store for me because somehow, He's orchestrating my return to Korea. Can I really go home again in my heart? I don't know, but some thirteen hours later, we are landing in Korea.

I don't remember any of this, Korea. It is not the bombed-out terrain of the past, and I see no raggedy urchins looking for food. Instead, Korea of 1989 is a country on its way to political and social democracy. The optimism is high because the 1988 Seoul Olympics have been a success, and indeed the feeling of *Arirang* is in the air. Was this hope finally here to stay? Arriving in Seoul, Gary and I clear customs. Standing outside baggage claim is a woman with a sign. My eyes zoom above the sign to the woman holding it. It's Molly! Totally forgetting about Gary, and with no idea what the sign says, I make a beeline toward her. I'm seeing Molly again for the first time in thirty-one-years, and as I run toward her, time and space evaporate. I'm all choked up. Molly, who'd placed my hand in Mama's at the San Francisco Airport, is here before me at the same airport from which I left Korea. I imagine she greets many adoptees who return, but it still feels so special that she's there to greet me. The joy of being reunited with a loved one overcomes us, and what could have been an awkward greeting melts into a warm embrace. I'm home again, and dear Lord, I remember these arms so well.

Finally, Molly introduces Gary and me to Reverend Lee. Gary, who's been standing right behind her, steps in closer. They look at each other as she rattles off my background to the Reverend in Korean. Some things never change, even if they go in reverse. Here is Molly speaking the only language I knew when I arrived in America, and here she is speaking it again, but this time I don't understand. Gary joins Reverend Lee in the front seat of the car as he drives us to our destination. Molly and I are in the backseat talking nonstop.

We are staying at the orphanage in her house. Molly introduces us to *Jaegoni,* known as Jake. He came to the orphanage not too long after I left, she tells me. Unfortunately, because of Jake's cerebral palsy, he was never adopted and so became a permanent resident of Il San. Now he's the cook for Molly and her guests. He's the one who needed the pectin for his homemade jams and jellies. Jake immediately bonds with Gary and me, and we with him. Physically he's obviously disabled, but his actions and his finished product are proof of his *ability,* minimizing the *dis* in front of it.

Molly and I talk and talk and then talk some more. I'm riveted when she talks about the Korean War history of which I'm a product and its devastation on the country and people. Molly takes me into the records office where my file has already been pulled. Over the thirty-one years since I left Korea—and, lived a lifetime in between—my memory is sketchy. I know I came to the Holt Orphanage from another orphanage, and indelible in my memory is being near the sea. Indeed, the records corroborate that I came to Hyo Chang Park from Mah San Infant Orphanage in Masan, a seaport. She tells me my last name/family name Chang comes from the lady who ran the orphanage. As I flip through the pages, I recognize some of the children, and indeed all their last names are Chang like mine. Molly tells me she was on the trip when I was picked up from Masan. She looks further at my papers and says nothing is known about my birth family or me and that there was no one associated with dropping me off.

I ask her, "Well, do you think my name was really Bang Sun since Chang is not my real family name?"

"I would say yes," she replies. "That's probably your real name because you were old enough to be verbal."

"What about my birthdate. Where did that come from?"

Molly answers, "Since you didn't have a date assigned, I'm probably the one who determined what I thought your age was based on your teeth development and verbal maturity."

"But Molly, why of all dates, April 1?" I ask.

She shrugs, spreads her palms upwards, and gives an "Oh, well" smile.

I smile, too. I tell Molly about the boy who took care of me and the lady with red lipstick. She tells me the war devastated countless families beyond belief and that so many were splintered forever to the north and south. "If you think the boy was perhaps your brother, your mother might have been widowed. To provide for her family, she could have had no other choice but to be a *Kijichon* woman to the soldiers. So many women tried to take care of their babies but just could not and mercifully gave them up to orphanages. So, consider yourself 'chosen' and 'blessed,' Bang Sun. You said you remember so many babies dying while you were here. Well, that could have easily been you. The women had it so hard, and they still do."

I'm silent, soaking in and reflecting on Molly's every word. That evening, I look at the moon. I realize it's the same moon I saw in Decatur, Georgia, and for some reason, that moment reminds me of the scripture, Hebrew 13:8, "*Jesus Christ is the same yesterday, today and forever.*" That same moon provides the glow of night everywhere like the omnipresent Christ who brought me from darkness through His guiding light, still showing the way today, and I rest assured that I can depend on that same light tomorrow. I am comforted.

Gary is enjoying the physical trip, but he is reluctant to hear about my past. "Don't bring me no bad news" is his motto, and therefore he rebukes hard-luck stories seeping into his spirit. Gary prefers to be like the ostrich—head in the sand—when it comes to things like this. That next morning, Molly takes me to the Korean Folk Village. Gary decides to hang back at the orphanage with Jake. The folk village is where time stands still in Korea as this is the place that preserves Old Korea, highlighting the best of its culture and traditions. Five others from the orphanage accompany Molly and me to the village. Our motley crew consists of one Caucasian, one albino Korean, one Black Amerasian, and four disabled Koreans. You can only imagine the attention we draw.

The moment I step inside the village, I'm transported to the past. Again, I'm on Sonyeon's back, mesmerized by the smells, sights, sounds, and activities of the village. The only things missing from this walk down memory lane are the uniformed soldiers and the stench of the dung and spoiling fish. I see the fun seesaw that I remember. Unlike seesaws in the United States where one sits on each end pushing off with their feet to go up and down safely, the one in Korea, they stand on each end, and one jumps on the platform dangerously catapulting the other into the air. It's truly a skill of balance, concentration, and guts. Giant urns of aging soy sauce are neatly lined up. From the thatched-roof huts that house the buried kimchi, a fermented smell wafts in the air. For so many years, I questioned myself about these memories because Mama had convinced me I couldn't possibly remember such details of Korea. But here I am, in time and space that confirm I have been right all along.

The moment I see the man coming toward me with a pair of big clacking, shearing scissors selling taffy-like candy, I start boohooing. It's the *Yeot*-*jangsu*! And it's as if he knew he had an appointment with me. Today, instead of stealing, I'm a paying customer. I'm buying enough *Yeot* for me and to take back to my children. I think about Sonyeon and give the *Yeot-jangsu* extra money for his ancestor who probably chased after Sonyeon and me. I close my eyes and place a small bit of the candy in my mouth. The sweetness reaches the north, south, east, and west of my mouth as I remember. I'm remembering, too, the choking dust of spring and the bitter cold of winter and the searing heat and humidity of summer being relieved by the cool blue waters. The shunned memories of a boy called Sonyeon are all being validated, and I want now, more than ever to find him, for he was real. The grasshoppers were real the ocean sea morsels were real, as was the lady with red lipstick.

Old memories that have been lost to time evoke emotions that have me reliving every moment of my life kept in my secret compartments that I was forced to suppress. But I'm here, a Korean in Korea, even if a forgotten one. I'm home and I'm sobbing. Sobbing for the lost child, sobbing for the found child, and sobbing for the adult with deep down self-doubt of her worthiness to be loved. I probably appear mentally challenged to passersby, but I don't care. Molly can see I'm overcome and takes me to a nearby bench to sit. Through tears, I share with her how much this trip and this moment mean to me. Even though I may never find Sonyeon, I at least know that my memories of him are real. I begin to tell Molly the story of my friend RJ who had also been at Holt orphanage. On his return to Korea, he finds his mother. To his disappointment, it caused quite a commotion and created confusion in his mother's current life. I'd never thought about trying to find my mother, and I certainly don't want to upset her life in any way, but I want to find Sonyeon. I want to see him face-to-face. I want to thank him.

We tour the DMZ, the 38th parallel dividing North and South Korea. As Molly is talking, I'm reading about the horrendous war. I think about my birth father. Who could he be or have been? Are his footprints in the history of this dirt? Could his blood have been shed in this field? Did he kill someone? Did he even survive? If he is alive, did he think of me, the child he left behind? Did he even know I existed? When I tune back in, Molly is telling me about families now permanently separated between the north and south and how hard it is on them. If they see each other again, it will be as strangers. Could my mother's family have been separated? What happened to her? My mind strays. Was she married? A widow? Did she feel sad, or had time healed her wounds? Did she hate the North Koreans, the perpetrators of the war? And what of the American soldier who impregnated her? Did she ever think of him or me? It seems the sky over Seoul is ready to cry with me as a droplet of rain lands on my arm. The droplets of rain are coming faster now. We tarry away to find shelter. Now pouring, the rain squelches the incessant questions to which I have no answers.

That evening at Molly's home, all of us close our visit to Korea with a Bible study. I glance at her with admiration. The idea that she has committed more than thirty years of her life to helping forgotten children is heartwarming. The impact of her love and care is evident in the rapport she has with the children and residents. The bible study is in Korean, but she opens her Bible to follow along in English. The message is about God's covenant with us from Deuteronomy 4:9–10:

*Only be careful, and watch yourselves closely so that you do not forget the things your eyes have seen or let them fade from your heart as long as you live. Teach them to your children and to their children after them. Remember the day you stood before the Lord your God at Horeb, when he said to me, "Assemble the people before me to hear my words so that they may learn to revere me as long as they live in the land and may teach them to their children."*

These words make me reflect on Grandma's advice to tell my children my story because it's their story, too, and they'll know how good God is. The verse right then and there inspires me to take action. I lean over and whisper to Gary, "When we get home, we must plan to come back with the children."

That's exactly what we do. I start preparing our children for their trip to Korea. Gibran and Ravi remember Grandma Holt's visit from a few years earlier when we attended Holt's thirtieth celebration with her. They've also seen the film about Holt International adoption, and now I need to personalize my involvement with Korea and the Holts by telling them my story. I pull out my original passport from Korea.

All three ask, "Who is that little girl in the picture?"

"That's me."

I begin telling my story, abbreviated and child friendly. Sprawled on the floor, they are listening intently, much like spellbound kindergarteners. After I finish, they have lots of questions.

Gibran asks, "Well, Mommy, are we going to Korea to help you find your family?"

"No. I mainly want you all to see the land that I came from and meet the lady who took care of me. She is like family," I respond.

"Is Grandma Holt going to be in Korea?" Ravi asks.

"No. She lives here in the United States of America like us, but her daughter Molly will be there. It's possible that she might visit her at the same time we'll be there. We'll see." I look over at Amir, deep in thought. "Well, Amir, everyone has asked a question. Do you have one?"

"Mommy, did you really eat sea morsels and grasshoppers?" he asks.

"Yes, and I'm going to kiss you and put sea morsels and grasshopper juice on your cheeks," I say, grabbing him. Immediately the room clears as they run in different directions. I give chase, reveling in hearing the joyous laughter of my children—medicine for my soul.

Because we've traveled often to visit friends in Bermuda, the children already have passports. So, a month later, in the spring of 1989, our family returns to Korea. Springtime with the cherry blossoms in bloom should be wonderful. The children do very well on the long thirteen-hour flight. Before landing, I tell them about my first flight when I wondered what the fluffy white stuff outside the plane's window was.

Amir, a little tongue-tied, says, "Mommy, you didn't even know it was clouds?"

We all laugh, but more at him rather than at my not knowing.

After clearing customs, Molly is again at the airport to pick us up, this time in a van. We're staying a few days at the orphanage before seeing the rest of what is now called the Miracle on the Han River (the developed Korea post-war). The kids are in awe of the beautiful vast campus of Il San. I let them know this isn't the original orphanage I lived in, but Molly was my caregiver much as she is to the children today. Most of the residents now are special-needs children, and it amazes my kids to see a child with a severe limp pushing another child in a wheelchair. They observe a teen turning the pages of the Bible with her toes because she doesn't have use of her hands. They see a blind young person easily maneuvering with a stick. They're learning resilience and grace. Gary and I talk with them later that evening about what they saw and how they feel. Ravi and Gibran say they were feeling sad about the children's condition, but then they saw how happy they were and how they helped each other, so they felt better. Amir says he was still feeling sad that kids need to be in a wheelchair or can't see. We agree everyone will pray for them. It is a teachable moment in faith, compassion, and resilience.

At breakfast, Molly, Gary, and I chitchat over coffee and tea. Jake has prepared porridge, toast, and the jam he's made for breakfast. Before eating, the children begin singing sweetly the grace. It is the same song I'd sung as a child before eating. I join in with them:

*nahl-mah-dah oo-ree eh-geh yang-shik-eul joo-shi-neun*
*eun-heh-ro oo-shin hah-nah-neem jeul-gam-sah-hahb-*
*nee-dah. ah-men*
For the meal that you provide for us daily
We joyfully thank our gracious God.
A-men

I always wondered about my pronunciation of the song lyrics when I would sing it in America, but after all these years, and to my surprise, my melody and words are right on point. My kids get a kick out of hearing me singing in Korean. Enjoying the song, I wonder out loud to Molly what she thought I would be doing if I'd never been adopted and was still here in Korea, speaking Korean but not looking Korean. Molly says the odds are extremely high that my life would have been pitiful. On any scale, it would never measure up to the life I'm enjoying in the U.S. She tells Gary and me about a word the Koreans use to identify dark-skinned people. She said they call us *geomdungi.*

Molly remembers how much I loved the Korean Folk Village, so we decide to take the kids there. We take the train, which is very crowded, but the kids enjoy it. I'm glad when we finally arrive at our stop because I'm simultaneously trying to hold on to the kids, bracing and balancing against each other while I'm holding on to the rail. The kids who are making a game of it are enjoying themselves when the train pulls into a stop and wants to continue on. As soon as we arrive at the village, we're drawn to the performance of a folk-dance called Farmer's Dance. The dancers' costumes are brilliant colors of blue, red, and yellow over a white garment. They can make the long white ribbons attached to their headdress twirl in unison. While standing and watching them dance, some school-age students on a field trip are filing into a straight line. One of them starts pointing at us and begins shouting, "*Geomdungi, Geomdungi.*" The other students look over, gasp, and they too start echoing "*Geomdungi, Geomdungi,*" as though they are doing a vocal warmup. I look at Molly, amazed that she'd just told us about the term, and here we are being called "Blackies!" I whisper to Gary some things never change. We come all the way to Korea, and we are being called the N-word. I don't know if the Korean word holds the vitriol or if it's even equivalent to the meaning of the term in America, but it feels like it. Yet, after all, wasn't my Blackness the reason for my expulsion from Korea? Not really. It was my mixed blood, much like the mixed blood of White soldiers' children who, too, were deported. Thank goodness my kids don't understand what's going on. They are beaming, feeling like celebrities from America. Amir starts dancing, and a small crowd forms, cheering him on.

At five years old, he's already drawing attention and making others notice him. After all the fanfare, I take the kids to my favorite exhibits and narrate as if I'm a tour guide. The finale is when the *Yeot-jangsu* comes clacking his scissors. I tell the kids how much I'd craved this candy as a child. I let them know the sound of the scissors clacking is like the ice cream man's blaring tune announcing his arrival in our neighborhood. I buy them some *Yeot* and rice candy before leaving the Korean Folk Village. Like me, the children experience the explosion of the sweet candy that permeates the insides of their mouths—north, south, east, west.

Back at the orphanage, we tour the beautiful modern gymnasium. Molly tells us the Paralympic teams practiced at Il San for the 1988 Paralympic games. That afternoon, we wrap up our stay with Molly. We spend our last day in Itaewon, now a commercial area for shopping, complete with the Korean War Memorial statue. During the war, Itaewon, close to the headquarters of the United States Forces Korea (the combined Army, Air Force, Navy, and Marines) was mostly known for its seedy bars and prostitution catering to foreign soldiers and serviceman based in Yongsan.

Ravi, who hasn't been eating much since we arrived as only sushi is being served, is starving. On our way, she pulls my coattail and says she's starving. She doesn't starve much longer because not only do we see a McDonald's, but a Denny's, too. The kids are in seventh heaven, and so is Gary, who is eager to shop. He has items of clothing made, picks up goods like silk scarves for his side hustle of selling women's wear, and gets the kids' starter jackets and athletic shoes. All the loot is packed, and we finally head back to Atlanta after another wonderful trip to Korea.

Since my layoff, I've been interviewing here and there for corporate jobs however, my inclination is to return to teaching. With our travel over, I turn my attention to my career. Discouraged by the regulations around teaching when I'd first moved to Atlanta eight years back, I'm excited to try again. Pleasantly surprised, I learn that Atlanta's school superintendent is none other than Dr. Alonzo A. Crim, my school's superintendent back in Compton. Crim was the one who'd handed me my high school diploma. Hired away to Atlanta, he becomes the first Black superintendent to integrate schools. His accomplishments in Atlanta have him now rubbing elbows with giants such as Benjamin E. Mays, Andrew Young, Julian Bond, and Maynard Jackson.

I make an appointment to see him and am honored to be in his presence. During our meeting, I share an in-depth social studies unit I'd developed on my trip with Gary to Haiti and Jamaica. Dr. Crim steers me to the curriculum department head but is emphatic I check in with the state Department of Education to get certified to teach in Georgia. When I arrived in Atlanta, I'd assumed that getting my Georgia teaching certificate would be a breeze as I was already licensed in California, Nevada, and Texas. To my utter shock, when I submitted my application, I was told Georgia didn't recognize any of my certificates nor my master's degree in education from USC. How dare Georgia, when nationally they ranked at the bottom in education? To be certified I would need sixty additional credits, which meant going to school all over again.

I make my Caribbean history presentation to a few high schools and cultural centers but quickly recognize I have zero passion for entrepreneurship as a lifestyle. It so happens that my church, Greenforest Baptist Church, is one of the fastest-growing churches in the country. It provides a one-stop-shop environment for all family needs. Besides spiritual fulfillment and family meals before Bible study, kids can enroll in sports, cheerleading, and even take exercise and diet management classes. The church decides to open a school, and I become a part of the inaugural opening committee and planning team. After launching in August 1989, I begin teaching sixth and seventh grades. I also teach elective Spanish and realize how very much I enjoy it. With the Spanish program's success, I see the need to teach a foreign language in other church schools without the hassle of state certifications, so I pitch my idea.

I begin teaching Spanish at three different churches, which is great because I can negotiate my pay, set my own schedule, and still see my children off to school and pick them up. It's the best of both worlds. I'm a quasi-entrepreneur, just like with my encyclopedia job. My passion as a teacher and educator again makes it easy to sell a foreign language program's benefits to enhance each school's curriculum. While my career is budding, my marriage is deteriorating and has been on the decline for years. Misery sets in like a dark shadow. Our path to love was never traditional. I've always cared for Gary, loving him the best I knew how, but he's not once made me his priority. Lucky for me, I see married life as par for the course, and as they say, children live what they learn. Our marriage is closer to Mama and Daddy's relationship rather than the Bacon family in Detroit.

I think back from the very beginning of our relationship. We skipped courtship altogether and never developed a friendship. Gary has never seemed satisfied with my physical appearance so much so that when we're at the beach, he's always zooming in on voluptuous women in their bikinis with his video camera. He would title his tapings T & A (Tits & Ass). Gary's insensitivity reaches the pinnacle when one day, he invites a few of his co-workers over and plays his T & A videos for them. It's not as though he's in his private man cave; he's in our family room. Amir and I have to walk back and forth through it to get to the kitchen. I'm quiet, but not Amir, who stops in front of the men on one of our trips.

"Daddy," says our six-year-old in a reprimanding voice, "is it right to be showing that? How do you think Mommy feels?"

Out of the mouth of babes. A mere six-year-old gives a teachable moment on respect and morality to his father and his friends. The men flush, and I can see they're feeling awkward and embarrassed. I think a lot about that day. There has always been, it seems to me, a sense of Gary wishing for something more. I'm not one for tears of sorrow. I'm one who for sure can rise up.

Gary's fear of financial debt is his idea of the ultimate nightmare of a ball and chain holding him down. Totally driven by financial caution and restraint, he's a penny pincher. Many red flags were now flying high and without restraint. I should've heeded the second red flag when we decided to get married and he didn't buy me a ring. When I bought myself a three-dollar jade ring from the swap meet to have something to symbolize our marriage, he felt no embarrassment. Of course, a wedding ring is no indicator that a marriage will be successful, but it is a universal love symbol. When we arrived on the island of Jamaica with no plans, the first red flag I'd ignored has now led to many red flags.

The third red flag—this one blood-red—is when Gary lowers the boom when I'm left to go through my prenatal visits with Gibran alone. He's afraid to show up because the hospital might look to him for any financial obligation. I've never depended on Gary for a single financial need, including the time I was laid off. Red flag number four shows up when he begins badgering me about not working, reminding me I'm a Stanford graduate, and continuously comparing me to my friends who are doctors as if to say my career is insignificant. I just can't understand why Gary isn't more supportive and why he doesn't feel blessed to have me home to nurture our family. Even though his respect, friendship, and emotional support are missing in our relationship, I'm tolerating this mistreatment because it's when I lost both my parents and desperately needed his support. The final and glaring red flag I ignored and the one that cracks our foundation wide open is when Daddy died, and Gary uses my father's death as a bargaining tool. I know then for sure the true nature of my husband.

Imagine how distraught I was, and all Gary can think of is how to leverage his flying privileges to control when and if I can go to plan my father's funeral. My daddy is dead. I needed to be in California to help my family, and Gary is feuding with me, telling me I need to stay back and help figure out how and when we'll meet a one-time payment obligation on our house, which is due five months from now! He knew Mama was distraught and depending on me to plan the funeral, and here I am on hold because all Gary can think about is punishing me for never being enough. I arrived home in Los Angeles four days later than was expected. That was the beginning of the end. I would never forgive him. His cold and mean-spirited action ignites a fire that began to turn my tolerance into resentment before it finally erupted and detonated our marriage.

The marriage is over unless we get help. I still want things to work out, not because I love Gary but to keep my family intact, so I set up marriage counseling. We went—Gary reluctantly, as is true of most males, especially Black males. It seems helpful at first because we are given assignments to write down: How do we feel? What are our expectations of each other? What are our turn-on and turn-off triggers? And so on. One of my pet peeves is that Gary travels often because he can, which isn't a problem. The problem is, I don't know where he is because he doesn't communicate with me when he travels. I'm always worrying if he's arrived safely, where he's staying, and what will happen if there's an emergency with one of the kids. It seems a reasonable request. Why wouldn't he want to be contacted if something happens to our kids? After several months of counseling, Gary goes out of the country, and again I don't hear from him. Right then and there, we stop the counseling. It's pointless if he's not going to honor the goals we've set to improve our relationship. The point of no return is near.

And then it arrives. One day, leaving work early, I race home to get something I'd left behind and needed. I go into our bedroom to find that Gary has returned from one of his trips. His wallet and a bunch of things I'm sure not meant for my eyes are strewn on the bed. Naturally, I see what isn't for my eyes and confront Gary. He begins blaming his brother. It's such poppycock. How can his brother make *him* a philanderer? At this point, I've had enough. The emotional abuse I'm tolerating has to stop. I'm through blaming myself for being me. If I'm not enough for Gary, so be it. Any psychological obstacle or remaining self-doubt that halts my forward progress will be squashed from this day forward.

I move with the kids to a friends' house. While staying with Terry, I begin negotiating to have a townhome built. Though it's inevitable, I still don't want a divorce. I tell Gary maybe we can start over. Maybe we can court each other this time. Maybe we can be friends and be there for our kids. To close on the townhouse, I have to show papers of separation. I tell Gary this, and unbeknownst to me, his lawyer friend tells him that rather than separation papers, she will draw up divorce papers to include child support to him as the custodial parent. I'm served divorce papers at work on my thirty-ninth birthday. I'm having a hard time and wish I were closer to Lolo, who returned from London a few years earlier and is having marital woes as well. After mama and daddy passed on, the bond that held us kids together, had weakened. Not wanting to burden her, I suck it all up.

Devastated, I leave the church school in utter shock. To add to my distress, I now can't close on the townhome because of the monkey wrench introduced of having to potentially pay child support. Back to square one and reeling in chaos, I need to find a place to live. I'm livid. Knowing his intention now, I feel stupid having told Gary that we could use the townhome as a rental property if we reconciled. The thought makes me even more furious. Maybe all his emotional abuse and slights are intended to drive me away in the first place. At this point, I don't appreciate that hurt people hurt people and that damaged people know how to survive, but I know I will survive. Livid, I lawyer up. The builder of my townhome is sympathetic to my situation. Through his kindness and the grace of God, he allows me to move into one of his previously built townhouses that backs up to a golf course. It is beautiful and more spacious than the one I intend to buy. Best of all, he allows me to live there rent-free for months until I can close on my unit.

The kids are shaken. Especially our youngest, Amir. Hurt, he's acting out because of the divorce. First, he tries to jump out of my moving car; then he takes to running off from me in crowded places. When his frustration is high, he lashes out at Ravi and Gibran and becomes very agitated. I decide to resume counseling, this time with the kids, so they can have an outlet to deal with this family trauma. I must get it together and prepare for life as a single parent. The truth is I've been a single parent all along. For years, I've been the one traveling alone with the kids, going to church alone with the kids, and ripping and running, triple timing it to get them to every scheduled event or activity. My job with the churches, which I love so much, is on the chopping block because I need to get a job that offers benefits. Since my layoff, we've been on Gary's benefits as I must be assured that the kids have the health care they need, but other than that, I want nothing from him anymore. It doesn't take long for me to make up my mind: I will go back to teaching public school.

I've walked in faith since the day I was born. Eleven years before, I'd applied for and had issues with getting my teaching certification for Georgia. I decide to reapply. I submit the same teaching certificate application, the same college transcripts, and to my surprise and delight this time, everything is accepted. Job interviews are pouring in from all over metro Atlanta. I decide to only interview within the Atlanta Public Schools system because of the offered pay and benefits, which are my priority. Fortunately, I receive offers from every school where I interviewed. My decision about where to go is helped along because I'm a Girl Scout leader at my church, and Ms. Bazoline Estelle Usher, now 106 years old who started the Black Girl Scout Troops in Georgia, is someone I admire. I choose her namesake school, B.E. Usher Middle School, to begin my public-school teaching career in Atlanta.

I'm in action mode, determined to make sure my children adjust and that their lives aren't materially affected by the divorce. My lawyer tells me I can easily get child support because it's obvious I have been the kids' primary caretaker since birth. Because I know Gary, it's a certainty that pressing for child support will be an ongoing source of stress in our lives and may turn ugly. I don't need this. Plus, the problem is with Gary and me, not with the children, and I want to keep it that way. Knowing I'll land on my feet, I agree to a six-month custody sharing offer on the table, opting out of child support. My children love their father, and the boys, especially Amir, want their dad's approval. They need his presence in their lives, and this, I feel, is a good compromise. When each of my children was born, I promised with all my heart to protect them. I'm being called on to do that now. Seeing their father and continuing a relationship with him is protecting them, no matter how miserable it might make me.

As an educator and one who majored in psychology as an undergraduate, I know the importance of men being involved in their children's lives, especially at my kids' vulnerable age. Defaulting to the familiar of pulling up my big girl pants, I keep my issues with Gary in check for the children's sake.

The divorce is finalized in October 1992. When visitation starts, I find it very difficult to be away from my kids as this is the first time we've ever been apart for this length of time. The void is palpable. Gary doesn't seem to get it that he can't just run off when the kids are with him and leave them when he feels like it. As my kids have never been left alone without supervision, at first, I get a kick out of Amir, a fan of the recent movie *Home Alone* who is continually calling to say, "Mom, we're home alone."

On Valentine's Day, when Amir is continuously calling about them being alone, I realize it's not just a minute or two, so when the calls don't stop, I go over to Gary's house around 2:00 a.m. and stay the night with them. Gary returns with his date in the morning, not a single word of apology. I'm furious that he would stay out all night, especially since Gibran isn't old enough to be considered of legal age to supervise them, and leaving underage kids alone is against the law. I try not to overreact in front of the kids, but I'm fuming. Instead of going off the rail, I do what I usually do to get myself centered: I reach out to Mama Lee (Mrs. Bacon in Detroit). She tells me to let go and let Gary be in control of the kids during his time with them. I still can't relax when the kids are with their father, but I relent to the circumstance over time.

To fill up the time, I finally decide to try dating. I meet this man who seems to have a lot going for him. Like me, he's going through a separation and divorce, and of course, I can relate. When he tells me he has cancer, my heart goes out to him. How could a wife leave her husband when he's so ill? Our meetings are sporadic, but I understand because of his illness. Then I begin to see red flags waving furiously (and I should know about red flags by now). When we are together, it's not hard to overhear his calls that do not remotely sound like business. When I ask him about his divorce timeline, he's reluctant to talk about it. When I press hard, he gets aloof. When the truth, which always finds the light of day, comes out, the deceiver is neither separated nor going through a divorce. He is such a boldface liar that I question if he even has cancer. How much more of a fool can I be in the choices I keep making in men? Still, I'm making progress because, without hesitation, I keep on walkin' and don't look back. This time around, I'll be the victim of no man.

Rearing its head again is the doubt I feel about why I'm not worthy of a real loving relationship. Immediately catching myself, I ask God for forgiveness. After all He's done for me. I need to stay present to His grace and believe the path He is leading me on is the right one.

But it's hard. Scars from abandonment and rejection can hide and only show up as involuntary actions, much like a knee-jerk reaction, because they are deeply embedded in the marrow of pain and loss. To combat my fear, I decide to try again with a new man. I'm ready to look fear squarely in the eye, but this time it's not fear but my children who sabotage the relationship. Amir, the ringleader, plots with Ravi and Gibran how they can make life unpleasant for the man I'm seeing. Since my children are always my priority, they need not have. I'm already done with this new guy when he doesn't want to include my children on an outing that includes his son. Done. That's it for him.

During Gary's six-month custody stint, he makes it a rite of passage to manhood for the boys to mow the lawn, rake leaves, wash dishes, and wash their own clothes. I agree with this because they have to help with dishes and laundry at my home, but our together time is focused on academics, emphasizing homework, school projects, school sports, and activities. At his house, they must still do homework but not with an unrelenting monitor like me. The boys especially don't look forward to going to Gary's because they're butting heads with their father and rebelling against his house rules. Ravi, named after the transcendental meditation sitarist Ravi Shankar, has always been the Zen child, and she adapts well and makes the best of both situations.

By the time Gibran is in high school, the struggle becomes real, and Gary kicks him out. Gibran decides without telling me to move in with some other teenagers who have no adult supervision in their house either. When I find out, I protest, but Gary insists that I should let him handle the situation and let Gibran become a man. When one of the teens accidentally has a gun go off, Gibran, pretty shaken, calls me and is ready to come home. The same thing happens with Amir. He is kicked out and is staying with one of his friends. At least this time, I know the parent because we serve on the parent-teacher association and as band parents. It all seems so crazy, and like Gibran, Amir eventually moves back home. That is the end of the six-month visitation swap for the boys. Gary makes no fuss about it, and neither do I. Everyone who knows our children would say they are good kids, but children will be children. Ravi decides to keep up her six-month stint with her dad.

Gary doesn't have the patience to endure parental responsibilities. Sometimes I wonder if he's capable of extending himself beyond himself. My conclusion: Parenting causes stress, and Gary aims to be stress-free. With Ravi, he's stress-free. I think back to the advice my parents and mentor, Mr. Freeman, gave me. Maybe Gary was indeed a good-time Charlie—all the fun but none of the responsibility—how right they were. If you ask me how I feel in hindsight, my answer is: I wouldn't have done anything differently. I still know our meeting at that reunion dance was orchestrated, so I have no regrets. How could I with my three beautiful children? Sure, any woman wants to feel desirable and be loved, and I didn't have that with Gary, but life is what it is, and I'm more than content with my children.

By the time the kids get to be teenagers, I'm praying I'll be able to keep the promise I made to them when they were born—to protect them and support their dreams. The challenges I now face are no longer just the daily morning whirlwind breakfast, taxi service to school, after-school activities, and home but are coming-of-age problems—trying coming of age problems! When Ravi and Amir were in elementary and Gibran in high school, I'd drop them off and then dash to work thirty miles away to meet my students by 8:30 a.m.

Amir turns out to be a pretty good athlete, and he's very popular with the girls. He starts to feel his oats and becomes mouthy and testy with me. One morning, we are all in our mad dash routine except Amir. He's still asleep. I wake him and plead with him to hurry because attendance is a part of my evaluation as a teacher. After so many tardies, the principal can place me on probationary status, eventually leading to termination. I've always been a conscientious employee, and a key staff member noted for writing the school plan, assisting with meeting accreditation standards and writing proposals for grants. I want to keep it that way. Even as a key employee, whenever I'm late, I have to sign in with a red pen, which is effective in deterring tardiness. On this particular morning, Amir, even after waking up late, has no sense of urgency. He's taking his sweet time ironing his pants.

"I need you just to put on something—anything—so we can leave in five minutes. I can't be late."

"That's not my problem," he says.

I head straight for his mouth to bop it for him being smart. Well, wouldn't you know, he grabs my hand, and automatically my feet start kicking him. He at least has the good sense to let go. I get the other children, and we leave without Amir. For the first time in his life, he must take public transportation, and because we don't live in his school zone, it's a trek. Amir gets to school rather late. He's in the magnet program, which is a close-knit small learning community. He's telling his classmate why he's late and shows him the bruise on his shin. His math teacher overhears the conversation and immediately sends him to the counselor who reports me to a social worker. Amir is sent home to Gary, not me. As far as I'm concerned, he needs some reflection time, so I'm okay with it. That evening, when I get home, my doorbell rings. I open it to two hefty, tall police officers looking straight over my head and not seeing me.

"Yes?" I say.

In unison, their heads lower and land on all four feet, eleven inches of me. They look at each other and begin chuckling.

"Ma'am," one of them says, barely able to keep a straight face, "we're here checking on a potential child abuse case. Can you tell us what happened with your son?"

I tell him my side of the story, and he says, "Sorry for your troubles." The officers go on their way, still amused, muffling their laughter. When all of it blows over, my cheeky son starts bragging, "Don't mess with my mama 'cause she'll karate chop you with her feet." From that day on, my children teasingly call me Chang Bang to emphasize my Korean side, which they associate with karate.

All three children do well in school. Both Ravi and Amir are always on the honor roll. Gibran maintains being a B student with little effort. Amir is the only one Gary and I have a few parent conferences about because he talks too much in class. None of my children are fighters or disrespectful to adults, but Amir can't stop talking. They are all active in sports, band, cheering, Beta club, etc. To afford all the fees, dues, and uniforms for them to participate in these activities, I accept the job of being the basketball and track coach at my school. Mind you, I've never participated as an athlete in my life, only as commissioner of athletics in junior high and in high school as the girl who held the tape at the finish line of the track meets.

I did watch lots of sports with Daddy, and I did go to many Stanford football and basketball games, so I can figure this coaching thing out. From years of watching UCLA win basketball championships with Lou Alcindor/Kareem Abdul Jabbar who had the "winningest" basketball coach, John Wooden, I'm confident. I take the basketball coach position very seriously and check out John Wooden's videotapes from the library. In earnest, I study his practice drills. I also bring on an assistant coach, and with our consistent practice regiment, great defense, and fast-breaking offense, we win nine of the ten games, the most the school has ever won, just missing the championship. One doesn't have to be tall or be an athlete to win.

In the summer of 1996, while school is out, I'm selected to be a hostess for Atlanta's 100th Summer Olympics. My friend Dorothy, a co-worker at B.E. Usher Middle School, partners with me in hosting the dignitaries from Equatorial Guinea. We are given a new BMW for six weeks and given access to all the Olympic sites to transport the dignitaries to events they desire to attend.

Even though the men we're transporting speak Spanish, they studied in Barcelona. It is challenging to understand their Spanish because it's different from the Castilian Spanish I learned. However, my Spanish is enough to communicate with our dignitaries, and we thoroughly enjoy the six-week experience. Almost immediately after the Olympics, it's time for school to start again. I have active children who are participating in numerous school activities requiring much money. I need a part-time job besides my teaching job to afford all this. I run into someone who recruits me to deliver newspapers in the middle of the night. Daily, after picking up my kids from school, around 7:00 p.m. from their practices, I feed them and go to bed around 9:30 p.m. to get up at 1:00 a.m. to begin working from 2:00 a.m. until 6:00 a.m. rolling newspapers and delivering them for my route. Amir comes with me a few times to help.

By the fourth month of working two, grueling twenty hours a day jobs, I am tired beyond reason. I'm elated and energized, however, when I learn that I've won the honor of being the 1996 Atlanta Public Schools Middle School Teacher of the Year for the district. The school has a huge celebration on my behalf, and my pastor, along with Gary's father and my dear friend Marilyn, my old friend from Vegas, fly in from California. That night, I'm honored at the district-wide gala where I give a speech. My family and staff who attend are enormously proud of my recognition, and it's a happy moment for me. One of my friends who attends knows that every night I deliver newspapers to make ends meet. He confides as he is watching and listening to me give my speech and seeing my children's glowing pride in me that he is moved and wants to make me an offer: If I quit my job with the newspaper, he'll supplement whatever I'm making there until the end of the school year. The offer is very generous and a testament to how true a friend can be with no strings attached. I thank God for his merciful intervention. That night, I get in from the event late, but I still go to my newspaper job at 2:00 a.m. I give my two-week notice, finding it hard to believe I've been working there night after night, seven days a week, for four consecutive months.

During Gibran's senior year, my quiet, independent child works multiple jobs to save money to get a car. He even changed his birth certificate to work at Popeye's chicken inside the Kroger grocery store near his dad's house when he was too young to work. His many jobs include selling newspapers on the weekends, working in the food court at several malls, and being a lifeguard. As a student, he passes all four of the required graduation tests in his first sitting and earns the Hope scholarship, which will pay his tuition if he attends a state school in Georgia. Fortunately, he decides to go to the University of West Georgia, but I must still pay for his room and board. To make ends meet, I continue working extra jobs. At the end of his freshman year, Gibran tells me he doesn't want to continue at the university, but instead, he wants to go to technical school to get his barber's license. I've never lived vicariously through my children, so I'm in support of Gibran's passion.

Along with his barbering, Gibran is also learning the art of being a good deejay from my friend and colleague, Rambo, a renowned deejay. I'm still coaching track at the middle school and am now also teaching Spanish at Crim Evening School for adults and students who need to make up or catch up. Keeping up with college expenses so far is proving doable.

I can't believe how time flies. Two years have gone by, and now it's time for Ravi to go to college. She's also earned the Hope scholarship but wants to attend either Howard University or Clark Atlanta. She chooses Howard in Washington, D.C., so her in-state scholarship is void. I'm trying to avoid applying for student loans to pay the exorbitant out-of-state tuition fees, but since God knows I want to support their dreams, I pray He will help make a way. Ravi and I take the train to D.C., and I help her move into her dorm. I'm feeling all kinds of emotions leaving my daughter, but I'm very proud of her for choosing to leave home. To see her stepping out of her comfort zone reminds me of when I left Compton.

Now it's just Amir and me at home. From the day he was born, Amir has been his own person. He is spunky and driven to achieve. An all-around athlete playing baseball, basketball, football, and track, he's always under the tutelage of a coach. Between his schoolwork and his extracurricular activities, he's swamped. I'm grateful to his coaches for being such great support and especially to his godparents, my church members, the Dossmans, whom Amir loves and who could command his attention when I had difficulty reaching him. For me, it's a win-win situation. When it is time for him to go off to college, I'm not sure what I will do with all the free time on my hands. Amir chose to leave the state like his sister, Ravi, and heads, to Florida A&M University in Tallahassee. I take my last trek southbound to see my baby off to college. I'm so proud of all three of my children.

Aware I've been running hard, I haven't fully processed my buried emotions because my priority was to create a home for my family. Determined to make sure my children have every opportunity to shine and that I'd keep my promise always to protect them, I've kept moving, doing what I had to do. Through all the sacrifices, I came face-to-face with my own strength and my capacity to strive. Now, as an empty nester, I have no idea what to do with myself.

One thing that doesn't stay buried for long when one is idle is anger. For years, I've simmered in my resentment for Gary. His lack of support of me and for dropping the ball on co-parenting has been stuck in my craw. Even as a devout Christian, I can't approach the idea of forgiveness. I don't know what to do with this anger. They often preach sermons and lessons on forgiveness at church, but it's easier said than done for me. One day after church, I'm walking up the hill to my car. Suddenly, I'm overcome because I hear God's voice as clear as a bell telling me, "Forgive, and set yourself free." I, who have faith in God, must obey. From that day forward, I begin to feel a sense of peace within. The proof is since then, I've always extended an invitation to Gary to join us for family gatherings at my home. He attends from that point forward and, on occasion, even brings dates to whom I feel no animosity. I'm truly set free. Gary and I are products of our past, and we've both come to learn that loneliness or running away isn't the basis of love. In freeing myself of this anger, I begin to appreciate that a lot of my happiness stems from my three beautiful children, and they exist because of him. I thank him.

Home alone, my education career takes off. I've been a key teacher for years, but now I can take positions with more time commitments, such as interim instructional liaison and department chair. After getting my leadership certification at Georgia State, I transfer to Therrell High School as a teaching and learning specialist. My specialty at all the schools where I've been, besides writing school plans, is to provide data to effectively determine how to use the student information system to advance our programs and services. Easy-to-understand graphs inform our faculty's understanding of our ranking and show them where we need to go with our student achievement. This position is heavy on data management. If you remember, I wanted to become a computer scientist, which fits well with my nerdy, data geek personality. Eventually, I'm asked to interview for the assistant principal position. I get the job, and it's a huge undertaking. At the time, I'm the only assistant principal, and every day I pray nothing catastrophic happens. The school has more than fifty exits/entrances, and daily after school, it's a challenge keeping intruders out and students in. I form a great working relationship with Officer Davidson who is the after-school resource officer. I have to meticulously come up with IDs and systems to determine who should be in attendance. We establish rapport with the students, set expectations, and do everything to keep them in a safe environment. Somehow, we do it.

During my time at Therrell High School, I lose two of my favorite people, Papa Wil Bacon and my beloved Nanny. At least with Papa Wil, he knew his last days were near, so he and Mama Lee came to visit me in Atlanta, and I went to Detroit to see them. Losing Nanny is hard. As a kid, I'd always thought of Mama and Nanny as immortal. When I learn Nanny had diabetes and is losing her sight, it dampens my spirits. My admiration for her determination to never give up or give in garnered even more respect. As terrible as her sight becomes, she finds ways to get close enough to the TV to cheer on her Dodgers and Lakers. Because I never saw her deathly ill, I still envision her spirit—strong, defiant, and loving her family. I also gained two – new family members extending, my bloodline. I become a grandma to Gibran's two daughters, my M and M's—Mariah and Mackenzie, on whom I dote. They both carry hints of their Korean ancestry.

My accomplishments over the years apparently haven't gone unnoticed. I'm called to meet with the associate superintendent. He informs me that one of our district schools has been given a $3.2 million School Improvement Grant (SIG) and wants me to help implement the plan with fidelity. This will require that I transfer to Alonzo A. Crim Open Campus High School, a school named for the superintendent from Compton who handed me my diploma almost forty years earlier. The staff doesn't receive me warmly when I start in the summer of 2010. This troubled school is on the news all the time as the "dump school" for dropouts from other high schools that want to get rid of students who negatively impact their data. The stipulation of the SIG grant is to boost Crim's academic and graduation rate.

When I arrive at Crim, the previous principal has been removed, and a new principal has been appointed. Unfortunately, he doesn't show restraint for what comes out of his mouth or his actions. By November 2010, I go to Boston, Massachusetts, to the Harvard Graduate School of Education Principal's Center to attend a rigorous, intensive four-day program. I connect by phone with my Stanford classmate Charles Ogletree, a renowned attorney and Harvard Law professor, mentor to President Barack and First Lady Michelle Obama, and head of the Charles Hamilton Institute for Race & Justice at Harvard. Though I'd seen him recently at an event he hosted for *Before they Die*, a documentary about the Tulsa Race Riot Survivors. It would be good to see him again. Charles is also always in the news as he'd legally represented the survivors from the documentary. We usually see each other every five years at our Stanford reunion, but I am excited to get together with him in Boston.

I'm looking forward to seeing Charles, but on the day I can, he has an event with the cast of HBO's *The Wire*, which is on a timeframe out of his control, so we're playing it by his availability. I complete my closing assignment, which is a letter I write to myself that Harvard will mail to me sixty days from now. After completing my assignment, I head to the airport when Charles calls looking for me. As we chat, I'm surprised when he tells me he knows my son Amir. I shouldn't be shocked, though because Amir has the gift of gab, which has broadened his contacts all over the world. Charles included me in the content of his last book, *All Deliberate Speed,* and now he tells me he's sending his latest book to Amir. I hate that Charles and I miss each other, but I look forward to seeing him at our next reunion.

I get back to Atlanta and continue working my usual twelve-to eighteen-hour days. On January 21, 2011, I'm called into the office of Mrs. Crawford's, the high school executive director. She lets me know something has happened, and the district is sidelining the current principal of Crim. To my shock, she asks me to take over as the interim principal. I accept. I'm ready to take the helm. The next day, when I check my home mailbox, I see a letter from the Harvard Graduate School of Education. I'd forgotten about the note to myself I'd written sixty days prior. As promised, they mailed it. When I open the letter, I'm amazed at how prophetic and timely my response is to the second question below:

**Sandy's Five-Finger Letter to Herself:**

November 7, 2010

- Thumb—What gives you support?
- Index—Where do you want to go?
- Middle—What makes you unique?
- Ring—What promises are you going to make to yourself?
- Pinky—What are you going to improve on?

Of course, my answer to this first question is my family, especially my grandchildren, who inspire me. My faith, which always sustains me because I have a track record with God who has brought me through. The second question, Where do you want to go? I answered like this.

Professionally, I'm still unsure–principalship–I know I can do it if I'm placed in that position. I see more of a divine intervention or providence of that happening rather than my pursuit. I want to travel and see places I've never seen (Japan, China, back to Korea, Australia,

Europe, Canada, places in the U.S. (Maine, Chicago, and places like Disney with my family). After reviewing all the questions, I ponder my future. How foretelling.

My school improvement specialist Dr. Woodley and I are going to Washington, D.C., for a conference, April 14–16, 2011. There's a wave of tornados moving violently eastward, leaving a path of deadly destruction. Because of the frequent lightning strikes, Dr. Woodley says she is afraid to travel. As tired as I am, I, too, can easily cancel, but for some reason, I feel I might get better rest if I'm out of town. I check with my district office to let them know I will make the trip and request they ensure that my district credit card is working. They assure me that it is. Because of lightning strikes, we are grounded for a while, so the plane is delayed in its arrival to Washington, D.C.

By the time I arrive at the Hyatt Hotel, it's 2:00 a.m., and I'm exhausted. At check-in, the young lady tells me my credit card doesn't work. I can't believe it after I asked them to be sure there would be no problems. The credit card is issued through Bank of America, and because my private banking has been with Bank of America for years, I call them, and they vouch for approval based on my personal accounts. As I head to the elevator, I wearily look up at the events board, and what do I see but a message scrolling by about Holt Internationals 55th Celebration. I can't believe it. I know right then that God has again played His hands in my being in D.C despite all the reasons I had not to come. Holt is here. I'm convinced, whatever the reason, that's why I'm here.

The next morning, during a conference break, I go to the rooms hosting the Holt gathering. There is Molly in her Korean *hanbok* listening to the speaker on stage. It so happens, after the speaker, they're taking a break. During the break, I bogart my way to see her even though she is surrounded. I walk straight to her, greet her, and she immediately recognizes me. In her group are two people who she starts speaking to in Korean. She is telling them about me being an early adoptee and visiting her years ago. She introduces me to a medical doctor and Mr. Kim, director of Holt International Orphanages. Lo and behold, he was the same David Kim who had come to Mah San to escort us to Holt and who had also accompanied the baby lift flight that took me to America. Molly says that the doctor, too, was probably the one who had cleared me to come to the U.S. I finally get the opportunity to thank them. We take pictures, and Molly invites me to attend their events. I tell her I will work it around my conference. I also mention I'm now a principal, and this gives Molly bragging rights as she introduces me to several of their big donors. When I head back to Atlanta, I'm blown away by this unexpected reunion and how my circle has filled in a bit. I am so pleased to have met Molly, the doctor, and Mr. Kim again. I hope my presence and the outcome of my life are tangible proof to the donors that their generous contributions get results.

In my fourth year at Alonzo A. Crim, I'm honored as a Turnaround Principal by the State of Georgia Department of Education and the United States Department of Education. One of the things I required during my tenure is that every student who attends Crim must register for regular college-bound course work in addition to completing a career pathway that can lead to post secondary options. I'm awarded Principal of the Year by the district Career, Technical, and Agricultural Education Department for this. I attribute my success to having a great administrative team and staff and my desire to see the children succeed. Satisfied with my career accomplishments, I decide to retire. My staff gives me a memorable farewell. My children also host a wonderful retirement celebration, which includes representatives of family and friends from all parts of my life—Compton, Las Vegas, Stanford, Texas, and Atlanta.

I'm looking forward to spending time with my granddaughters, M&Ms, but my first action when I get home is to turn off my alarm clock, which for as long as I can remember, has been set for 5:00 a.m. The Monday morning after my retirement, I wake up, to God's gentle nudge easing me into a new day. I relax with a cup of coffee, greeted by the morning sun.

# CHAPTER THIRTEEN

## Lost

Now that I'm retired, I can take care of a problem most people didn't know I had. I've lived with functional double vision since 1977. Years ago, I'd learned when driving and drinking my on-the-go coffee that if I raised the cup to sip, as soon as it reached my eye level, my double vision triggered. Often I'd have to focus in split seconds to avoid accidents, which was unnerving. The remedy: I began drinking my coffee with a straw. For some reason, my last year of work worsened my visual acuity, especially working late every evening in my office, which has always been my most productive time. The past year, it was not only from a raised coffee cup, but I'm seeing double in front of the computer screen and struggling to correct it. I knew it was time to retire and save my sight.

Immediately following the last workday of my career, my ophthalmologist sets me up for surgery. Lolo, who has moved to Atlanta, takes me to an-early morning outpatient surgery. Since I've lived with this disability for years and functioned without missing a beat, it's hard to imagine that with a few slits here, or a stitch or two there, they will be able to fix what I have acutely experienced over the past year and chronically lived with for more than forty years. But the surgery is a resounding success. My double vision is gone, and it's liberating. After all those years of drinking coffee with a straw, *poof!* I can lift my cup to my mouth all I want, and I do. Why didn't I have the surgery sooner? With my sight corrected, I think, *I could have worked even longer*. As they say, be careful what you wish for!

No sooner do I think this, my phone rings. It's the associate superintendent, my most recent boss, David White.

"Saundra, I hope you are enjoying retirement," he says, "but I'm wondering if you would be interested in working part-time as an experienced principal retiree who can support our schools and principals."

Guess what I do? Naturally, say yes. I want to keep moving because I'm still full of life, and working part-time gives me ample time to be with my granddaughters and work in my yard. Mr. White also hires the former principal from Usher Middle School, Mr. Kenner, a fellow church member. We make a great team. Together, we use our Christian principles and years of experience dealing with students, parents, staff, and community to serve in a meaningful way as retirees. For the next two years of retirement, things are going pretty well. I can see, I'm working part-time, and I'm enjoying the fringe benefits of being the mother of grown children. Amir, Ravi, and Gibran are all so different, and they add so much meaning to my life. Ravi, who returned home after graduation, is involved with the arts in Atlanta, so I'm culturally and aesthetically enriched. I visit museums, go to symphonies and arts festivals, and I love the experiences. Besides being a barber at The Mall at Stonecrest for many years, Gibran is also known as DJ Polo throughout the metro Atlanta area. He is the sponsor of an event called Keys to the City for aspiring entertainers and musicians to showcase their talents and get feedback from known stars in the industry.

Just before retiring as Principal from Crim, I invited Gibran to speak to the students at my school who are interested in barbering. One of the reasons I insisted that students take a dual-track, college and career pathway, is that Alonzo A. Crim Open Campus High

School had students who need to reset their school experience because of circumstances interrupting or causing them to fall behind. Both Ravi, an arts and culture curator, and Amir, a music and entertainment executive, are regularly invited as career day speakers. This would be Gibran's first time as a career day speaker.

At Crim's career day, using himself as a testimonial, Gibran speaks of the reality that a four-year traditional college degree may not be for everyone. He speaks of leaving traditional college to pursue what he'd always wanted to do, become a licensed barber, which he did by completing the curriculum at the Atlanta Area Technical College. This is music to the ears of many Crim students already taking the trade curriculum in culinary arts, construction, early childhood care, nursing, graphic arts, business and engineering. Gibran provides further inspiration that a degree from technical school is within their reach and has value in the real world. Gibran's motivational speech sparks a fire in him too to move forward and obtain his barber's teaching certification. With his certificate, he can become an instructor as a vocational educator at a few high schools. I am delighted to see his vision expanding and that he is taking action toward seeing what the fruits of his labor can yield.

Gibran, in his twenties, has many challenges. He is the one who has had brushes with the law for not having either his driver's license or car insurance. He's the one who got a DUI, which leads to me having to bail him out of jail. Gibran being eye candy to women of all ages and ethnicities with his perfect blend of Asian/Black (*Blasian*) mixture has resulted in two unplanned babies. In reality, he's hustling for money to make ends meet and pay child support because he's already had to spend a few weeks in jail for child support violations. My quiet child has harbored secrets and fallen into the perfect storm for a life of disaster. I'm glad he's decide to move forward.

Amir, who initially found success in the entertainment industry as a music executive, is invited to be a speaker/mentor at

Gibran's Keys to the City event. As usual, Amir is charming, creative, and has the gift of gab. It seems to me everyone in Atlanta knows him, which makes him very suitable for his career choice as a film producer and Grammy-Award-winning record executive. He keeps me hip to the new music as he works with some pretty big names in the music industry, such as Pharrell, Bruno Mars, and Kanye West. His work with Pharrell on the song "Happy" in 2013 earned him platinum status as a music producer and made me happy. In 2014, I travel to Ireland with Amir to one of his speaking engagements. Watching Amir deliver his remarks fills me with pride, and I remember our trip as one of my favorite and most memorable excursions. He deserves his stripes. I'm a proud mother.

By the time 2016 rolls around my daughter, Ravi has married and divorced a young man who I never felt deserved her in the first place. Amir has been in a long-term relationship, and even though alarms are blaring, and red flags are waving, slapping them in the face, they get married anyway. Gibran derailed again by making some bad choices is again in resolution mode. He is talking to me about getting his affairs in order once again because he is on a mission to restore his buried dignity as a man and as an active father. Gibran wants his regular driver's license back because the temporary license only allows him to drive to and from work. He also has an opportunity to join the state's Fatherhood program in which he can go from being classified as a deadbeat dad to becoming an engaged, upbeat father. To accomplish this, Gibran solicits Amir and me to help him get a notarized letter from his daughter Mariah's mother. He'll need this release to waive his back-child support and clean up his records, a constant flag that prevents him from getting his driver's license and qualifying for the Fatherhood program. He is non-negotiable. He says that this is the year of stepping up and stepping out.

Mariah's mom refuses to waive his back child support even though I assure her I will be the intermediary to making sure she gets monthly funds while Gibran recovers his footing. This is definitely more assurance than the zero amount she is receiving through the system. Gibran, is not giving up. Plan B is to go to Washington, D.C., to establish residency and apply for a license there. He's doing well with his loyal clientele for his barbering services, his DJ Polo persona is known and sought after, and his Keys to the City has become an annual event, but he still can't get ahead because of his child support obligations.

Gibran has also experienced the death of two barbers recently. As I go with him to the funeral of the elder barber, Mr. Rush, whom he saw as a father figure, our family is also rocked by the sudden death of our beloved Chucky, Gary's brother who lives near us. This shook us to the core, especially Gibran, who at thirty-four, has experienced too much loss in his life. I'm very much aware that the impermanence of things is still something with which he grapples.

Over the next few weeks, Gibran is in a whirlwind, traveling back and forth to D.C. then to California to work with renowned record producer Zaytoven on a San Francisco concert. He is on a mission to meet requirements for an upcoming court date that will either move his life forward or continue to keep him in arrears. Before leaving the Bay Area, he is looking forward to seeing Mackenzie, his Mac Baby. He and his uncle Ronald, Gary's brother, are planning to get together. Gibran expects Ronald would be his ride to see his daughter. Unfortunately, Ronald has an unexpected family obligation. Since Gibran hadn't planned in advance a visitation with Mackenzie's mother and great-grandmother, by the time he tries to make alternate arrangements, his window for any other travel to reach Mackenzie has passed. He comes back home plagued with feelings of failure as a father.

On June 3 2016, the breaking news is that Muhammad Ali has died. The next morning, Gibran and I text back and forth because he remembers I'd seen Ali at the 1996 Atlanta Olympics. He wants me to send him a picture of Ali. I share my Ali stories from high school, in Houston, and at the Olympics. While Gibran is cutting hair that day, he is sharing my Ali stories with his clients. He can't seem to let go of death, and I worry that's at the root of his derailment.

The next day is Sunday. As usual, I go to early church service and Fulfillment Hour (same as Sunday school). One of my class members who is in rehab after knee surgery has the blues because of her slow recovery. I decide to visit her after church. When I get there, another church member is there. We're having a lively visit that's boosting all of our spirits when I get a call from Gibran. He wants to take Mariah and one of her friends to the movies as a reward for her all A's report card and overall great fourth grade school year. I tell him I know all about it because Mariah called earlier wanting to know what time he'd be picking her up. He said he is trying to figure it out and ends the call sounding so stressed. It so happens that Mackenzie is also in town but is not able to join him. I say my farewells at the rehab center and am on the freeway when Gibran calls again and asks if I can pick up Mariah and her friend and take them to my house, saying it will be a huge favor for him. I never seem to have any time just to chill, and I'm thinking about the long drive to Lawrenceville to pick them up, but the sound in Gibran's voice cautions me. He is letting me know that he needs me (his mommy) to put aside my needs because his are greater at the moment. At birth, I had promised my children to be there for them, so I reluctantly say okay. "I'll get the girls, and I'll see you later."

Gibran comes over around 5:30 p.m. to get the girls. As they head towards the door, I'm feeling concerned because Gibran, in person, looks even more stressed than he sounded, and it shows on his face, which looks fatigued. He gathers the girls, takes a few steps towards the door, then turns around and moves swiftly toward me, standing next to the family room couch. He embraces me with such lingering firmness. "I love you, Mommy," he says, and I say, "Love you too, Brano."

By 11:00 p.m. that evening, I'm tired but have to stay awake to let Mariah in from her outing. She has Vacation Bible School in the morning, so I call Gibran. He tells me he's just dropping off Mariah's friend and will be on his way. By 11:30 p.m., he and Mariah are at the door. I can tell she'd probably fallen asleep in the car by the "I can't wait to get in the bed" look on her face as she dashes past me and up the stairs. Gibran and I say goodnight, and I watch him as I do all three of my children when they leave from my door. I must see them get inside their car. When I go upstairs, the oddest feeling comes over me. Mariah has already climbed into my bed. I know she is tired, but for some reason, I make her get up, and I say, "Let's get on our knees and pray." This is out of the ordinary, but I feel compelled to pray. At midnight we are on our knees, and Mariah is praying for God to bless our family and the world.

A couple of hours later, the phone wakes me from my sleep. It's a call from Gibran's friend T saying Gibran has had a seizure and is in an ambulance on his way to the hospital. My clarity is a little foggy from waking up, so I'm making sure I heard correctly. While at school, I've seen many students have seizures. They quickly come out of them, so hearing seizure, even though Gibran has never had one, I expect him to be okay. I wake up Lolo and ask her to watch Mariah until I can call her mom or someone to come and get her. I get in my car and head to Piedmont Henry Hospital. On the way, I call Gibran's number to ask him if he wants me to let his dad know because sometimes when things happen, he would ask me not to call his father. His friend T answers his phone. I ask to speak to Gibran.

"Just ask him if he wants me to call his dad."

She replies, "Ma'am, he's NOT RESPONSIVE."

What the heck does that mean? I hang up, and immediately, I start praying for Gibran. In a panic, I hit the call button on my dashboard. "Siri, call Ravi," I command my phone." I need to tell her that something is wrong."

I don't remember driving anymore–my mind is racing, and my heart is racing, and somehow, even with my GPS acting crazy, I arrive at the hospital. Gibran's friend T and her family are in the emergency room when I walk in. I ask her what happened.

"I don't know. All of a sudden, he puts his hand over his left eye, saying over and over, it feels like a pin in my eye. It feels like a pin is in my eye, and then he begins convulsing and vomiting blood."

The doctor finally enters, and his report is not good. He is telling me it seems to be an aneurysm that has ruptured. He then corrects himself, saying it was probably more likely a hypertensive hemorrhage that burst in the worst area of his brain, the pons (the largest part of the brain stem), and that it's inoperable. He gives extremely low odds of survival. Ravi arrives. She calls Gary, and I call Amir, who is out of town but on his way back to Atlanta. I also call his wife, Cidney, who happens to be a nurse. This nightmare starts at 2:00 a.m. on June 6, 2016, and I'm in shock. Ravi and I go to a quiet spot and start praying. Our mantra becomes, "Dear God, choose us for a miracle."

When they wheel Gibran into the room, that stress I'd heard in his voice on the phone twelve hours before and the stress I'd seen on his face when he'd picked up Mariah has taken a toll on his body. What I didn't know at the time was that my son had been walking around with stroke level high blood pressure.

I look at Gibran closely. His eyes are slightly open. Does he see me? Does he know what is happening? The flurry of activity is intense as medics connect him to tubes and put needles in his arms to administer IV drips. They are also hooking him up to machines that are continually flickering and beeping with numbers representing his heart rate, blood pressure, and oxygen levels. The respirator that is breathing for him and keeping him alive is making rhythmic sounds. Ravi goes on social media asking for prayer. I call my church asking for prayer and text family and friends asking for prayer. "Dear God, choose us for a miracle!"

Ravi, Gary, and I continually talk to Gibran, hoping he can hear us and know that we are with him. I look for any type of movement or sound from him. I see his foot shake a little. I hear him hiccup as he did all the time I carried him in my womb. His hands are so soft and warm. Amir finally gets in and is in shock at what's happening. He wants to make sure that the right doctors are seeing him, so he begins calling around. Cidney, who works at Emory hospital, sends Gibran's scans to a neurologist there to see if they can offer any hope for what can be done. They say no. Amir is not giving up.

**Day 2:** By morning, Gibran has been moved to a private ICU room, and word has spread as a steady flow of visitors come to the hospital to comfort us and to see him. There are so many visitors that the staff asks if Gibran is a celebrity. So certain are they that he wouldn't make it, we are approached by a team who talks to us about organ donation. The whole family is in the room when this happens. Cidney mentions a friend who needs a heart, and one of Gary's nephews needs a kidney. This is too much for me. I'm not ready for this type of conversation. I leave the room. My sister follows me.

"Sandy, let him go. You don't want him to suffer!" she says.

I reply, "I trust God enough to let me know when it's time! Gibran is still alive; his heart is still beating; they say he is not brain dead. Until I know that we have done all that is humanly possible on our part, I will not consider this. Then I'll let God make it plain."

Mariah and Mackenzie come to the hospital to see their dad. Mackenzie is seven, and Mariah is ten. Mack gives me a big hug because we haven't seen each other in a while. She tells me, "You know God is putting us through a test to see how strong we are. He may take Daddy away or not." She has a gift of insight and profound wisdom. Were we to prepare for the worst? Did this mere child understand death? I know of death, but I never expected to have to face it with my son. It's now time to take Makenzie and Mariah into the room to see Gibran. I ask Mariah to pray. She prays eloquently and earnestly to God to heal her dad and to be with our family come what may. It is my third generation—Gibran's babies—who are bringing us the word and comfort.

I've been up for nearly three days, and everyone is encouraging me to go home and get some sleep. I make it home late Tuesday evening; take a long, hot shower; and get in bed. I remember preachers preaching about that agonizing midnight hour when you lay in your bed of despair. For the first time in my life, I'm knowingly in this pit of darkness, wrestling with something that is overpowering my usual composed, controlled being. "NO, NO, NO!" I cry aloud over and over as my head tosses from side to side, and my body spasms. Trembling as if I were naked in the North Pole, I hear myself say, "Please, God, let me wake up from this nightmare. Please, God, let me wake up from this nightmare. Please, God, let me wake up from this nightmare." Tears are flowing. My mouth is dry from panting and pleading with God, who I'm told never to question, but now I want to know why this is happening to my firstborn. The God I know is just and kind, and I have faith, so, I'm begging, "Please, God, wake me up from this nightmare. Finally, exhausted, I drift away.

I wake up scared and hurting. Looking in the bathroom mirror at my disheveled and worn-out self, I ask God once more to please help me because I can't face this reality without him!"

**Day 3:** Amir is on the phone trying to find a doctor who specializes in this type of hemorrhage, one who may be able to do surgery or do something to influence a positive outcome. One of Amir's mentors, The Chairman of the 100 Black Men of America, Mr. Tommy Dortch, introduces him to Dr. Gustavo Pradilla. We now have three hospitals that will take Gibran, but Dr. Pradilla tells us to bring him to Grady Hospital. We are rejoicing because it is our first sign of hope that the door of finality is not being slammed in our faces. I ride in the ambulance with Gibran to Grady. Grady is known as the best trauma hospital, but it is also known as the hospital for the indigent. It also happens to be the hospital where Gibran was born almost thirty-five years before. There is no bed for him yet in the Marcus Stroke Center, so we wait as they settle him in a temporary room. Immediately the doctor relieves some of the pressure off his brain by draining the accumulated blood and fluids.

Ravi and I are trying to position ourselves in uncomfortable upright chairs for the night. Just as soon as we close our eyes, a rickety gurney with a large, black trash bag is being rolled in by a very young Black woman. She is not a staff member. She has on super short shorts and looks so frustrated and depressed. A security guard comes behind her and asks why she has the gurney and tells her she can't bring it in there. Her response is, "What I'm gonna do with all my shit?" Ravi and I look at each other, and for the first time in the last seventy-two hours, we crack a smile knowing being at Grady will be colorful and entertaining.

The next morning, Gibran's attorney, Rob, comes to the hospital. It hurt him to see Gibran this way. They were supposed to be in court today for his ongoing child support hearing, so he let me know that he'd already contacted the courts to let them know the circumstance. There is such an outpouring from friends, church, work, and even from out of town. My niece Stormee (Chucky's daughter), a doctor, flies in from Texas, as does my nephew Eric (Gary's deceased sister's son), from northern California. My Stanford friend Terry, who is also a doctor, is by my side. They all bring their God-given specialty, supporting us through nourishing our physical/spiritual needs, advocacy, humor, remember-when stories, sympathizing with tears and hugs and the power of expressing just silent presence.

**Day 6:** Gibran's condition is the same. The doctor is saying his brain stem is covered with blood. Ravi and I continue to pray, and she cries out, "But whose blood is it, Lord?" We stand in the hallway holding hands, and it seems God's rays surround us as we feel the warmth of the sunshine. We conclude our prayer with a thirty five-breath ritual in honor of Gibran's upcoming thirty fifth birthday. As soon as we are finished, we are told Gibran has been moved to a beautiful private room in the Marcus Stroke Center. It includes an attached family room with a restroom. This becomes home. I can shower down the hall and get coffee from a few hidden Keurig Coffee Makers I've discovered on the floor.

My daily ritual is to continually talk to Gibran. I massage his feet, exercise his legs, hold his warm hands, and clean his eyes from the respirator causing terrible gook to accumulate. What is unusual is that for the first time, his eyes are open. Though they are not vibrant, his eyes are open, and he's slowly blinking. I rejoice in this small victory despite the medical staff saying it wasn't an intentional action on his part. While Ravi and I are in the family room next to Gibran, we can hear some of what his visitors say to him. It reminds me of an old HBO series *Taxicab Confessions*. One night we hear a young lady is saying, "Gibran, you know that me and you used to get into some devilment. I tried to wait around for you, but I had to go on and get married." Another girl comes and cries the entire time. I feel bad for several of the young ladies who think they are in an exclusive relationship with Gibran.

**Day 8:** God is so good! He gives us comfort when we need it. Ravi discovers Gibran's Instagram or Facebook message that he recorded on May 27, a couple of weeks before while he was in San Francisco, and shares it with me. It is foretelling, and he is speaking to all of us saying:

*"I want to give a special thanks real quick to the Lord. He's really been in my favor this year. He's always in my favor, but it's really been a blessing for a lot of the blessings that have been shined upon me this year. I've lost a lot of loved ones and a lot of friends this year for some odd reason. I guess it's their time to go. But it just woke me up to let me know you're only here while you're here. So you have to LOVE the people around you that surround you, who love you, and who don't love you. You still gotta show that kind of LOVE, man. 'Cause if not, you'll leave this earth feeling a certain kind of way when you don't need to. So, I just wanted to give a thank you to the Lord again. It really dawned upon me to spread this message to people.*

*Peace*". It comforts me. This is what he has posted about the name that everyone calls him 'P.O.L.O: P.O.L.O means (Presence of the Lord's Omnipotence). He knows who he is and WHOSE he is!

An invitation is sent through social media and Gibran's high school mates decide to hold a candlelight vigil outside of his window in front of the hospital tonight. Ravi's friend Donice has painted a beautiful portrait of Gibran for the hospital staff to sign as well as tonight's attendees. Gibran's room has a huge picture window from his eighth-floor suite. We can see the people gathering on the corner. Love is carrying us through daily, and seeing the crowd below in prayer and support for our family is overwhelming. Gary has been having a hard time seeing Gibran like this, but the outpouring of love is sustaining him too.

**Day 10 – Day 14:** My friend Marilyn has come into town from California to be supportive. While I bask in the blessings of my strong support system, I run across someone who seems to have no one. It's the young lady who had her belongings on the gurney. She doesn't have the gurney this time, but she still looks distraught. This day, I speak to her in the elevator. We get off on the same floor, and I engage her in conversation. "I have seen you over the past few days and just want to ask how you're doing and who are you visiting." We sit down, and she tells me that she and her boyfriend are from South Carolina. They couldn't take care of their baby and had to leave her in South Carolina. She and her boyfriend came to Atlanta because he was supposed to start a job so they could go back and get their baby, but he suddenly had a stroke. That's the reason she's been at the hospital every day, all their belongings in black trash bags. From my understanding, her boyfriend is critical and has been in this state even longer than Gibran. I go downstairs and buy a card and put some cash in it. I'm certain I will see her again, and sure enough, I see the back of her in the lobby area early the next morning. I tap her shoulder. She turns around, and for the first time, I see her smile. I give her the card and a hug, along with my prayers for God to bless her and her family.

It's Father's Day, and Gibran has held on. Gary and Amir have the NBA championship game on the TV in front of Gibran, knowing he'd be watching it. The palliative care/hospice staff has been coming around to introduce themselves, and I don't want them to. I'm not ready for what they represent. I know it is unhealthy for Gibran to be on the ventilator for more than fourteen days; within two days, they will fully take him off. I'm forewarned that when the ventilator is removed, he may or may not breathe on his own. I have to sign papers for the removal and DNR (Do Not Resuscitate) paperwork. No one is around me, and I need it that way. It has to be just God and me. God reminds me, from Deuteronomy 31:6, "*Be strong and courageous. Do not be afraid or terrified because of them, for the Lord your God goes with you; He will never leave you nor forsake you.*" I sign the document.

**Day 16:** I call my longtime Sunday school leaders, Reverend Diann Ash and Deacon Mitchell. I need them to come and pray for our family today because they are taking Gibran off the ventilator at 3:00 p.m. When the time comes, my mind is in such turmoil, and everything is a blur. I know that family and friends, medical staff, palliative care pastoral staff are all in the room, but I can't see any of them. I can focus on no one except Gibran. The pastor prays before they remove the ventilator, and then just like that, they pull the tube out. I can hear noise coming from everyone. Gibran's body reacts to the sudden removal; he is gasping. I'm next to him, holding his hand and passionately coaching him to "Breathe, breathe, Gibran." Telling him to, "Breathe, breathe Gibran." Demanding that he, "BREATHE, BREATHE, GIBRAN!" Miracle of all miracles, Gibran begins breathing on his own. We cry in joy, shout hallelujah, praise God, hug and watch his chest go up and down, up and down, up and down on his own.

**Day 18:** Any moment now, they will be moving Gibran to hospice, two floors up. He has breathed three days on his own; his blood pressure has been good. For the first time, I decide to walk over to my job, which is about a fifteen-minute walk away. I have not been there an hour when Ravi calls me to come back because Gibran has taken a turn in his breathing and blood pressure. I race back. When I get to Gibran's room, they are already preparing him to go upstairs to hospice. We gather up our belongings and sadly hug and thank all the staff for all that they've done for Gibran and our family. We follow Gibran's gurney up to the hospice floor. The atmosphere feels like a place to die. While the attendants are transferring Gibran into his new bed and getting him situated, we stay in the hallway.

Gibran looks uncomfortable to me. His neck is slumping to one side. I try my best to straighten it. Around 11:00 p.m. Ravi and I are fitting snuggly together in the one lounge chair. We glance at Gibran whose breathing has been labored as if he's been climbing stairs all day. I look at Gibran and blink for clarity because I see that his upper body, left shoulder, and elbow are slowly rising. Other than foot spasms, he hasn't moved in nineteen days. I look closer, and his shoulder is being slowly lifted again. I loudly call out Ravi's name and say excitedly, "Gibran's left shoulder is raising up just like someone invisible is placing their arm underneath to lift him!"

Immediately, Gibran begins to labor even harder for his breath. I get close to Gibran; I hear little whimpers coming from him. Oh, God, I want to breathe into him so badly, but I can't. As much as I love him, I must love him enough to let him go. I've seen with my own eyes something supernatural lifting him. I'm sitting close to him on the bed. I can feel and hear him saying, "Mommy, I will be free and can do more for you all and my girls on the other side." I hear him make his last sound. I wonder which ancestor(s) have come to help him cross over. I saw him take his first and last breath right here at this same hospital.

Gibran passed away a week before this thirty-fifth birthday. On July 1, we have a balloon release ceremony at the mall near his workplace at the barbershop. While there, I see a little girl who looks like him. After releasing the thirty-five balloons, the girl's mother approaches me and tells me that her child is Gibran's daughter. I'm disappointed that I didn't know about her and inquire why she is just letting me know about her 8-year-old child. As a family, we'd already missed the critical early years of establishing a relationship. The mother tells me she didn't feel it was her place to tell me and that she could take care of her daughter. However, she requested a DNA test on Gibran before he was to be buried. Being through enough for the month, I just don't have the emotional energy to put out for this unexpected request. I tell her I will contact her after burying him and going through the grief period. She is amenable.

On July 7, I get a phone call on my cell phone. It's another young lady saying, "Hi I'm sorry for your loss, but I have a two-year-old daughter by your son." I tell the young lady, "I haven't buried Gibran yet. I mentally and emotionally cannot deal with this right now. I will call you back at a later time."

Gibran's well-attended homegoing service is held on Saturday, July 9, 2016, to give our out-of-state family and friends time to travel to Atlanta. The service ends with a Facebook video of Gibran's message to his friends about loving each other: "So, you have to love the people around you that surround you, who love you, and who don't love you. You still gotta show that kind of love, man. 'Cause if not, you'll leave this earth feeling a certain kind of way when you don't need to."

I'm still numb to the fact that Gibran is gone. I don't know if I'll ever accept what is so out of sync with the natural order of things. A mother should never have to bury her child. As Bob Marley says in his song, *Johnny Was a Good Man,* "Can a woman's tender care cease towards the child she bears?" I know I cannot.

I'm desperately trying to re-find normalcy. It is proving elusive. The distraction of taking fifth-grade Mariah to and from school is welcomed. I also return to my part-time job. My hectic routine offers a diversion from my pain. What I can't escape are the reminders that come through the mailbox that even though my son is no longer, life goes on. Gibran's medical and school loan bills come frequently. Fortunately, I'm not liable. What drives home that the world continues to turn and add salt to my open wound is the certified mail I receive in September for Gibran. It states his driver's license has been suspended due to noncompliance with his child support case. Do I dare go down the slippery slope of what ifs? What if this or that would or would not have happened? Would Gibran's outcome be different? In all honesty, probably not. We're all on a path of our own destiny.

By October, beyond my daily obligations, I have something to look forward to: my forty-fifth Centennial High School reunion. I'm asked to be the mistress of ceremony. Being back in California is usually frantic because it's "home," and I'm always trying to schedule time to see everyone I can. I have dinner with my brother, Virgil, and his wife, Gwen. I've always jokingly said, "When you reach your forties, the warranty starts running out on our body parts." For Virgil, who's now in his early seventies, he's had a reprieve, but now he's in a lot of hip pain and using a cane to get around. Impatiently, he's waiting to have hip replacement surgery. It warms my heart that his daughters, Monique, Veronica, and Latonya, come to join us.

As always, I see my friend Marilyn who, as usual, picks me up from the airport. I spend a few days with her. I also visit a few days with my high school Seoul connection, Jackie, and her husband, James. Since Jackie and I are a part of the reunion committee, we leave early afternoon for Long Beach to help with the event setup. We are barreling down the expressway when a ladder flies off a truck in front of us, heading directly toward our car. Thank God for Jackie's quick reaction to swerve; we avert a serious accident. We are grateful to get to Long Beach and to check into our hotel.

That evening, our reunion theme is "Still Super Fly." Yes, we are in our sixties but indeed *still super fly* as we, dressed to the nines, fashionably parade in, nodding to the rhythms of Curtis Mayfield and other soundtracks of our times blaring through the speakers. No spring chickens or cocky roosters anymore, aches and pains and all, this is one night when we can reminisce about our youthful adventures and the times and spaces we shared that shaped who we are today. Above all, it's a great pick-me-upper to see so many of my friends from my formative years in Compton.

# CHAPTER FOURTEEN

## Found/Full Circle

In 2009, Barack Obama becomes the forty-fourth President of the United States of America. At his swearing-in, I think of the many martyrs such as Dr. Martin Luther King Jr., and the thousands of civil rights protesters who have worn out shoes marching for freedom. I feel sure that on this auspicious day, Barack Obama's inauguration, angels of the movement are sounding their joyous trumpets for him for a job well done. Their fight has not been in vain for here, facing the very Mall on which they'd marched, at the Podium is the beneficiary of their struggle, *The First Black President* of the United States of America, Barack Obama. *Yes, we can, and yes, we did.* For some reason, too, I think about what a man like my biological father might have said on this historic day. *"Ahh, ahh, ahh. Who'd have ever believed it? A Black man in the White House fifty-six years after I suffered unimaginable racial indignancies as a soldier in the United States Armed Forces."* I'm sure wherever he is, he's beaming with pride.

Near the end of October 2016, four months after losing Gibran, it's unbelievable Obama has been in the White House for two terms. The world seems so peaceful and in such solidarity. We're heading for a new presidential election in a few weeks, and the calm of Obama will be gone. Over these past eight years, I've had many regrets about missing out on a few opportunities to see President Obama in person.

Amir hears of my lament and makes it possible for his wife, Cidney, and me to fly to Miami to see the president at a campaign rally where he'll be stumping for Hillary Clinton, his nominated successor. Fortunately, the hotel we're staying in is walking distance from where we are to pick up the rally venue tickets. Glad to be just breathing the same air as the President, I'm happy to sit in the nosebleed section of the arena as long as I can record into my memory banks that I've seen and heard President Obama in person.

On the way to picking up the tickets, I get a call from Amir. He gives me a number to call. I call it and speak with the young man who is in charge of the rally. He tells me, "Ms. Windom, you have a great son, and I'm going to make sure you have a memory you'll never forget." He tells me where to park and what time to be there. We get to the arena way early, and Mackenzie, Gibran's daughter's oldest brother, Mekhyl, who is in college at Florida Memorial, joins us. At the arena, a young man with the most pleasant face, a chirpy personality, and incredibly beautiful red hair comes over and introduces himself. He indeed looks like his voice, pleasant. We follow him to get positioned in line with a few people.

Directly in front of me is Trayvon Martin's mother. We are both grieving mothers—I who lost a son to failed health, and she who had to face the heartache of her seventeen-year-old son being gunned down while visiting his father. I acknowledge her in a moment of solidarity by sharing that I, too, understand the pain and grief of having to bury your child. We take a picture together, and she is then moved into another line. When we finally get inside the arena, I see the setup. Trayvon's mother is in the line for those who will be directly behind the president during the broadcast. I, on the other hand, am in the line that will be on the opposite side, in the front row that the president will face! My adrenaline is flowing. I'm so excited. I can't remember this type of anticipation since the first time I saw Smokey Robinson.

After several speakers, DJ Khalid pumps up the crowd in the filled-to-the-rafters' arena with his music and endless energy. Finally, I hear the introduction we've all been waiting for: "Ladies and gentlemen, please welcome President Barack Obama!" The cheers are through the roof. I pinch myself. Because of my wonderful son with the gift of gab, I'm not in the nosebleed section, but directly in front of and able to clearly see President Obama's face. I can even see the contrast of his black eyebrows against the gray edges of his hairline. I see his smile lines as he greets us so warmly. I see his perfect Colgate smile and signature ears. But more importantly, I feel his heart. I'm in awe. I, a girl from another land found tied to a tree, am directly in front of the most powerful man in the free world. Like I'd wished for a better life than the orphanage, I'd wished, just a few weeks ago, to see the president, and here I am. I'm in seventh heaven.

The crowd is enjoying every word of this master orator. The cadence of his delivery prompts cheers and chants, while the confidence in his voice is reassuring. When he pauses for his points to sink in, the crowd goes wild. His inspiring speech emphasizes his fierce belief in an America for all citizens is uplifting. When he finally ends his rousing rally speech for Hillary Clinton, he stands on the side talking to the Florida officials and politicians.

I'm beyond inspired and reluctantly readying myself to leave when a secret service man comes along the rail barrier of those of us standing in the front row and says, "The president is going to be coming over to the rail to shake your hands." The usually composed, mild-mannered me disappears as I blurt out loudly, "Are you telling me that he is going to touch me?" I'm now having an out-of-body experience. I feel like an excited little kid. Sure enough, President Obama comes down the line, and because of my small stature, someone jockeys me out of my front space. My aggressive side shows up as I push my way back up front just in time for the president to grab my hand. When I feel his hand on mine, I say loudly, "Obama." He looks me directly in the eyes, smiles, and grabs my other hand. I am full. Full of grace and gratitude like the man standing before me. Thank God Cidney's camera captures the moment. Like a teenage fanatic, I don't want to wash my hands. How long can I go before having to wash away the president's DNA? (Not long since I hadn't used the bathroom for nine hours.)

As Thanksgiving nears, the family reminisces about our last Thanksgiving as one of the best we've ever had. About how Gibran and my brother-in-law Chucky, now both gone, caused the most uproarious laughter in charades. Chucky's daughter, Stormee, suggests that we spend Thanksgiving in Texas with her. It's a last-minute decision, but since it would've been really hard for our family to have Thanksgiving at home without Gibran and Chucky, we all decide to head to Dallas. I make the homemade rolls my family loves and pack them in my luggage. We enjoy time with the lively Windom clan and even get to see Daddy's family.

The year 2016 can't leave fast enough. I'm eager to welcome 2017. I commit to focusing on Gibran's possible two other children. I reach out to the two mothers who had contacted me during the past year's trying summer. Next, I call several DNA companies to determine the validity of grandparents' DNA testing to validate paternity when the parent is deceased. There is no problem, so I call Aiyanna's and Skylure's mothers to share the DNA legitimacy information I've gotten. They agree to do the testing to confirm Gibran's paternity. Gary and I get swabbed at the lab, and the mothers take their girls to be swabbed. While we're waiting on the test results, my coworker, Mr. Kenner, suggests I check out AncestryDNA. I'd heard about it from Virgil's daughter Monique who joined it years before to trace her ancestry. She'd called me wanting to know more about our family. Just after Mama died, I learned through Uncle J.O., Mama's cousin's husband, that Virgil had a half-sister and was not Mama's and Daddy's biological child. He was the son of Uncle J.O's Navy buddy, and his mother might have been related to Mama. Virgil did not receive this information well, and as far as I know, never contacted his blood sister. I never mentioned this topic with Virgil again. I join AncestryDNA to see what would happen.

It is confirmed to Gary and me that we have two new granddaughters. I'm settling into having four granddaughters when I get a call from Ravi. "Mom, are you sitting down, and have you taken your blood pressure meds?"

"Okay, Rav, just tell me. I can take anything after what we've been through."

"Well, this young lady just contacted me and said she has a ten-year-old daughter that she feels could be Gibran's, too."

I'm in shock. I've known all along women are drawn to Gibran, but I didn't have a clue he was populating the family tree with so many progenies. All girls! I get her number and call with the DNA information to have her daughter take the test. She doesn't do it. I call her again after a few months, and she tells me her father has been ill, and she's still going to do it. We don't hear from her again.

With all this going on, I haven't gotten a chance to explore my AncestryDNA results. When I finally get around to it, I tool around the site, exploring what it has to offer and to learn how to read and understand the data. I navigate the site for several weeks. Finally, I begin to understand the results. The level of closeness in family relationships is based on something called centiMorgans(cM). The higher the cM, the closer the relationship. My results show one lady is considered close, one man is considered a first cousin, and several second cousins. There are hundreds of third-fifth cousins, This is overwhelming. I realize this is my family on my G.I. father's side because everyone is related to me through our African lineage. I'd never thought of finding my mother, but I always assumed being in the U.S., I might be able to find my father. Cautiously optimistic, I contact several of the people through the email provided by Ancestry. I don't get any responses, not even from DLangaigne, who is supposedly a close cM match. However, looking at her last sign-in date, I realize she hasn't checked her results since joining in September 2015. I believe she probably received the kit as a gift and never bothered to sign in to look at the results. Several of my second cousins who seem interested to learn more about how we are related in the beginning, for whatever reason, lose interest once I tell them I'm adopted. I lose interest, too, and go on to Ancestry less frequently.

Meanwhile, I'm trying to spend more time with my grandchildren. I learn close to Memorial Day, my daughter-in-law, Cidney, is pregnant. While I'm happy about the news, she and Amir have been experiencing marital woes since before they got married. All I can do is pray for God to intervene because I've learned to abide by The Serenity Prayer: "God grant me the SERENITY to accept the things I cannot CHANGE, COURAGE to CHANGE the things I can, and WISDOM to know the DIFFERENCE."

As I spend more time with my granddaughters, it tugs my heart that Mariah and Mackenzie have memories of their father, Gibran, whereas Aiyanna and Skylure do not. I want to get better acquainted with both girls. Aiyanna lives close by, so I call to see her as often as possible. One day I pick her up, and we decide to visit Gibran's gravesite.

"Did he ever ask about me?" she asks as we are getting out of the car. No matter what, parents are so important to their children. Looking over at her, I know I have to be honest, and I well up inside to have to tell her the truth. "I don't know because I didn't know about you until after he passed." It is then that I start having spiritual talks with Gibran. "Now, Gibran, you have four girls. They are struggling with your loss but more because they wished for more time with you when you were here. Skylure is young, but I assure you, all will ponder and feel disappointment about your lack of presence in their lives. I don't know what to tell them."

It's Sunday, and I'm at church sitting in the balcony as I usually do. Out of nowhere, I hear as clear as day my son's voice. As if he is next to me, he's saying, "Mommy, tell my girls to forgive me. Let them know that I can do more for them in my spirit life. Remind them that they have to believe in the Lord, who has allowed me to be their guardian angel." I am stunned. The mind is powerful. I don't know if I'm answering my own question or if Gibran is truly communicating with me!

To keep Gibran in our lives and to never forget, our family decides that every year on July 1, his birthday, we will make it a tradition to place flowers and release balloons at his resting place. All the girls are with me at his gravesite on our first July ritual. I share with them the spiritual talk I had with Gibran. Skylure is still too young, but Mackenzie is the only one who openly says, "Daddy, I forgive you." I can tell that Mariah and Aiyanna are still struggling. As a teacher my whole life, I know that children, especially those with trauma, having their feelings acknowledged and giving them tools on how to deal with change and circumstances forced upon them puts them light years ahead in their healing process. Learning forgiveness will be the best therapy to release their pain.

In October 2017, I have yet a new addition. Little Athan is born twelve weeks prematurely. My first grandson. Amir and I go daily to see my little *Guapo* (handsome), who is in the neonatal intensive care unit for two months and, thank God, everything seems to be all right with him. By the end of 2017, I'm a grandmother of five, maybe even six. Bang Sun's tribe continues to increase.

On March 26, 2018, a new eye issue sends me to a new ophthalmologist, Dr. Augustus Stephens. As a new patient, I'm asked to complete pages of medical history. Besides checking off my few ailments, I'm asked about my family history. This part of the form is always the easiest as for my whole life, I've scrawled in all caps, *ADOPTED, NO FAMILY HISTORY!* Back in the exam room, a distinguished-looking doctor comes in. He reviews my medical info, which looks like a rap sheet. He introduces himself, then continues to review my records. When he gets to my strikeouts and the message, *ADOPTED, NO FAMILY HISTORY,* he looks at me with a smile and says, "Oh, no such thing. You will know your family." I smile back, appreciating his cute and different ice breaker from all the other doctors I've ever seen. A quick exam and a couple of prescriptions, and I'm on my way to part two of my day's agenda, a Passover drama ministry rehearsal of the *Four Women Who Love Jesus.*

While waiting to do my part, I check my phone and look at my email. I see an email from AncestryDNA. I quickly glance at it, but it seems a little too deep to absorb while focusing on my lines. I grasp the gist, and the little I read had distracted me enough to botch my lines. I get home pretty late from rehearsal but decide to log on to Ancestry to read the full message which had been sent the day before from an Yvette Woolfolk.

> *March 26, 2018*
>
> *I am just getting started with Ancestry, and I'm reviewing my DNA results. It looks like we are a close match, and I was hoping you would be willing to share some information about yourself. Thus far, I have not come across your name in building my tree. I am 55 years old, born to parents, Harrison Woolfolk, Sr. and Hyon (nèe Choi) Woolfolk. My dad's family is from Virginia, and my mom's family is from Korea. I currently live in Northern California.*
>
> *Hope to hear from you.*
>
> *Thanks,*
> *Yvette*

It was after midnight, my time, and I replied.

> *Hello Yvette,*
>
> *I am overwhelmed and excited. I have a major project to get through tonight and will be able to enjoy sharing with you afterward. I will email you my number, or you do the same and let's talk around 7:30 p.m. your time.*

Yvette and I connected by phone the following day.

Yvette—*I recently joined Ancestry, and you showed up as a close match. I was talking with my dad about you, and he thinks that you might be related to his brother, my uncle "Buddy."*

Sandy – *Wow, you're the first person who has ever contacted me with any information. I was adopted from Korea and obviously fathered by a Black GI. Was your uncle in Korea?*

Yvette – *I'll have to ask my dad. He was known for surprising the family with other children, so we were speculating him as your connection to us.*

She tells me about her parents meeting in Korea and that she and her older brother were born there. Her youngest brother was born in the States when the family migrated. Yvette's mother passed away in 2010 at the age of seventy-three. I share my Korean story about being in two orphanages and my wish to find the young boy I imagined my brother and who'd helped me survive. Yvette tells me her mother told her about a little girl she wished she could have adopted back in Korea. When we end our phone conversation, we continue through text. She sends me pictures of her family. I see a warmhearted picture of Yvette with her mother when she is in her fifties. Yvette sends me one more picture that night. A young picture of her mom with red lipstick. I get goosebumps all over. Oh my God, I'm experiencing a flashback! My eyes widened. When Yvette and I spoke earlier, I never mentioned that the only visual I ever associated with the lady who could have been my Korean mother was red lipstick. It's late, but my mind is racing; I'm doing math in my head: *Yvette's mother was born in 1937. I'm not sure of my exact birth, but it's either 1953 or 1954, probably, so she would have been sixteen or seventeen. My high school, Crim, had plenty of teen moms, so this happens to young girls worldwide, so why not Korea, too.* The idea of finding my father through Yvette has just gone out the window.

I accidentally send a text meant for Ravi to Yvette sharing my thoughts about the woman with the red lipstick. I'm telling Ravi that Yvette said her mother wished she could adopt a little girl in Korea. I wonder if it's me to whom she is referring. After doing the math, I calculate that she could've been my mother as a sixteen or seventeen-year-old. How could I have made such a mistake? I'm annoyed at myself to have slipped up and sent such a text. If indeed this lady was my mother, this text could cause irreparable harm and disruption, and that was not my intent. I send an apology text to Yvette.

Sandy—*Sorry, Yvette, I meant this for my children. I'm glad I waited to speak to you because my mind was turning after talking with you, and I surely would not have remembered my lines. I'm now in the "what if" thoughts based on what I remember. When I saw your mother's picture at first, I was still thinking maybe she had a sister-cousin, but I woke up with the realization of a possibility that perhaps she could've been my mother, a young teen 16/17 (don't know my real age or birthdate). I'm curious to know her brother's age because a young boy was the one who cared for me—just wondering if he could have been her brother or family member. He's the only one I tried to find.*

Yvette—*I'm still in deep thought about it myself. My mom would have been 16 or 17 if she gave birth to you – obviously a possibility. We will probably not know the circumstances around your conception/birth. My uncle Chan is (I'm guessing around 7 to 8 years younger) and could know something. I'll need to talk with my dad about this some more as I know he is in overwhelm mode right now. I'm wondering if we can contact Ancestry to get further analysis on our DNA in hopes of them confirming if we have the same mom. I'll look into that today.*

After texting back and forth with Yvette, I start to wonder if my text was an accident or if it was divine providence. Was it my chance to find out who I am and to whom I belong? Yvette and I speak on the phone about how to download my raw DNA from Ancestry. "By the way," Yvette says, "you know, my mom's name is Sandy, too."

Have you ever heard something you think you didn't hear, and it doesn't sink in because it flies over you? I don't respond to this news because there is no place in my brain to register it. It is too much to comprehend. Finally, I send pictures of my family to Yvette, and she shares that her two brothers both have families, but she is single with no kids. Life is truly a miracle. If they are my family, they also live in California, a mere six hours away from Compton and nearly two hours from Stanford except one of the brothers who live in Ohio, where I was determined to go to school before Stanford came into the picture. What's the chance?

We finally get our raw DNA downloaded. Breaking news throughout the country is that Sacramento investigators have arrested the long-sought-after Golden State serial rapist/killer through his DNA. Yvette so happens to work for the Sacramento court system and knows one of the DNA analysts who'd worked on the now resolved cold case. He volunteers to work on our DNA on his own time. By May 2018, he concludes that our DNA match looks very typical of half-siblings. To be sure if our relationship is on the maternal side, he suggests we get a mitochondrial DNA test. At this point, I search to find this specific test. Yvette and I submit swabs through a company called BioGene. On June 6, 2018, exactly two years to the exact date that Gibran fell into a nineteen-day coma, I'm feeling the blues of the day as I'm driving on the freeway. My phone is on the dashboard, open to my emails. While waiting for the green light to merge on the highway, I see a BioGene email pop up. I pull onto the shoulder of the road and grab my phone. It reads, "***Here are the results of your recent DNA test. Your results indicate: Half sibling relationship confirmed.***"

Immediately, I mean at that very moment, as clear as day, I see my Korean mother and Gibran hugging, and it's as if she is looking directly at me and saying, "I'm giving him the LOVE I couldn't give to you." I start bawling. Deep sobs rack my body. Deep sobs that express the years of having no expectation, of no connection, of no family. How…just how…on this day? This unexpected experience leaves me emotionally sapped. I have been indifferent about the lady with red lipstick all these years because I never, in a million years, dared to hope that big. When I speak to Yvette, she tells me of an unusual occurrence that happened the moment she learns of our confirmed relationship. In their home is a large plant, nearly the height of the ceiling her mother had planted and nurtured for almost forty years, which mysteriously turns over and hits the ground. She concludes her mother was getting their attention to confirm that she had a hand in the news.

Our families decide to meet. Plans for us to go in August don't pan out because Ravi has an event to which she's already committed. For me, this uniting of our families is too important an event for all of us not to be there, so we move the date to September 12, 2018, when everyone's schedule is clear. Yvette tells me her mom's best friend, whom she has known since living in Korea, is looking forward to meeting me. Someone looking forward to meeting me still sounds foreign after sixty years of life. I wonder if she knew about me. I'm excited yet anxious, wondering how I'll feel and react at the moment I lay eyes on the family I never fathom existed.

I head west to meet my new family. The entire journey reminds me of going back to Korea to see Molly, coming face-to-face with someone I was certain I would never, ever see again. I'm in awe. As I buckle my seat belt, I keep thinking, *Life should come with a seat belt to hold one steady because God's plan in our ever-unfolding journey can be unpredictable with many jolts and twists and turns along the way.* While on the plane, I reflect on how looney I must have sounded to the few people with whom I'd shared my supernatural experience of seeing my birth mother and Gibran.

I look at the clouds outside my window, the magical clouds I'd first noticed at five years old as they floated by the window. Here they are again, ready to accompany me wherever my new fate takes me. I have to believe God's in those clouds. At this thought, my imagination turns on. All of this could have been orchestrated. My *Eomeoni* Hyon and Gibran meeting in their parallel universe could have gone to appeal to Mama and Daddy to get their blessings for God to align all that is happening to bring our families together. Mama, I bet, wasn't easy to deal with because her jealousy of meeting my birth mother, even in heaven, was probably rearing its ugly head. I bet Daddy and Nanny had to coax her to go along with the plan. I stifle a smile at the wild thoughts of my imagination and tune back into reality. How will Yvette feel when she sees me in the flesh? Our discovery of each other, more accidental than purposeful, has led to the unbelievable outcome of us being sisters rather than cousins.

I arrive at the Sacramento Airport around 8:30 p.m. My thoughtful son Amir calls to tell me a friend of his will be meeting me, and he'll be videotaping this first in-person moment when I meet my sister. As soon as I get past the security area, I see his friend Craig with his video equipment aimed at me. An officer approaches, letting him know filming in the area is prohibited. Craig is very respectful and cooperative, letting the officer know he's former military and understands rules and regulations. The exchange ends amicably. Craig walking alongside me, stops me for a moment and asks, "How do you feel?" I don't remember what I say because, again, I feel I'm having an out-of-body experience, and my mind is all over the place in la-la land.

As we head down the escalator, my phone rings. It's Yvette calling, wondering if she's missed me. I'm talking on the phone and looking lost when there she is, standing about four feet in front of me with a beautiful bouquet of pink roses. We've done a lot of texting and talking, but seeing her in front of me, my heart lurches. I'm not dreaming. She's real. My birth mother's daughter, who had shared the same womb that brought us into this world, is in front of me. *She is my sister!* We embrace. My voice cracks when I try to speak, and my eyes well. Fighting back the tears, I linger in her embrace. From that point on, I'm truly in la-la land. The moment is so surreal. I've forgotten about Craig, who is continuing to videotape us even as we head to the car. I wave goodbye to him, and we take off.

I'm operating on pure adrenaline because I've been up since 5:00 a.m. Eastern Standard Time, and this surreal moment has added even more of an adrenaline rush. Yvette sits with me while I settle in with Mackenzie's family's gracious home. Margie, aka Granny, Mackenzie's great-grandmother, insists on feeding us by fixing us a plate that would have put us in a coma had we eaten the all-you-can-eat buffet portion size. I appreciate the love and hospitality, but I'm marveling at the presence of my sister and trying to listen intently to everything she says so I can learn more about my birth mother and my new family. Surreptitiously, I look at Yvette to see if we have any features in common. She and my friend Jackie have the same tight slant to their Asian eyes. I sense we both are overwhelmed trying to take it all in.

Amir and my oldest granddaughter, Mariah, arrive from Atlanta at about 1:00 a.m. We're only waiting for Ravi to arrive now. Being in the Pacific time zone, I'm now feeling Eastern time zone fatigue. My son's arrival is like a shot of espresso and revitalizes me as I enjoy watching the natural unfolding of three generations of families interacting together. On September 13, I spend the day at my granddaughter's house. Amir wants to get a haircut and shave, so we go into Vacaville. It's a quaint downtown with specialty shops and dining. We go into one of the busiest barbershops I've ever seen. As we leave and head to the rental car, for some reason, I look down, and even though I inspected and admired the pedicure I gave myself, I didn't notice I'm wearing mismatched sandals. Not only different colors but different styles. I'm seriously in la-la land. Spontaneously, I burst into a hard, long belly laugh, which proves to be the best stress reliever. I take a picture and send it to my family and friends, texting them to be the judge of whether I'm a trend-setter or just senile. For the few hours we're out and about, I walk with a sense of purpose, sure I'm making a fashion statement. People, if they even notice, are probably wondering, *What's wrong with this lady? Does she know or even care about her mismatched shoes?*

When Ravi finally makes it the following day September 14, we're ready to meet our newfound family. Yvette meets us at our Sacramento hotel and takes us on a brief tour of the city before the light of the day settles into dusk. We end up at a Mexican restaurant. Before even looking at the menu, we launch into a conversation about our respective lives. I share that my godmother, Nanny, told me I had been found tied to a tree in Korea and taken to my first orphanage. If indeed I was tied to a tree, it could have been Yvette's mother who did so, and now it sounds a bit harsh. "When I first heard this," I continue, "I thought *how cruel,* but came to appreciate that in actuality, it might have been an act of benevolence. Being tied to a tree was probably assurance that I wouldn't wander off into danger and that I was strategically near sympathizers who would take me in." I'm now wondering if the story is true though it very well could have been.

I remember a scene from *The Joy Luck Club* and an earlier conversation Ravi and I had about the movie. It was around the backstory of one of the mothers as she fled her homeland in China. Riddled with dysentery, she could no longer make the journey with her twin infants, who she'd been pushing in a rickety wheelbarrow. Forced to leave her babies behind, she place them near a tree and leaves a note with her valuables wrapped in a cloth for the kind-hearted stranger who might find them. Years later, in America, after her mother's death, the Chinese woman's American-Chinese daughter discovers she has older twin sisters in China. She travels there to meet the babies, now adults who'd been left behind under the tree. Instead of being a harsh reality, it turns out to be a tender moment because Yvette, Ravi, and I confirm the movie to be a favorite of ours. In a way, our story parallels the film's ending. Yvette goes on to share that her mother's best friend, who was looking forward to meeting me, suddenly passed away. I was really looking forward to meeting her, too, in hopes of learning even more about my life in Korea, but alas, such is life's twists and turns. As we gush on, Amir is feeling left out because he is clueless about *The Joy Luck Club.*

On the afternoon of September 15, we gather at my brother Harrison Jr.'s home. Even though Yvette and I have been talking for over six months now and confirmed as siblings for more than three months, she's the only family member with whom I've had any contact. I know both of my new brothers were thrown for a loop to hear their mother had a child several years before them.

"Don't be discouraged," Yvette would say. "Be patient, and give them time."

I have no expectations, as understandably, the family needs time to digest the fact that the matriarch of their family had kept a secret. I'm unsure how I'll be received when I meet my new brother, but I'm hoping it's as fulfilling as meeting Yvette.

Before heading over to meet our new family, we meet up with my nephew Eric and his family who live in Tracy, California. He is my ex-husband, Gary's only sister's son. Unfortunately, she passed away from an aneurysm in her late thirties, similar to what took Gibran. As we visit, I observe the warmth and genuine familial love my children display and pray that in a few hours, that warmth will extend to our new family circle and grow even more. On the way, a few hours later, we stop at the florist to buy two beautiful orchids—one for Harrison's home and one for Yvette's home. When we arrive, I ring the doorbell and presumably Papa Harry, as Yvette calls him, opens the door. I look up at him, and before I can utter a word, he says, "I see my wife in your eyes." For the first time in my life, I feel a belonging I've never felt before. Papa Harry had been married to my mother for nearly fifty years, so his acknowledgment of me is the nod of approval I need, and the hugs begin.

I hug my brother Harrison who teases and playfully scolds me, "Now you show up after all these years of me taking on the burden of being the first-born."

Harrison's nickname is Dee, so Amir and Ravi immediately call him Uncle Dee. Yvette told me I'd instantly love them, especially Dee's wife, Brenda, and she is right. I can feel her genuine sweetness radiate when we hug. I also meet my nephew Christian and my niece Sydney who are both college students. It happens to be Sydney's birthday. I share with her that today is also my adopted Mama's birthday. There are so many coincidences around dates that I inwardly chuckle, thinking, *Yeah, Mama, your agreement to go along with this union is that it's happening on your birthday. You know*

*I'd be thinking about and honoring you all day, but you had to make sure. Thank you!*

To represent Gibran, his daughters Mariah and Mackenzie are with us. Even Mackenzie's family decides to attend the gathering. In honor of *Eomeoni* (my birth mother), Yvette and Brenda make a delicious Korean meal from one of Hyon's/Sandy's (as her family calls her) favorite recipes. The moment is dreamlike and emotional. I'm trying to take in all the stories Papa Harry is telling me about my mother. Indeed, she'd been separated from her family, as Molly had said. Yvette goes through the photo albums sharing their childhood. Dee tells me how his mother cooked for all of his teammates when he was in school. The outline of the beautiful lady with red lipstick I remember is now colored in. Before me, her life is being drawn on my canvas. My mother was intelligent, self-taught, an initiator, a dedicated wife and a wonderful mother who made many sacrifices for her family. She loved sports, especially baseball, and was a doting grandmother. She was a great cook, and she had a green thumb.

In contrast, in my world and not even for certain, she was the lady with red lipstick. I sit back and observe my new family. United, we all knew the same woman in different ways, understanding how circumstances can lead to different outcomes. In my case, the woman they all knew who made dinner for her sons' teammates was the same woman whose benevolence, under different circumstances, led to her having to make an enormous sacrifice and abandon her child. I might have been in la-la land for most of the weekend, but now I'm fully conscious and firmly planted in reality, knowing this incredible gift of validation and reconciliation isn't a dream and is now permanently implanted in my heart. The evening ends with a beautiful family picture uniting Bang Sun and her family with the family of Hyon Ok Choi Woolfolk. Almost a year later, we all meet up in Mason, Ohio, to complete the family picture with my brother James and his sons Carter and Kai.

I'm at the airport heading home from Ohio when I realize I've left my carry-on at security. When I go back, they are calling the bomb squad. They look closely at my suitcase and say, "It says, Sandy Windom." I shout, waving my hand, "Yes, that's me!" I am Sandy Windom. I am also Bang Sun. I now know who I am.

The eye doctor was right! I met my family.

# CHAPTER FIFTEEN

## Confirmation Voices Breathing Life into the Past

You've heard my story—from scavenging for food in the South Korean Peninsula to meeting my lost Korean family sixty years later. But wait, there's more. In an earlier chapter, you were introduced to my half Korean life-long friend Jackie, whom I met in high school. She recently found her Korean birth mother and was able to fill in the gaps in their lives. I wasn't as fortunate to meet my birth mother; however, her husband, my stepdad (Papa Harry) shared her story with me. These are their accounts. For many Korean children of war, listening to these voices may breathe life into your story as it did mine.

### Harry Woolfolk (My Mother's Husband, My Mother's Story)

*As a young man in Virginia, born to a deeply religious father and a mother who was a staunch educator, my two brothers and I looked forward to stepping outside of the walls of our upbringing. With a bag packed full of values, faith, and fortitude to face what the world had in store for us, my older brother led the way with his military service across the ocean in Japan on the island of Iwo Jima. I followed in his footsteps by joining the Air Force when I was just seventeen. By September 1959, my first assignment was to Japan also, and when I arrived, I was further assigned to Korea at Osan Air Force Base.*

*The country was recovering from the conflict through post-war efforts to stabilize the government and rebuild the devastated infrastructure. I was assigned to the organization responsible for developing radio and telephone communications for the entire area of South Korea. One of the first friends I made was an African American gentleman who was married to a Korean lady. I became intrigued with their relationship in how they related and communicated with each other. My new friend invited me to socialize at his home. At one of our social gatherings, a Korean woman I had already met named Kim insisted I meet her best friend. She told me her name was Sandy, and while she was incredibly beautiful, I was not interested in dating a Korean woman as Korea was just a stepping stone for me to travel the world. But Sandy was different from all of the other Korean women I had met so far. What intrigued me most was not only her ability to speak English well but her intellect. Sandy, like so many of the ladies, worked in the NCO (non-commissioned officers) club, the social club where we had drinks and dancing. It was like a sheltered society. I am intrigued by this young Korean woman named Sandy. I asked her how did she learn to speak English so well. She said she learned in school and taught herself. At the NCO club, it was an employment requirement to be able to speak English well.*

*We began dating, but there were not a lot of places to go to, plus I had to remember where I was. This is the country of President Syngman Rhee, an autocrat who promotes a purist society in the midst of needing the help of the United States military comprised of Black and White soldiers. Several times when off base, I'd hear a word sounding like* 'khamdinghy.' *I had no idea what it meant until my friend Fred enlightened me to the derogatory reference about my color. Being from Virginia, a segregated state, I was quite accustomed to being called out of my name. Sandy and I capitalized on the few base meeting places accessible to us. Over the days that became weeks, that became months, we enjoyed talking with each other. She was serious-minded, very aware of what was going on. I loved that she was opinionated about things. She had a unique ability with perception to figure things out. Most of the women on base thought I was stuck-up because I wouldn't get involved, but here I am with someone with whom I have a lot in common and I'm smitten, and I think so is she.*

*What I learned of her early life was that Sandy's Korean name was Choi, Hyon Ok. Her last name was pronounced phonetically as* 'Chae' *and not* 'Choy' *as we would say it in the U.S. I don't know what made her select and identify with the name Sandy, but that was how she was introduced the first day we met. She was born on January 1, but her parents said that it was bad luck for a girl to be born on that day, so they changed it to January 6. She was the eldest of seven siblings—three brothers and three sisters. Two of her brothers passed away when they were young. The youngest drowned in a water accident. Another brother suffered an accident while in the military and became a paraplegic. She also had a sister to die as a young child. When the Japanese occupied South Korea, they were known for taking many of the Koreans for labor. They took her dad to Japan and trained him to become a pharmacist. Sandy said she developed some kind of illness when she was young, and there were no doctors or hospitals to go to. It was fortunate that her dad was familiar with medicine because he was able to successfully treat her.*

*She was educated through junior high school. At some point in her teens, she was separated from her family. There was never any detail about the family's separation. I didn't press it because I knew how horrific war could be. She alluded to the fact that she and her family and all of the Koreans in the Seoul area were forced to march South as the Chinese and North Koreans were pushing south from North Korea. They left Incheon, went into Seoul, then across the river into Pusan all the way down to the peninsula's southern tip. She never alluded to anything happening to her because, apparently, their family, was able to reunite at some point.*

*Sandy and I spent a lot of time together. Our personalities really meshed. That frightened me, so I'm thinking I'd better get out of here before getting too serious and going off-track from my military goals. So, in 1960 it was time for me to apply for an assignment. I applied for Europe, but I got Okinawa, and I was going to leave Korea, but it turned out around that time, Sandy became pregnant. I had to make a quick decision. I was so aware of how many military men who had impregnated women and left. I was in love, and I said, we're going to get married. The military had to investigate her to make sure she wasn't communist (they went through records to see if her name or family's name was on a list); she had to take the physical. The process took about a month. Plus, she had already been cleared to work for the military. We got the Korean government's approval, and on May 4, 1961, we were married in Seoul city hall. I don't think Sandy's father ever approved of our marriage. Her mother was very cordial and loved her daughter dearly. Both of her younger sisters did not speak any English. The youngest sister spent a lot of time with us.*

*Sandy and I were extremely fortunate to acquire a home from an American Air Force person who was married to a Korean. He had built it in the Osan Air Force area. When it was time for our baby to be born, I had already made plans. I had contacted ambulance drivers that I knew to be on call for that day. We traveled up to Seoul to the Army hospital because the Osan hospital did not have OBGyn doctors. The doctors indicated it's going to be a while before delivery time. I needed to return to Osan to change into a proper uniform. The doctors assured me I'd have enough time. By the time I got back to the hospital, my son was already born, so much for "you have time." The nurse said, "Do you want to hold him?" They wanted me to put on this protective gown. I had just proudly put on my uniform. I figure I don't need the gown, so I refuse. My son had on a cloth diaper, and he had already been fed. I guess my little fella said, "Since you didn't get a chance to see my official entry, let me give you something to remember." He had his first bowel movement all over me!*

*We are all doing fine with the baby, but Sandy is extremely particular about who Dee was around. She kept him away from most of the Koreans. I believe Sandy was cautious because there was a lot of raw sewage that probably contributed to rampant diseases like TB and dysentery. Perhaps she was also thinking of her little sister, who died at an early age. Sandy becomes pregnant again, and while we are waiting for our next baby to be born, I realized it was time for us to leave Korea. I wanted our children to be exposed to western culture. Yvette was born in March 1963, and I set up for our departure to be in May 1963. Before Sandy gets out of the hospital, she had to receive a blood transfusion due to an episiotomy that caused her to excessively bleed while giving birth to Yvette.*

*Our family leaves Korea, and we stop in Virginia to visit my parents and on to Pennsylvania as my next assignment. She adapted very quickly to western culture, considering she was quickly removed from her way of life in Korea and her immediate family. There was no mother or family to call on. Our third baby, James, was born in Pennsylvania. As a parent, Sandy was absolutely outstanding in managing three small children. Dee basically only knew Korean. I suggested that she start speaking predominantly English so the children will be able to fully communicate in English.*

*Her best friend Kim, who'd introduced us, was also married to an African American soldier named Andy. They were stationed in New Jersey and had invited us up there. When we visit, it is the same time that President Kennedy was assassinated, so our country is on high alert, and I know that I could be called at a moment's notice to report to a special duty. Kim and Andy moved to California and were lifelong friends.*

*Eventually, Sandy helped her brother Chan Il come to the United States. He moved to New York, and her mother, father and one of her sisters would visit Chan Il, but it was disappointing that they never came through California to visit her. She would go to New York to see her family but never went back to Korea. She never expressed any desire to go back even though she knew she could have. When Sandy had a medical physical in 1968, we learned that she was exposed to Hepatitis C from the blood transfusion received from the American Red Cross when she gave birth to Yvette. She took medication that cured the Hepatitis C. Later, a physical showed she had signs of early diabetes, and her blood analysis showed that her creatine and protein were abnormal—her kidneys were failing. She started dialysis proactively early at Travis Air Force Base in 2001. Going three times a week exhausted her. The doctor made arrangements for her to take dialysis in Sacramento, which was closer to home. In 2006 I bought her a new car, the wrong car—a Buick. She was only five-three" and couldn't comfortably see the end. She had an accident backing into somebody, so I got her a Ford Taurus, which was easier for her to handle to drive herself to dialysis. Her health was deteriorating rapidly, and she ended up in a wheelchair. In 2010, Sandy eventually decided she couldn't take anymore. The entire family was present at Sandy's bedside to say goodbye. The beautiful woman I have loved and been with for fifty years, who had given her all to her family, was ready for her eternal rest. She was semi-conscious, giving us a last glimpse of the gift of her presence in our lives, and we all accepted her spirit into our hearts as she gave her soul to God. 'Til this day, we miss her. I have changed nothing in the house. It is the same as it was since Sandy left it ten years ago. I vowed to maintain a couple of plants—a Hawaiian sugar cane plant, and there's a tree that is now the height of the ceiling I've kept alive.*

*To find out that Sandy gave birth to a daughter several years before I met her was a shock. I wished she would have said something. If she had, I would have insisted that we try to find you. She never said anything, never gave any indication. One thing I will say, if you were found tied to a tree, I can assure you it was an act of love. I would find it impossible for Sandy to do anything harmful to anyone; she has always cherished her kids and other people's kids.*

*It's interesting, though, how things have a way of naturally presenting themselves to either give credence or discredit speculation. I spend a lot of time in the veteran's facilities. After I heard about you, and without trying to eavesdrop, I listened to some Korean vets who'd married Korean women share how they had discovered that their wives had babies in Korea prior to meeting them after years of being married. My ears perked up. I couldn't tell if they were widowers or how recent this information was revealed to them, but I could tell that both men had a resolve, that the timing was right in their lives to accept and not be judgmental. I left that day feeling a resolve too, that my wife had to make a hard decision of what was going to be best for her child at that time, and knowing what I know now, coming face-to-face with meeting you Sandy 2, she's smiling because "it is well with her soul.'"*

## Jackie

Like my friend Sandy, I've gone for over sixty years, not knowing who my biological parents were. I, too, am Asian and Black. Sandy told me about Ancestry.com and that through them, someone had contacted her. At the time, she was waiting on confirmation to see if they were siblings, and it was unbelievable to me. For my upcoming birthday, Sandy gifted me an Ancestry kit. I procrastinated, then finally sent it off. My results came back, and by August 2018, I'd discovered who my now deceased Black father was through a new cousin. I'd also found one contact on my mother's side who I couldn't reach. Sandy, not giving up, decides to help me find my closest match—a person named Joe. She searched unsuccessfully, but I discovered she was looking for a half-Black person. Joe was half-White. With that information, Sandy finds him and passes on his information.

I contact Joe, who, according to the amount of DNA, is my sibling. Of course, he is shocked and proceeds to tell me his (our) mother is alive, but she obviously kept me a secret all these years. Three months passed, and I'm patient, but Sandy pressures me to ask him if he has told his mother about me. He finally gives her my information, and at first, she reacts with silence. A week after he told her, she tells him, "I'm ready to come straight" and acknowledges me to him. I call her, but she doesn't respond, though I know it is her on the other end of the line. She finally gathers her inner strength and calls me. Even after all of the empty years, there's no judgment. I'm frozen with disbelief when I hear her voice. Yet, at the same time, there is a feeling of healing. The first thing she tells me is that she's never forgotten me and has always prayed for me and loved me.

My husband, James, knows how monumental this is. He decides that for our upcoming wedding anniversary, a week away, he'd take me and my only daughter, Jessica, to Baltimore, where my birth mother now lives. I would meet my mom and my siblings. My birth mother, now in her eighties, shares her story of war and how I came to be, a story of so many of us children who were victims of the Korean War. Out from the shadows for so many women bearing secrets, hear this account in her broken English from my mother, Jung Ok.

**Jung Ok**

*I am from Incheon, Korea. As a young girl, I can remember soldiers in my country all of the time. First, it was the Japanese, then Chinese, Soviets, North Koreans, and the U.S. I didn't know who was friend or enemy. I know that the Japanese soldiers were very mean and cruel to us. One of my worst memories was when my best friend and I were walking home from school. All of a sudden, a missile went past us. Terrified, we stopped in our tracks, our bodies stiffened from fear. The missile hit a tree; the tree came down fast—crashing on top of my friend, just missing me. I look down, and my friend is crushed and immediately dead. I am crying and running home to tell my parents and then we had to sadly tell my friend's parents what happened to her.*

*Another time, the soldiers come to our home, put a gun to my father's head, asked him, Are you communist? They did not care if my father says yes or no because they make him dig a grave for himself, but miraculously, something happened that they had to rush away and did not kill him. We find a place to live high in the mountain area where we can see the soldiers coming. When they come again, we have time to hide. We have to be very still, barely breathing because if they find us, they take us away. They don't care if you are a woman or a child. Where and why they take us, I don't know, but we always live in fear.*

*Somebody always keeps our lives upside down. Now we have to live through the war between North and South Korea. The Chinese and North Koreans are demolishing our people and land, forcing so many families, including ours, to flee south from our homes. My father tells us we must separate quickly. We grab only what we can carry. My little brother and me go with Mother in one direction, and my father and my older brothers go in another direction. If we survive, we know where to reunite. We are fortunate because we survive.*

*Our country was devastated. Our people lived very poorly. I started working in a snack store as a cashier near a U.S. base. A Black American soldier named Ross started coming in. He was always looking and smelling good, dressed well, and always trying to flirt with me. We finally start dating, and I got pregnant with you, Jackie. Your father called you Lavonia, after his mother. His duty was up in Korea, and he left right after you were born. He promised to come back for us and, after a year of not hearing from him, I contact the Red Cross to get in touch with him. He tells them he was not coming back because he got married. I was very hurt and told my mother, "He no come back." I must face a hard life but especially you, because Koreans, especially the men, don't want brown babies in our country.*

*I continue to work, and my mother, your* halmeoni, *take good care of you. During that time, soldiers would come around in trucks they would grab children and take them away. She protect you by carrying you on her back everywhere. That's why you got bow-legs today. I was still very young and got pregnant again. This time I have a mixed White and Korean baby boy. It does not work out with that soldier either. Your* halmeoni *take care of both of you. Soldiers still come and scare us because they take children away like you. You know to hide when you see strange man or soldier come to the house because we always afraid they will take you away. One day, I find you with a rock rubbing your arm, scraping it until you bleed. You tell me in Korean you want to be like me, like my color, so you won't have to be taken away.*

*I meet another White U.S. soldier who fell in love with me and wanted me to go the U.S. with him to get married. He knew I had a boy baby half White, but I didn't know how to tell him I had a brown baby, too. Once he find out, he say he can take care of my little boy because he is half White, but not my brown baby. My mother and me cry a lot because we love you so much, but we know that you will have a bad life in Korea, so I decide to give you up to the orphanage in Seoul, where the American man finds homes in America. I could not do it, so your* halmeoni, *with all her love, find the courage to drop you off at the orphanage. She tells them your Korean name is Hyo Ja. I had to keep you in my heart from that day and promise to never forget you.*

*When I get to America, I do get married in Texas, but my husband is still on duty in the military. I stay with his family in Baltimore, Maryland. They treat me and your brother very bad. I have no money, and they keep us in the basement of the house. They know that your little brother is not the child of my husband, so they make like accident, and they push him down the stairs and break his arm and damage his hip. I don't speak English and can't defend myself. The only peace I have was when I take my baby outside across the street to the park. A Black lady named Dorothy notice me sitting sadly on the bench every day and begin talking to me. I tell her I don't speak English. She tell me to come to her house, and she will teach me English. I learn all the bad words first, like "bitch." That is the word that I feel like calling my husband's mother and sister the way they treat me and your brother. Dorothy also called the authorities on the women for abusing me and my baby. They come to the house to investigate and also discover my husband had been sending me money all that time, and they never give it to me. This is when my life get better because the authorities get my money back for me, help me move out and get my own place and a job. My husband finally come home. I help my family come over from Korea and settle in the U.S. They move on and forget about me and my family. My father doesn't want to come to the U.S., and it's okay because, like so many of the Korean men, he was very mean.*

*Life was cruel in Korea, and I never want to go back; it is much better here in the United States. My husband and I have five more children and are together until he dies. This is when your brother Joe finds out that my husband was not his dad. Joe used Ancestry to search for his real dad and finds you, which turns out to be our blessing. Many Korean women like me live our whole life with secrets about our past, and it haunts us because we never forget our babies that we had to give up. But we never stop loving them and always hope and pray we made the right decision for their lives. I am happy that God let me see you and know you before I die.*

After listening to my stepfather's and Jackie's story, I want to imagine what my *Oma* would have said to me if she was able to give me an insight into my life. So, in the still of quietness, I sit down with pen and paper, and this is what came through my fingertips from my mother, **Hyon Ok Choi Woolfolk**

*Dearest Bang Sun,*

*Witnesses of real accounts have been shared with you, allowing you to surmise some of the missing fragments of your past.*

*Life does not always spell out things you want to know. You have heard the voices of Jackie, Jung Ok, and my dear Harry, and can now weave the common threads to the tapestry of their story to yours. You have had spiritual connections your whole life, so continue to be ready and discern when our Father enlightens you. Your life has been orchestrated since the day you were born. Take that in, YOU WERE BORN, and YOU ARE STILL HERE over six decades later! What happens in between are a series of predestined "IF THEN" actions,* the ***ORCHESTRATIONS****. Many are seemingly logical and predictable, but many are extreme. For example, IF this terrible thing happens, THEN this wonderful thing happens. A real example is: IF thousands of homeless and hungry children are orphaned in a war-torn country and destined to die. THEN a retired couple from Oregon sees a video about children of war, hungry and homeless, and decides to adopt a few foreign children. This led Harry Holt to Korea to gather his eight adopted children and discovered his heart couldn't leave the remaining thousands behind until he found them homes, providing food, shelter, and a loving family.*

*On June 6, 2018, you were not delusional. Our heavenly Father allowed you to see me with your baby, my grandson Gibran. Yes, we were jubilantly celebrating and hugging that you and my family unquestionably confirmed that I am your mother and my children and grandchildren are your brothers, sister, niece, and nephews. Yes, the most important part of your vision was telling you that I am giving Gibran the love I couldn't give to you—KNOW NOW, it wasn't because I did not love you! I knew that as a mother, it would give you a peace about Gibran and, at the same time, an unexpected resolve about me.*

*Writing this memoir has made clear to you that my actions were predestined.* ***IF*** *you are orphaned (my part),* ***THEN*** *your humbled spirit will always remember your launching pad (your part) that propelled you for* *your chosen path and purpose that had to begin with the Henderson family in Compton—James, Clemmie, Virgil, and Loretta. God knew when the timing was right for you and Yvette to meet. You both thought you were seeking DNA to reveal more about your paternal side, not expecting that this was my way of breaking the decades of silence and uncovering the truth. Sandy, that first night you and Yvette talked, and she sent you my picture, you gasped after years of not seeing me, but your God-given instincts told you who I was. You already have thoughts about the identity of Sonyeon. It really does not matter whether you find him, learn his name or his fate. The gift you have been given is that you have always carried him in your heart. There, he will always be alive and well. My dear Bang Sun, we helped get you to that launching pad. Turning our backs to walk away was our love that propelled you forward.*

*With all my LOVE,*
***Your Oma Hyon***

# Epilogue

In sharing my story, I've come to understand the larger stories of the many who've sacrificed for Korea's prosperity. I also understand but not necessarily accept the history of a third world country, finding a way to rise up by sacrificing its people. Yet, Korea's story is the story of many nations. Today, South Korea, now called the Miracle on the Han River, is one of the world's fastest-growing economies. Still, it has yet to formally address the abandonment of its children and the denial of citizenship to mixed-race G.I. babies. This conversation remains but a whisper in political and social circles when in reality, a large part of Korea's wealth, much like from the sex workers during the war, was built on the backbone of adoption. Ballooning to include full-blooded Korean orphans in the 1960s, adoption was so lucrative that all around the United States, big headlines began appearing:

Korea Makes Them, America Adopts Them.

A *Life* magazine article explained the phenomenon this way: "Bringing Korean children to the U.S. is proving to be a great way to assuaged both the guilt of the Americans and the Koreans. They both see it as a way to pull off a win-win of a most unpopular war, considered at best a stalemate, and at worst a loss."

In addition to racial cleansing and financial incentive for Korea, the U.S., aware of widespread racial tensions—prejudice, antagonisms, lynching, and Jim Crow saw it as a way to soften the perception of the U.S. as racist. The atrocities of history the world over are often mind-boggling, but to look back at and rectify the past mistakes is the right thing to do. There is evidence that in the ever-rising global and culturally savvy world, that change might still come to the Korean society. In fact, in 1991, a door cracked open after the release of a movie called *Arirang*. It's about the life of a Korean adoptee in Sweden. After it aired, Koreans began to feel the guilt and shame of a past they wish they could forget, and it prompted President Kim Dae-Jung to invite twenty-nine adoptees from around the world to the Blue House. He publicly apologized to them for South Korea's inability to raise them as children. Adoption, a cultural embarrassment, and not wanting to be seen as a baby exporting nation anymore, the government-sanctioned baby adoption quotas were expected to be eleminated in 2015. They are still looking toward that goal.

In 2020, it is alleged that the government will allow Korean adoptees to have dual citizenship. That Korea's soft power, namely K-Pop, is an adaptation of Black hip-hop is interesting. I've even seen on the K-drama *Itaewon Class* a storyline about a Black Korean looking for his parent. I have faith that at the speed at which Korea's wealth was built, the country will rapidly become an inclusive society. As for America, in 2020, it's reached another inflection point where equality is not being asked for but demanded. Yet, like with the pushback of the seventies, it is severe. As Bob Marley says, "None of them can stop time," and the time for global cultural equality has come.

The year 2020 was when my new sister and I planned to return to Korea to search for my mother's sisters/family. I know my mother has a brother, Chan Il, who lives in New York. Yvette and I made numerous attempts to reach out to Uncle Chan and his family, but we got no response. I'm sad to say, I feel my mother's family still lives under Syngman Rhee's influence of a pure race. I hope they prove me wrong. I reflected that even thirty years ago in Korea, my children and I were identified as *Geomdungi* (Blackie). The 2020 pandemic has sidelined us but I am eager to see how inclusive and receptive Korea will be when normal travel resumes and we finally get there. I'm looking forward to going back to a more welcoming Korea and turning more pages in the family history book.

What I know today is that I was baby number 213 on a flight to America from Korea. Only years later do I find out from an excerpt in one of Bertha Holt's books, *Bring My Sons From Afar*, why the journey to America was such a challenging one. It states that *halabeoji* notices that one of the plane's propellers has stopped turning midair in flight. *Halabeoji* began praying for our lives at that moment. We were saved. I validated even more that nothing could have kept me from the destiny orchestrated for my life. God has revealed that my mother is Hyon Ok Choi Woolfolk from Korea. I'm close to knowing more about my biological father, whose last name is Kelley.

When I laid eyes on the picture of the beautiful woman with red lipstick, in my heart, I knew she was the one. I felt the same way when I saw my mother's picture with her little brother, Chang Yeng. I feel he is my Sonyeon. If he was, Chang Yeng is not here for me to confirm this because he succumbed to the sea that we loved. But his memory is immortalized not only in my story but in my heart.

My story does not end because I am sure there are more Orchestrations to unfold. Stay tuned…

I leave you with a quote from Albert Camus: "No matter how hard the world pushes against me, within me there's something stronger, something better, pushing right back." I know I pushed back.

# Acknowledgments

There are many along the way who have impacted my life. Some of these encounters have been momentary, some for a season and some for a lifetime, but all have helped to steer the course of my life.

I owe deep gratitude to my parents (James and Clemmie Henderson) for raising me. To my older brother, Virgil, whom I looked up to and my younger sister, Loretta, still in my corner. To my grandfather, Papa, whose fiery temper defended our family and to my godmother, Nanny (Berneatha), who was always my cheerleader. Thank you for the consistent love from the Allen/Wade/Windom family.

To my lifelong friends, Jackie Deary Hyatte, Lynda Randle, Marilyn Gavin, Jeanie Banks, Tony and Steve Bacon, Tony Rambo, Ester Gutierrez and my mentors Dr. Lawrence Freeman, Dorothy Lassiter, and Mr. and Mrs. Bacon who along the way supported and shared the highs and lows of my life's ebbs and flows. Thank you. Thank you, too, for the forever friendships forged through my academic paths at Centennial High School (Reunion Committee): Ann Bradley, Cynthia Machen, Pam Lambert, Sondra Johnson and Reggie Pierson. From Stanford (my SOS—Sistas of Stern); Bev Anderson, Darlene Beaubien, Paris Brooks, Melonie Gibbs. From the University of Southern California (my Mod Squad team); Sheila Cassidy, Michael Lewis, Amy Perez, Aurelia Trujillo. To all of my students, colleagues and special family/friends from Compton, Las Vegas, Houston/Dallas, Detroit and especially in Atlanta (Usher Middle School, Therrell High School and Alonzo A. Crim Open Campus High School and APS District Office).

Where would I be without my Greenforest church family? Thank you to my pastors and Fulfillment Hour Class, which has provided thirty plus years of soul-stirring spiritual food that sustains and recharges me to my power source—GOD. Knowing Him makes it easy to acknowledge my need to Love God and others, to forgive and be forgiven. Though divorced, I am grateful for the good relationship with my ex-husband, Gary, as we continue to celebrate our children, Gibran, Ravi, and Amir. I am particularly grateful for Ravi's mature wisdom and inspiration and for Amir's gift to put laughter and a smile within the hearts of all he encounters. A special thank you to my first-born Gibran, no longer with, us but whose memory will never be forgotten and will live forever through his daughters and my grand-children, Mariah, Aiyanna, Mackenzie and Skylure. To my precious only grandson, Athan, the caboose of my love train. My once absent bloodline has now increased to a third generation.

To my biological mother (Hyon Ok Woolfolk) for leading me to my Korean family, Yvette Woolfolk, Harrison Jr., and James and their children, Christian, Sydney, Carter, and Kai and my step-father Papa Harry. To my sister-in-law, Brenda, and to my biological father wherever he is.

Finally, thank you, Amir, my wonderful son and Marva Allen of Wordeee Publishing, who encouraged me to turn all my years of accumulated memories and stories into this tangible project—with years of hearing from friends, "You need to write a book." As we now know, all happens in the timing of its **ORCHESTRATION**.